CONTEMPORARY CHINESE POLITICAL THOUGHT

CONTEMPORARY CHINESE POLITICAL THOUGHT

Debates and Perspectives

Edited by
FRED DALLMAYR
and ZHAO TINGYANG

UNIVERSITY PRESS OF KENTUCKY

Scholarly publisher for the Commonwealth,
serving Bellarmine University, Berea College, Centre College of Kentucky,
Eastern Kentucky University, The Filson Historical Society, Georgetown College,
Kentucky Historical Society, Kentucky State University, Morehead State
University, Murray State University, Northern Kentucky University, Transylvania
University, University of Kentucky, University of Louisville, and Western
Kentucky University.
All rights reserved.

Editorial and Sales Offices: The University Press of Kentucky
663 South Limestone Street, Lexington, Kentucky 40508-4008
www.kentuckypress.com

16 15 14 13 12   5 4 3 2 1

Library of Congress Cataloging-in-Publication Data

Contemporary Chinese political thought : debates and perspectives / edited by
Fred Dallmayr and Zhao Tingyang.
    p. cm.— (Asia in the new millennium)
  Includes bibliographical references and index.
  ISBN 978-0-8131-3642-4 (hardcover : alk. paper)
  — ISBN 978-0-8131-3643-1 (pdf) — ISBN 978-0-8131-4063-6 (epub)
  1. Political science—China—Philosophy—History—20th century. 2. Political
science—China—Philosophy—History—21th century. I. Dallmayr, Fred R.
(Fred Reinhard), 1928- II. Zhao, Tingyang.
  JA84.C6C66 2012
  320.0951—dc23   2012010814

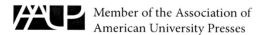 Member of the Association of
American University Presses

Contents

Preface

The present volume is a result of the collaboration between a Western political theorist and a Chinese philosopher. I first met Professor Zhao Tingyang some ten years ago at a conference held at Capital Normal University in Beijing. At that time, we had extensive discussions, and we both discovered an affinity or compatibility of our views on many topics. Like me, Zhao Tingyang is neither a universalist nor a narrow particularist, neither a devotee of abstract principles or formulas nor a supporter of an exclusivist identity politics. It is in the interstices of these positions that dialogue and communication flourish.

Since our first meeting we continued our intellectual exchanges. One idea that emerged in our communications was the desirability of putting together a volume presenting the spectrum of political ideas and intellectual debates in contemporary China. As we both agreed, there is still—at least in the West—a woeful lack of knowledge of these ideas, accompanied by an often gross misunderstanding and a tendency to resort to simplistic stereotypes. One of the central ambitions of philosophical thought everywhere is to combat stereotypes and to reduce the likelihood of misunderstanding. Philosophy in its best sense thus is a means of conflict resolution and a pathway to peace, here the peace between "East" and "West."

Regarding the spelling of Chinese names, we enlisted the help of Professor Cai Daliang.

Fred Dallmayr
October 2011

Introduction

Fred Dallmayr

During the past two decades or so, China has been emerging into the limelight of global economics, global science, and global politics. Having been consumed for nearly a century by the strains of internal and external troubles, the Asian giant is at long last assuming its rightful place in the global community of peoples. Yet, behind staggering growth rates and levels of productivity, something else at least equally impressive is happening: the steady burgeoning of Chinese intellectual life and its solid integration into the global market of ideas and philosophical arguments. For political pessimists, this intellectual emergence is only another stepping-stone in the direction of a looming "clash of civilizations." From another, more hopeful and dispassionate angle, the same development is able to lay the groundwork for a genuine dialogue between the "East" and the "West," a dialogue conducive to a mutual learning process and a loosening of rigid ideological positions. Ever since the onset of the Cold War, political thought in the West—especially in America—has been in the grip of liberal individualism and neoliberalism, with its accent on private autonomy, profit making, and public deregulation. On the other hand, roughly since the same time, China has experienced the fortunes and misfortunes of political and economic collectivism, sometimes abetted by a heavy-handed traditionalism disdainful of individual freedoms. Under these circumstances, a genuine encounter between "East" and "West" carries with it the prospect of greater mutual attentiveness and a dismantling of ideological straitjackets.

The present volume brings together essays by Chinese intellectuals written (with one exception) in the first decade of the twenty-first century. The arguments of the writers, of course, are not advanced in a vacuum but make sense only when seen against the background of Chinese history, especially developments in the past century. By and large, Chinese intellectual life in recent times has been dominated by a dialectic of radically opposed positions: anti-Westernism and pro-Westernism—

a dialectic sometimes tempered by efforts of mediation or reconciliation. The Opium War (1840–1842) and the imposition of "unequal treaties" during the nineteenth century triggered a virulent opposition to Western-style imperialism and colonialism. At the same time, the realization of Western military and industrial superiority produced an equally intense desire to "catch up" with the West—a desire additionally fueled by the humiliating defeat in the Sino-Japanese War (1894–1895). The entire cauldron of competing factors led ultimately to the collapse of the last Chinese dynasty, the revolution of 1911, and the establishment of a fledgling constitutional republic. The republican regime did not so much resolve festering intellectual issues as profile competing positions more neatly. One of the leaders or "presidents" of the regime, Sun Zhongshan (Sun Yat-Sen), exemplified the existing tensions by being at the same time a progressive "liberal" reformer and a defender of Chinese nationalist traditions. During the same period, a sternly Westernizing movement arose—the so-called May Fourth Movement (1919)—led by philosopher Hu Shi, whose chief commitment was to Western-style "science and democracy." This orientation, however, was one among many, contested from the beginning by an attachment to Chinese nationalism and Chinese intellectual traditions (like Confucianism). The regime came to an end with the Japanese invasion of 1937, the ensuing world war, the retreat of the nationalist "Kuomintang" to Taiwan, and the victory of communism in 1949.

During the first half century of Communist rule, intellectual life in Mainland China was stabilized and streamlined under totalitarian auspices. To some extent, this stabilization was facilitated by the retreat of both progressive-liberal and traditional nationalist thinkers to Taiwan (and Hong Kong). Yet, even during the rule of Mao Zedong (Mao Tse-tung, 1893–1976), mainland communism was marked by profound rifts and tensions. This may have to do with the fact that, as an offshoot of Marxism, Chinese communism or "Maoism" was both Western in origin and, at the same time, distinctly anti-Western or Chinese in character (a distinction that was accentuated by the Cold War). The conflict between Chinese traditionalism and progressive antitraditionalism repeatedly erupted during Mao's rule, especially in the so-called Great Leap Forward (1958–1960) and the Cultural Revolution (1965–1976), the latter aiming at the radical destruction of all traditional Chinese vestiges. Since the death of Mao, the rigidity of the Communist ideology has been softened and, in fact, has made room for a (still-limited) plurality of intellectual orientations: while aspects of liberal progressivism have been allowed to enter the economic arena, strands of traditional Chinese thought—especially Confucianism—have experienced a resurgence in the cultural and religious domain. This pluralization of the earlier ideological structure continues and is reinforced in the present century. Basically, one might say that Chinese intellectual life today revolves around a debate among disparate, and not easily reconcilable, perspectives: mainly Western-style liberalism (in the economic sphere), Confucianism (in culture and religion), and a post-Maoist "New Leftism" (especially in politics). The situation is additionally complicated, however, by multiple crossovers and overlaps. Thus, liberalism ranges from republican to radical-individualist, Confucianism varies from staunchly reactionary to democratic and progressive, and New Leftism spans the spectrum from "cadre" bureaucrats to democratic socialists.

The first essay in this volume dates from 1992 and seeks to introduce the reader to prominent intellectual figures and discussions of the twentieth century as a prelude to more recent debates. The essay reminds readers of the critical and near-desperate situation into which China was plunged as a result of a series of misfortunes, from the Opium War and the "unequal treaties" to the Japanese invasion. The author, Ji Wenshun, singles out nine major political thinkers of the twentieth century: Kang Youwei (1858–1927), Liang Qichao (1873–1929), Sun Zhongshan (1866–1925), Hu Shi (1891–1962), Zhang Junmai (known as Carsun Chang, 1887–1969), Zhang Dongsun (1886–1976), Liang Shuming (1893–1988), Chen Duxiu (1879–1942), and Mao Zedong (1893–1976). As the author shows, Kang was one of the most radical thinkers, who ideally wanted to do away with all traditional social distinctions in favor of a one-world ideal labeled "great harmony" or "great unity." A disciple of Kang, Liang more moderately advocated constitutional reform along Western liberal lines and, after 1911, became an ardent supporter of constitutional republicanism. Sun Zhongshan initially supported the revolutionary overthrow of the Manchu dynasty but later became the spokesman for a model of republicanism summarized in the three principles of "nationalism, democracy, and the people's livelihood." Although in accord with republicanism, Hu Shi was culturally more radical and innovative, seeking the virtual replacement of Chinese traditions with modern Western ideas. To some extent, this perspective was supported by both Zhang Junmai and Zhang Dongsun, who, as devotees of the British government, sought to introduce parliamentary democracy in China. In opposition to radical Westernization,

Liang Shuming placed his hope instead in the revival of Chinese Confucianism—though a revival attentive to the need for social and economic reform. Chen Duxiu was torn throughout his life between conflicting commitments, first to democratic reform and later (for a time) to the agenda of proletarian revolution—an agenda pursued with relentless fervor by Mao Zedong and the Communist Party.

The persisting influence of the preceding political conflicts needs to be kept in mind when turning to more recent intellectual debates and controversies. In his essay "The Debates in Contemporary Chinese Political Thought," Zhou Lian draws attention to two major contested issues: first, the contemporary status of Chinese political thought and especially its presumed uniqueness (summarized under the label "the China Model"); and second, the great diversity of political perspectives in China, resulting in part from the competition of Western and traditional Chinese influences. In the first rubric, the author first pinpoints the rough meaning of such phrases as "the China Model" and "the Beijing Consensus": namely, the combination of mixed ownership, individual property rights, and heavy government intervention in the economy and politics. This sets the stage for a discussion of different interpretations of the "model," focused on the very possibility and legitimacy of a distinctly Chinese political philosophy. Turning to the second topic, Zhou first adopts the broad scheme shared by many observers: that Chinese thought today can be loosely differentiated into the strands of liberalism, leftism, and conservatism. However, he immediately demonstrates the looseness of this differentiation by examining a number of writers whose work escapes neat compartmentalization. One of these writers is Gan Yang, who is well known for his idea of the "integration of the three traditions"—of communism, liberal socialism (in the manner of Deng Xiaoping), and Confucianism. In Gan's view, what the integration ultimately yields is a "Confucian socialist republic" that reconciles the Confucian preference for "social harmony" with Mao's motto of "common wealth" and the liberal trust in a functioning market economy. Even more "integrationist" is the thought of Zhao Tingyang, who strives to overcome all distinct attachments, loyalties, and traditions and, by adopting the "nonstance" position of "all-under-heaven," to usher in a universal world society. As Gan observes by way of conclusion, a strange (or exotic) version of conservatism in China today is a strand inspired by the work of Leo Strauss and Carl Schmitt—a strand upholding certain Western texts but hostile to Western modernity.

In the essay following Gan's, Zhao Tingyang elaborates in consider-able detail on his perspective of "all-under-heaven" (*Tianxia*). Taking his point of departure from the ancient Zhou dynasty, he shows how during that dynasty the effort was not so much to construct a rigidly unified "state" (or *polis*), but rather to cultivate a comprehensive, multidimensional politi-cal framework in which different tribes and ethnicities would be able to live together in peace and harmony. According to Zhou policy, the goal of harmony meant seeking reasonable solutions to conflicts and building a network of reliable correlations that in the long run would benefit all participants. In Zhao's view, this policy rested on a number of metaphysi-cal, philosophical, and epistemological premises. In terms of epistemol-ogy, preference was given to methodological "holism" or "relationism" over methodological individualism; in terms of social philosophy, the accent was placed on interdependence over atomistic independence—where interde-pendence governed all levels of sociality, from family to larger commu-nity to the "world" as a whole. Philosophically and metaphysically, Zhao's piece opposes a "relational rationality" to an egocentric rationality and a cosmic holism to an anarchical atomism. According to Zhao Tingyang, the Zhou vision of "all-under-heaven" needs urgently to be revived in our time (though also reconceptualized) as an antidote to self-centered indi-vidualism and hostile clashes between nation-states and civilizations (sup-ported by Hobbesian statism and Carl Schmitt's "friend-enemy" formula). He reviews a number of prominent "international" theories—from Martin Wight and Wallerstein to Alexander Wendt—and finds them all lacking a genuine notion of "world." As Zhao makes clear, "all-under-heaven" is not a synonym for empire or imperialism—because it is based on the well-being of "all." It is also not necessarily uniform or homogenous but allows for a differentiated or "compatible" cosmopolitanism (what sometimes is called "transversalism").

By contrast to Zhao's emphatic cosmopolitanism, Zhang Feng's essay returns to the dimension of interstate or international relations, with the specific aim of exploring the role of Chinese intellectuals in that field. As Zhang points out, the study of international relations (IR) is a new aca-demic field in China, having emerged some thirty years ago, and from the beginning has patterned itself on American ideas and scholarship. This means that, although far removed from the European background, Chi-nese practitioners have tended to subscribe to the traditional "Westpha-lian" paradigm of interstate rivalry. The issue that long preoccupied many intellectuals was how to introduce a Chinese dimension into this para-digm; efforts in this direction led to the formulation of an "IR theory with Chinese characteristics," to the project of a "Chinese theory of IR," and finally to the agenda of a "Chinese School." Zhang's essay traces the his-torical development of these efforts, pointing out the role of the conflicting tendencies of globalization and "Sinicization" in that development. After reviewing the debates surrounding an international theory "with Chi-nese characteristics," Zhang turns his attention to the ambitious idea of a "Chinese School," discussing in detail the arguments of some of the idea's leading proponents and critics. According to Zhang, the central conun-drum afflicting the idea is the unresolved tension between globalism and localism, between universalism and historical-contextual particularism. On that issue, Zhang aligns himself with the critics of the "China School" and with the defenders of academic universalism. As he might acknowl-edge, the defended universalism is ultimately that of the Westphalian para-digm (as supported by Morgenthau, Huntington, and others); more than a superficial localism is needed to contest that paradigm.

As it happens, many Chinese intellectuals in recent times have tried to revive and reinvigorate the deeper cultural and intellectual resources available in Chinese history. One of the main resources is the tradition of Chinese Confucianism, which of late has experienced a remarkable resurgence. As Liu Shuxian points out in his essay on contemporary New Confucianism, the Confucian tradition in China has developed through a number of prominent stages, from the founding period of Confucius and Mencius; to the "Neo-Confucian" reformulations of Zhu Xi (1130–1200, learning of principle) and Wang Yangming (1472–1529, learning of heart-mind); to the recent resurgence of the tradition, frequently labeled "New Confucianism." In his essay Liu guides the reader from the Song and Ming dynasties to the fall of the last Qing dynasty in 1911–1912 and from there to the May Fourth Movement and the final victory of communism. In the aftermath of that victory, Confucianism was marginalized and even attacked; however, in 1986, it was reelevated to a major national "research program" in Mainland China (alongside such perspectives as communism and Western liberalism). In terms of the evolution of the New Confu-cianism, Liu distinguishes among three generations: the generation of the founders, including Liang Shuming (1893–1988) and Xiong Shili (1885–1968); the generation of their students, including Tang Junyi (1909–1978) and Mou Zongsan (1909–1995); and a still younger generation, including himself and Du Weiming (1940–). While the first generation worked on the mainland, many members of the subsequent generations developed their ideas in Taiwan, Hong Kong, or overseas. In his essay, Liu ponders the question of how the New Confucianism could emerge in China, given extremely unfavorable external conditions. In this context, major attention is given to the work and thought of Liang Shuming and his effort to synthesize Chinese and Western traditions. By way of conclusion, Liu reflects on the significance of New Confucianism, with special reference to a famous manifesto of 1958 (drafted by Tang and Mou).

Turning specifically to political philosophy, Chen Ming in his essay asks what role Confucianism can play in the context of a modern and globalizing world. He highlights first of all a basic distinction between traditional Western and traditional Chinese thought, arguing that the former was from the beginning state centered (or centered on the *polis*), while the latter was basically family centered or clan centered (what he calls "kindredom"). The main part of Chen Ming's essay, however, is devoted to a discussion of the diversity of political perspectives covered by the broad umbrella notion of "New Confucianism." For purposes of illustration, Chen Ming differentiates among three main perspectives: a very conservative and even reactionary version hostile to modernity, a more "liberal" version seeking to blend traditional Confucianism with basic tenets of Western modern life, and a strongly nationalist version using Confucian values chiefly as a means to bolster the legitimacy of the Chinese state. The intellectual chosen to represent the first version is Jiang Qing. As Chen Ming's essay shows, Jiang's main concern is with the preservation and reconstruction of Chinese identity; Confucianism is assumed to encapsulate this identity and to provide a shield against all forms of Westernization and modernization (including liberalism and Marxism-Maoism). The second version is represented by Chen Ming's own work. Here Confucianism is assumed to play its role mainly in the domains of culture and civil society, while politics and economics are opened up to the demands of liberal modernity. In addition to strengthening social ethics, Confucian values for Chen Ming also can serve as a "civil religion." The nationalist strand is represented by Kang Xiaoguang, for whom Confucianism provides not only cultural glue but also a state ideology in the form of "benevolent" but strongly authoritarian government. Ultimately, benevolent rule means the autocracy of Confucian scholars. In Kang's words: "When Confucianism replaces Marxist-Leninism as state ideology and

Confucian scholars replace communist cadres, the process of creating a benevolent government is complete."

The autocratic tendency in some versions of Confucianism brings to the fore the problem of the relation between Confucianism and democracy. In his essay dealing with this topic, He Baogang elaborates on the complexity of this relationship: a complexity deriving from the fact that both Confucianism and democracy can be interpreted in multiple ways (in the case of Confucianism from conservative-authoritarian to more liberal readings, in the case of democracy from liberal and deliberative to social and populist variants). Regarding the relationship between the two terms, Baogang distinguishes among four main "models" or ideal types, which he labels "conflictive," "compatible," "hybrid," and "critical." Advanced famously by Samuel Huntington, the conflict model stresses the supposedly antithetical qualities of the two terms, thus pitting a heavily autocratic Confucian ethos against democracy's liberal egalitarianism. This stark antithesis is rejected by the "compatibility" approach—favored by such writers as Fukuyama, Theodore de Bary, and Liang Shuming—which construes Confucianism as a flexible and open-ended perspective readily congruent with an ethical and socially responsible democracy. While the first two models still treat the two sides of the relationship as relatively self-contained and distinct, the "hybrid" model starts from the premise that the two sides are already overlapping and interpenetrating today in many ways. An example given by the author is Chinese local democratization during the past decade, giving rise to village elections, deliberative forums, and intraparty democracy. Whereas in most discussions of this relationship, Western democracy is taken as a standard by which to evaluate Confucianism, Baogang's fourth, or "critical," model reverses this stance and critically evaluates features of Western democracy—such as the axiom of liberal neutrality and the overly "individualistic" theory of human rights—from the vantage of Chinese traditions, an evaluation that brings into view the possibility of a genuinely "Confucian democracy."

The issues involved in the relation between Confucianism and democracy are also explored in Ni Peimin's essay. Without directly invoking Baogang's argument, Ni Peimin's essay elaborates chiefly on Baogang's "conflictive" and "compatible" models, where the relation is seen respectively as one of "water and fire" and of "water and fish." As Ni Peimin acknowledges, the predominant view is still that of "water and fire," where Confucianism is held to be authoritarian and repressive in contrast to democracy's goal of equal liberty. In recent times, this view has been challenged by many scholars postulating as a minimum the possibility of peaceful coexistence ("water and oil") and, more hopefully, the prospect of a mutually beneficial compatibility. In line with Baogang, Ni Peimin agrees that much depends here on the meaning of Confucianism (autocratic versus flexible) and also on the definition of democracy (liberal-individualistic versus ethical and contextual). In this respect, his essay endorses the arguments of Roger Ames, Henry Rosemont, and others stressing the Confucian preference for an "embodied, relational, duty-bearing" personhood—a preference they consider as quite compatible with an ethical democracy balancing human rights and responsibilities. "If we define democracy," Ni Peimin writes, as involving the right and duty of every member "to participate in public affairs and take the welfare of all other members as one's own," then Confucian teachings are "fully in accord with the spirit of democracy." The essay also discusses critical objections raised to this compatibility model: that it idealizes the Confucian tradition, neglecting its frequent cooptation by political power; and that it exaggerates the distance between Confucian personhood and liberal individualism. For Ni Peimin, however, these and other criticisms are open to successful rebuttal.

As the authors of the preceding essays are acutely aware, Confucian democracy does not operate in a vacuum, but has to find resonance in a social context marked for half a century by the revolutionary policies of Marxism-Leninism and Maoism. How can or should both Confucian and non-Confucian Chinese intellectuals relate to this revolutionary past? This question is at the heart of "New Leftism" in post-Maoist China. In his essay "The Dialectic of the Chinese Revolution Revisited," Ci Jiwei discusses the development of China during the past half century in terms of the dialectic between idealism and materialism, between socialist utopianism and pragmatic reformism and consumerism. Supplanting the Hegelian-Marxist notion of "dialectic" with Freudian vocabulary, Ci Jiwei speaks of the "desublimation" and "resublimation" of the initial utopian élan—with desublimation ushering in both consumerist euphoria and a social and personal "crisis of meaning." At that point, while public values may still be externally proclaimed, the actual situation on the ground is one of a "moral vacuum" (*Daode Zhenkong*) or "crisis of belief" (*Xinyang Weiji*). In an earlier study, entitled *Dialectic of the Chinese Revolution*, Ci Jiwei traced the descent from socialist utopianism into nihilism and "hedonism," where the latter means the "guilt-free pursuit of wealth and pleasure." That study distinguishes among three dimensions of desublimation: epistemic, moral, and corporeal—a distinction the essay here reaffirms. In Ci Jiwei's view, desublimation has occurred in China in all three dimensions—despite efforts to reverse the downward slide. As he points out, while condoning and even promoting corporeal consumerism/hedonism, political leaders have attempted to achieve "resublimation" on the epistemic and moral levels—with predictably dubious results. Such "partial resublimation," he observes, is likely to be perceived as a mere verbal exercise or as "resublimation out of context."

If this assessment is correct, then the task of Chinese intellectuals, especially intellectuals on the Left, is to articulate a "meaning" structure that is at odds with both liberal consumerism and an officially imposed communism. Cui Zhiyuan, a leader of the Chinese New Left, outlines precisely such a meaning structure for China's future, namely a "petty bourgeois socialist theory." As Cui writes, evoking the language of the 1848 Manifesto: "A specter is haunting China and the world: the specter of petty bourgeois socialism." The reason is that both Marxism and old-style socialism have lost their momentum, while the appeal of neoliberalism is likewise fading. The difference of the new agenda from communism is that it does not seek to perpetuate the proletarian status of the workers (and peasants) but to foster the classlessness of the "universal petty bourgeoisie." The economic goal is a "socialist market economy," the political goal that of "economic and political democracy." Pointing in the direction of these goals is China's land-ownership system, where land is owned by village collectives (an idea inspired by Proudhon). A similar orientation is manifest in the "modern enterprise system" anchored in workers' and shareholders' cooperatives (an idea favored by John Stuart Mill). A major inspiration in this field comes from Nobel laureate James E. Meade and his promotion of a "liberal socialism" based on the two pillars of "labor-capital partnerships" and of "social dividends" provided tax free to all citizens. Cui compares petty bourgeois socialism with the kind of "oligarchy capitalism" that emerged in Russia after the collapse of the Soviet Union—and finds the latter seriously flawed. Apart from Meade, Cui's program also draws inspiration from Silvio Gesell's modified Keynesianism, from Piore and Sabel's emphasis on flexible specialization, and from Roberto Unger's concern with "petty commodity production" and his understanding of property as a "bundle of rights."

Cui does not reflect on the viability or sustainability of "liberal socialism" or especially on the compatibility between rapid economic growth and political stability. Frank Fang, however, resolutely takes up these issues in his essay "Taking the China Model Seriously." As Fang points out, many people in the West believe that a Western-style liberal market is required for economic growth and that the sustainability of such growth depends on the functioning of liberal democracy. Fang considers these assumptions untenable. As his essay tries to show, political stability ensured by a strong "state" is precisely a requisite for sustainable growth (which is the key tenet of the "China Model"). Reviewing China's economic development during the past half century, he critiques the neoliberal mantra of privatization as "disappointing if not disastrous" for developing countries; he also subjects to critical scrutiny the "open-access logic" extolled by many Western social scientists—finding it neglectful of historical-political context. As an antidote, Fang proposes a "property-rights theory of the state," where the state is viewed as a property owned respectively by monarchs, oligarchs, party rulers, and democratic leaders. In terms of this concept, China since 2002 can be seen as a "dominant-party" rulership and ownership, with a progressive shift toward a democratic "common property regime" (as defined by Elinor Ostrom). Democratization here still maintains strong state-centered stability as a warrant of growth. Fang presents the "China Model" as a form of "one-party constitutionalism"; he also speaks of a "three-tiered, effort-based" institutional approach where the tiers of the state, the economy, and popular participation interpenetrate and mutually reinforce each other. By moving in these directions, he concludes, China cannot only catch up with the West but also challenge the preeminence of the liberal model of democracy.

In a similar spirit, but from a slightly different angle, the next essay, by Wang Shaoguang, insists on the need for strong state institutions as a requisite for the development of democracy. Departing from liberal "third-wave" models, Wang holds that the success of democratization depends not only on economic advances and a vibrant civil society and civic culture but also, and quite crucially, on a coherent and well-functioning state apparatus. Seen in this light, "democracy" for him means not only a political regime but a form of public authority endowed with "infrastructural power." To be effective, the state must perform a number of critical functions: it must be able to monopolize the legitimate use of violence, to extract needed resources, to shape national identity, to regulate social and economic life, to distribute resources, and to maintain an efficient bureaucracy. For Wang, a state endowed with these critical capacities is not an end in itself, but an enabling context allowing for the emergence of a sustainable democracy: only such a state can protect citizens' basic rights, maintain the rule of law, energize civil society, and meet peoples' basic demands. In all these respects, state effectiveness contributes to (what is often called) "democratic consolidation." To corroborate his argument, Wang next turns to a discussion of five Asian democracies (Indonesia, the Philippines, Thailand, South Korea, and Taiwan), showing how different levels of state effectiveness lead to different levels of democratization. By way of conclusion, the essay spells out the implications of the argument for China, making a plea for the strengthening of state institutions as a gateway to democratic reform.

The preceding essays, especially those by Cui Zhiyuan and Frank Fang, are unconventional and prominent examples of "New Left" thinking in China today. This does not mean that there is no room for more traditional Marxist thought; the essay by Cheng Guangyun is a case in point. Cheng presents Marxism not simply as an economic theory (in opposition to capitalism) nor as a mere ideology (in opposition to such "isms" as liberalism and conservatism), but rather as a full-fledged political philosophy. Taken seriously, such a philosophy provides foundational reasons justifying the preeminence of workers and peasants (the "proletariat") in political life and thus gives meaning to the notion of a "democratic politics of socialism with Chinese characteristics." The core of Marxist thought, especially its conception of "historical materialism," in Cheng's view, is the tenet that the world and its "objectifications" are the result of human creative action, production, and communication; given the central productive role of workers and peasants, this tenet supports the Marxist accent on "proletarian" practice. Traditional Marxism developed two basic "logics" to support its central tenet: a logic of the production and reproduction of ordinary human life and a logic of historical or natural "laws" determining (as "iron laws" of necessity) the processes of production. In this context, Cheng clearly favors the "humanistic" or life-centered version of Marxism over the pseudo-scientific or deterministic version; agreeing with earlier "Western" Marxists, he finds the latter version prone to slide into sterile dogmatism. Instead of celebrating inexorable laws, the humanist version places at center stage the role of human struggle, that is, the practical effort to overcome prevailing conditions of oppression and human suffering. Seen from this angle, the "proletariat" is the preeminently oppressed and suffering segment of society; the goal of its struggle is to remove the dichotomy between oppressors and oppressed and thus to establish "communism" seen or understood as the "democratic politics of socialism." The latter goal is not just an empty chimera, but a real possibility especially in countries previously subject to colonial or imperialist domination.

The present volume provides an overview of intellectual trends and perspectives in contemporary China, paying attention to the interlocking arenas of politics, economics, and culture. The overview is by no means exhaustive and does not claim to cover all possible modes of political thought. Relatively sidelined or marginalized are approaches that simply replicate customary liberal, libertarian, or neoconservative perspectives; most Western readers are liable to be sufficiently familiar with the gist of these approaches and hence readily able to reconstruct imaginatively their arguments. As indicated at the beginning, the hope of the editors is that the volume may stimulate a broadening of horizons and encourage a willingness to learn on all sides, across vast distances and often seemingly irreconcilable premises. To this extent, the volume hopes to make a contribution to global pedagogy—a pedagogy that, under favorable conditions, may be a stepping-stone to a grand vision: the harmony of "all-under-heaven."

1

Contemporary Issues
and Debates

1

Ideological Conflicts in Modern China

Ji Wenshun

China has undergone greater changes in the past hundred years than in the whole preceding historical period, and the greatest changes have been concentrated in the past thirty-odd years. Prior to 1800 China was a populous country that enjoyed political stability and economic self-sufficiency and was admired by many European scholars. China was also a country that proudly regarded her civilization as the highest in world history and her position as being at the center of the world, surrounded by barbarians. It is possible that the Chinese viewed themselves as existing in a stage approaching a peaceful one-world kingdom, though such a view was based on an imperfect understanding of the scope of the globe. The Chinese devoted their energies more to civil and cultural activities than to military concerns. And because they were free from any serious external threat prior to 1800, they saw no necessity to provide for proper protection against external aggression.

China's relative stability was disrupted beginning with the Opium War of 1840–1842. The crisis began when the British forced the sale of opium on China under the pretext of trade. During the same period other foreign powers arrived and fought the Chinese in their own territory with superior weapons and gunboats that the militarily ill-prepared Chinese were unable to overcome. China then began to suffer humiliation after humiliation as she proved unable to defend herself against foreign aggression.

As one of the consequences of the Opium War and other wars that followed, China signed a number of treaties—generally known as the unequal treaties—with foreign powers. These treaties deprived China of the conditions necessary to retain her independence. Sun Zhongshan (Sun Yat-Sen) once described China's status at that time as that of a subcolony, for China was not subject to the oppression of a single country, as was Korea under Japan or Indochina under France, but suffered the oppression of most of the strong countries of East and West. The unequal treaties eroded China's prestige and abridged certain political and economic rights.[1]

The following quotation from R. R. Palmer may help to give an American reader a sense of the deep psychological shock the Chinese suffered from foreign intervention:

> If the reader will imagine what the United States would be like if foreign warships patrolled the Mississippi as far as St. Louis, if foreigners came and went throughout the country without being under its laws, if New York, New Orleans, and other cities contained foreign settlements outside its jurisdiction, but in which all banking and management were concentrated, if foreigners determined the tariff policy, collected the proceeds and remitted much of the money to their own governments, if the western part of the city of Washington had been burned [the Summer Palace], Long Island and California annexed to distant empires [Hong Kong and Indochina] and all New England were coveted by two immediate neighbors [Manchuria], if the national authorities were half in collusion with these foreigners and half victimized by them, and if large areas of the country were prey to bandits, guerillas, and revolutionary secret societies conspiring against the helpless government and occasionally murdering some of the foreigners—then he can understand how observant Chinese felt at the end of the last century, and why the term "imperialism" came to be held by so many of the world's people in abomination.[2]

Fighting imperialism has been a slogan of the Communist Party for years. Imperialism is considered one of the three great mountains on the backs of the Chinese people. In his "Three Principles of the People," Sun Zhongshan warns the Chinese people of the dangers of the imperialist economic and political pressure that menaced the existence of China, and in his will, he called for the abolition of unequal treaties. Anti-imperialism was a major objective of the Kuomintang's Northern Expedition of 1926–1928 against the warlords and their foreign backers. It is clearly true that foreign invasions did serious damage to China and that they marked the decline of Chinese prestige and power. But placing the blame solely on foreign pressures for China's historical problems—the effect of her own internal inconsistencies, which would emerge eventually—cannot be justified. An objective and dispassionate study of China's problems would include careful consideration of both the impact of foreign powers and China's own internal shortcomings.

The Chinese had always regarded themselves as the most civilized people in the world, but now, with repeated failures in war, the Chinese were suddenly labeled and treated as barbarians. Western thinkers who had once shown deference to China were now contemptuous. The Chinese began to lose confidence in their country and felt the loss of national pride. Chinese public opinion now exalted as advanced those countries it had once considered barbaric and began to regard China as a backward country. The Chinese further realized that China was not now and never had been the geographic center of the world. China, suddenly a prey of the colonial powers, was now confronted with the danger of partition— being cut up like a melon, as the Chinese referred to the situation—and her survival as a nation, as well as a culture, was in peril. The possibility that China faced the threat of extinction as a country and extermination as a race frightened and appalled the Chinese.

This situation was really an unprecedented challenge to the Chinese people as a whole. It could be viewed as an unfortunate situation, but it could also be viewed as fortunate, for according to Toynbee, there are virtues in adversity. He holds that it is difficult conditions, rather than easy ones, that produce civilization; that man achieves civilization as a response to the challenge of a situation of special difficulty that rouses him to make a hitherto unprecedented effort;[3] and that a sudden crushing defeat is apt to stimulate the defeated person to set his house in order and prepare to make a victorious response.[4]

Toynbee's concept of challenge and response finds a parallel in Mencius's famous aphorism: "Life springs from adversity and death from ease and comfort."[5] To many Chinese thinkers, the salvation of China politically and culturally became the cause to which they were anxious and willing to devote themselves. The programs provided by these thinkers vary in approach, but their basic great goals are the same—to maintain China's national existence and cultural identity.

The latest serious threat to China's existence was the Japanese aggres-

sion, beginning with the Mukden Incident of 18 September 1931 and culminating with the War of Resistance against Japan between 1937 and 1945.
This was the gravest disaster China had encountered since the Opium
War. The Chinese realized that they had reached a critical stage, where
they would either fight on to victory and survive or go down to defeat and
extinction. Programs for national salvation took on a new immediacy and
urgency. During the course of the war, the surviving thinkers mentioned
in this study and intellectuals in general became ever more acutely aware of
the conflict between the Kuomintang and the Communists in their struggle for political power and the ideological allegiance of the people. The
United Front in fact prevented neither an intensification of this conflict nor
the polarization of the supporters on either side.

The purpose of this chapter is to provide a brief overview of the programs for China's social reconstruction, those programs that were only
proposed and those that were actually undertaken by men concerned with
saving China from extinction, both as a nation and as a culture. It surveys
the social programs of nine modern Chinese thinkers: Kang Youwei, Liang
Qichao, Sun Zhongshan, Hu Shi, Zhang Junmai, Zhang Dongsun, Liang
Shuming, Chen Duxiu, and Mao Zedong. The thoughts of these nine men
represent the major trends in Chinese ideologies of social reform during
the past one hundred years.

Kang Youwei was the first thinker in modern times who advocated
a radical and complete change in China. His one-world ideal—variously
translated as "great harmony" or "great unity"—consists of a much more
radical vision than that of a communist society. He advocated not only the
abolition of private property and national governments but also the complete dissolution of families and even the elimination of personal names,
which were to be replaced by numbers. However, Kang warned, this ideal
was to be realized in the distant future. For his own time, he advocated a
constitutional monarchy after the model of Great Britain.

Liang Qichao, a disciple of Kang Youwei, was more influential though
less creative than his mentor. Politically, Liang first advocated constitutional monarchy and later supported constitutional republicanism when
the Chinese Republic was founded in 1911. A prolific writer whose complete works have been estimated to run to at least sixteen million characters, Liang achieved a tremendous and sweeping influence on the Chinese
mind, an influence due perhaps as much to the magnetic attraction of his
style as to the Western ideas and proposals for change that he introduced.

Sun Zhongshan advocated a revolution against the Manchu government and its replacement by a republic, whereas both Kang and Liang
had advocated peaceful change in China. Sun's activity in the early years
before 1911 was primarily focused on a nationalist movement, aimed at
overthrowing the Manchu government by force and mainly motivated
by nationalistic considerations that treated the Manchus as foreigners.
By 1924, Sun had elaborated his revolutionary theory and formulated
his "Three Principles of the People" into a system. These three principles
are nationalism, democracy, and the people's livelihood. The principle of
nationalism seeks equality among all peoples in China and China's equality with all foreign nations. The principle of democracy seeks to establish a
democratic form of government, mainly after the U.S. model, with certain
modifications, The principle of the people's livelihood is a kind of socialism
that provides programs for the regulation of capital and the equalization of
land ownership.

Although the republican political system effected a great change in
theory and form, China's difficulties nevertheless remained, and the problem of China's modernization still had to be solved. In the years subsequent
to the establishment of the republic in China, three different ideals, represented by four scholars, emerged and became important.

Hu Shi was a protagonist of China's new cultural movement. To his
mind, the new cultural movement meant the creation of a new Chinese
culture. Actually, the new culture Hu envisioned was virtually a replacement of Eastern civilization by Western civilization. Thus, he emphatically
maintained the position that the complete Westernization of China, particularly in relation to the two outstanding features of Western civilization—
science and democracy, was the way to save China.

Zhang Junmai (known in the West as Carsun Chang) represented the
line of thinking that advocated parliamentary democracy in China. The
dream of his life was to draft and put into effect a national constitution and
to organize a workable parliament, based principally on the British model,
with certain modifications to suit China's particular conditions. Zhang
Dongsun, a close friend and colleague of Zhang Junmai, followed the same
line of thinking; thus, the two Zhangs may be grouped together. Hu and
the Zhangs were strong opponents of any kind of dictatorship of whatever
variety, be it the Kuomintang's one-party dictatorship or the Communist
Party's democratic dictatorship.

Liang Shuming, who based his program on his own analysis and comparison of three patterns of world cultures, concluded that Chinese culture was supreme. He was convinced that the revival of true Confucianism would save China and even the world from decline and destruction. Interestingly enough, although Liang Shuming advocated Confucianism as a philosophical ideal, his proposed practical reform was what he called rural reconstruction, whereby intellectuals would work alongside farmers in the countryside. This was a program with obvious parallels to the communist program, yet it was based on a very different ideology.

Chen Duxiu was another protagonist of China's new cultural movement, whose political thought had a checkered history. Prior to the May Fourth Movement, he was purely a bourgeois thinker who dreamed of making Western democracy and capitalism a perfect model for China. He was converted to communism in 1920; during his communist period, he believed in Marxism and favored the dictatorship of the proletariat. But his god of Soviet communism failed after some twenty years of bitter experiences with the Comintern, the Soviet Union, and Stalin. Shortly before his death in 1942, although he still believed in socialism, he reverted to his original belief, seeing democracy as having an intrinsic value that transcends time, classes, and social systems.

The last but most influential of these thinkers is Mao Zedong. Unlike the others mentioned above, except Sun Zhongshan, Mao was both a thinker and a revolutionary. He envisioned a communist society to be effected by a revolution. At an early stage in his revolutionary career, he organized a peasant army to seize political power from the Kuomintang. After that had succeeded, he led a continuous revolution, divided into various stages, toward the building of socialism and communism. In theory and practice, Mao was different from all the other representative people in their various approaches to China's reconstruction.

The nine thinkers included in this chapter differ in their programs of social reconstruction, but there is one important dividing line that sets Mao Zedong off from the rest. Mao, representing communist ideology, advocated violent revolution; the others favored a more gradual approach. Sun was a gradualist, in that once the Qing dynasty was overthrown, he intended to proceed by peaceful and gradual means. Mao advocated a command or administered economy; the other thinkers advocated a free-enterprise economy with varying degrees of socialism.

Communist power prevails over whatever other political parties exist in China today, as well as over all other schools of thought. Mao stated:

"Everything else has been tried and all failed."⁶ By "everything else" he included Kang Youwei's ideal of the Great Harmony, Sun Zhongshan's Three Principles of the People, and the democratic and liberal ideals of other scholars. In a sense, Mao was right in saying that all avenues except the communist way have failed, because the Communist Party is the political party in power. However, it is not true that everything else has been tried, because many democratic and liberal programs have had no chance to be carried out. For instance, the Kuomintang had neither the opportunity nor the ability to put Sun Zhongshan's principles into practice, partly because of internal strife among the warlords and the Kuomintang's fighting with the Communists and partly because of the circumstances of the Japanese aggression. The social programs of the other thinkers remained only theories on paper and were never put into effect. The reformers were never able to go beyond aspiration, inspiration, and persuasion in their programs of social reconstruction.

Since the introduction of communism into China at the turn of the twentieth century, it has been an increasingly powerful and widespread current of thought. Although noncommunist thinkers with independent ideas for national salvation opposed communist theory, they were nevertheless forced to regard communist theory as a powerful force to be dealt with. The choice was either to go along with communism or to oppose it; it was impossible to ignore it. Thus, we find that the intellectual history of modern China is a history of the struggle between those who support democracy and gradualism and those who support the Communist revolution. Communist writers are wont to categorize noncommunist thinkers of the past hundred years as reformists, while viewing themselves as revolutionaries. To use communist terminology, it is the struggle between two lines—the bourgeois line and the proletarian line.

Representative communist intellectual historians hold that all thought struggles (including national struggle) are an inseparable part of class struggle, developing in accordance with the development of social, economic, and political struggles. Furthermore, all modern Chinese thought struggles focus on the solution to the problem of the Chinese revolution. Since the modern Chinese revolution is a revolution of the masses against imperialism and feudalism, it follows that the history of modern Chinese thought is the history of the genesis and development of anti-imperialist and antifeudal thought among the masses for the past hundred years. At the same time, it is the history of the genesis, development, senility, and final decline of bourgeois and petty-bourgeois thought, and it is also the history of the growth and ultimate victory of proletarian thought. The modern revolutionary history of anti-imperialism and antifeudalism in China can be divided into two stages: the old democratic revolutionary stage and the new democratic revolutionary stage. Hence, the development of Chinese thought should also be divided into these two stages.[7] In a slightly different form, the development of modern thought is seen as a process by which reformist thought is replaced by revolutionary thought, and the revolutionary thought of other classes by that of the proletariat, ending in the proletarian victory over imperialism and feudalism in China.[8] What communist writers refer to as the bourgeois line, or the reformist line, is actually the democratic movement that began at the time of Kang Youwei.

Whether it is called the bourgeois line, the reformist line, or the democratic movement, it has been the liberal trend of Chinese political thought in the past century. The actions and beliefs of Kang Youwei and Liang Qichao, in their advocacy of a kind of constitutional monarchy aimed at the creation of a parliamentary form of government patterned after the British and at making the Manchu emperor a titular head, marked the beginning of the democratic movement in China. Politically, Sun Zhongshan's ideal government was also a form of democratic government. Other scholars, such as Hu Shi, Zhang Junmai, and Zhang Dongsun, together with a large group of intellectuals, also strongly believed in democracy. Liang Shuming, although his central emphasis lay elsewhere, was definitely in favor of democracy. Chen Duxiu began as an ardent advocate of democracy, was converted to communism for a time, and rejoined the democratic movement in his last years. But the communists claim that such people and their visions are gone.

Since I am a native Chinese of the generation born in the early years of the twentieth century, I grew up in an atmosphere of grave social upheavals, and I share—with both joy and sorrow—the concern for the destiny of China that resulted in the different programs for social reconstruction brought forth by the thinking of the men reviewed in this book. Thus, my understanding of their ideas is more intimate and direct than the understanding of either a non-Chinese or a member of the younger generation could be. In general, I believe that my understanding of these thinkers' ideas corresponds, to a considerable degree, with the great majority of Chinese intellectuals' understanding and that my aspirations for China similarly agree with theirs.

It is my belief that ideas dominate human minds and that their influence is long lasting. The present ideological conflicts in China are the outcome of conflicting ideas rooted in the past; the present political struggle in China is basically a reflection of past ideological differences. That is why thought reform or thought struggle has been tremendously emphasized in contemporary China. To even begin to understand modern China's problems and their possible solutions, it is necessary to have a precise comprehension of the ideological conflicts between the communist and noncommunist thinkers who competed for dominance during the twentieth century.

Notes

This chapter is reprinted from Ji Wenshun, *Ideological Conflicts in Modern China: Democracy and Authoritarianism* (New Brunswick, NJ: Transaction, 1992), pp. 1–10, with the permission of the publisher.

1. For a detailed account of the unequal treaties and their effect on modern China, see Jiang Jieshi (Chiang Kai-shek), "Zhongguo Zhi Mingyun," in *Jiang Zongtong Sixiang Yanlun Ji,* 4 vols. (Taipei: Zhongyang Wenwu Gongyingshe, 1966), 4: 11–23 (translated by Philip Jaffe as *China's Destiny and Chinese Economic Theory* [New York: Roy Publishers, 1947]).

2. R. R. Palmer, *A History of the Modern World,* 5th ed. (New York: Knopf, 1978), 637–38. I do not mean to suggest that this is a strict comparison; e.g., China never integrated Indochina as the United States did California.

3. Arnold J. Toynbee, *A Study of History,* abridgement of vol. 12 by D. C. Somervell (New York: Oxford University Press, 1957), 358.

4. Ibid., 360.

5. *The Works of Mencius,* Book 6, part 1, chap. 15, sec. 5, in *The Chinese Classics,* trans. James Legge, vols. 1 and 2 (Beijing: Wenzhe Chubanshe, 1970). All translations of the Confucian classics cited here are by James Legge, except where otherwise indicated.

6. Mao Zedong, "Lun Renmin Minzhu Zhuanzheng," in *Mao Zedong Xuanji,* 5 vols. (Beijing: Renmin Chubanshe, 1969–77), 4: 1361. Henceforth all translations of quotations from this work are based on the *Selected Works of Mao Tse-tung* (Beijing: Foreign Languages, 1967).

7. Shi Jun, Ren Jiyu, and Zhu Bokun, *Zhongguo Jindai Sixiangshi Jiangshou Tigang* (Beijing: Renmin Chubanshe, 1957), 9–10. This is a collective work by the faculty of Peking University, supplying an outline for teaching the history of modern Chinese thought. It represents, in general, the official line of Communist historians.

8. Ibid., 17.

2

The Debates in Contemporary Chinese Political Thought

Zhou Lian

Since the 1990s there has been a spate of interest in understanding why political philosophy is so fashionable in Mainland China. Since the viewpoints of the most influential political philosophers are very different and contradictory, more and more Chinese intellectuals have engaged in heated debate about whose theory is the most relevant to the current reality of China and its future. Because some realize that political philosophy should be assessed not only in terms of moral desirability but also with regard to cultural acceptability and socioeconomic feasibility, we should not be confused by the kaleidoscopic appearance of contemporary Chinese political philosophy, but rather penetrate the inner logic of the various theories and comprehend the ways in which they correspond to the reality of China today.

This chapter has two aims. The first is to provide an account of contemporary Chinese political philosophers' unique contributions to political theory. I will pay particular attention to one ideological trend and two scholars, respectively. Due to Chinese economic success over the last thirty years, especially after the Olympic games, the world financial crisis, and the sixtieth anniversary of the founding of the People's Republic of China, more and more Chinese scholars have recognized the ongoing revival of the national confidence of ordinary people. What has confused Chinese scholars most, however, is how to figure out a coherent and reasonable interpretation of the history of People's Republic of China, especially the relationship between its first thirty years (from 1949 to 1979) and the next thirty years (from 1979 to 2009). In order to explain the positive role of Chinese political institutions in the country's economic development, some scholars coined the notion "the China Model." The idea of the "China Model" or "Chinese characteristics" raises many related questions. For example, is China still under a form of socialism? What is the political legitimacy of the Chinese government? How can we understand socialist democracy? Can China offer another version of modernity? What kind of contribution will Chinese culture bring to the world? I do not intend to explore all those topics here; instead I will focus on two special issues: the discourse of political legitimacy in China and the unique understanding of democracy in China. Besides the "China Model," I will explore professor Gan Yang and Zhao Tingyang's ideas. Both specialize in Western philosophy, without, however, merely echoing Western ideas or repeating traditional Chinese concepts. Both are committed to the arduous task of transforming Chinese traditional thought, so as to develop original and debate-provoking ideas.

The second aim of this chapter is to give a general picture of contemporary Western political philosophy in China in the twenty-first century. More than one hundred years have gone by since Chinese intellectuals first introduced Western political ideas into China. Although the process was interrupted for nearly thirty years in the middle of the twentieth century, for well-known reasons, the trend of introducing Western thought was resumed in the 1980s. After Tiananmen Square, many Chinese scholars began to reflect upon the whole intellectual process of the twentieth century. On the one hand, some advocated a gradual and evolutionary approach to change and called for a "Farewell to Revolution"; by contrast, others chose to go back to studying classical texts. These two approaches have developed very distinctively. Among those who advocate a gradual, evolutionary approach, there are two competing positions. Some, known as the "New Left," have argued that the goal of national strength and stability should be put above any absolute commitment to the "rational autonomy" of the individual. On the other hand, those proponents of a gradual approach who advocate a free market and the limitation of governmental power are called "liberals" or "liberalists." These two gradualist sides have long debated how to maintain a balance between issues of equality and economic development, their members including political scientists, economists, socialists, and political philosophers. While the present essay will not go into this debate in any detail, this is not because it is no longer important or influential in today's China, but rather because many introductory and analytical articles examining it have been published in the West since the 1990s.

In comparison with the gradualist group, there is less diversity among those who advocate a return to classical studies. Most of the proponents of this approach are philosophers and humanists. Even though they could all be labeled as "conservatives," what they want to conserve and the resources they depend on are very different. Some have moved from criticizing Chinese tradition to researching it, especially Confucian texts. Others have resumed the translation of Western classics; among them, the Straussians possibly have been the most popular, the most organized, and the best-funded group of the past ten years in Mainland China. As a result, many Chinese intellectuals are confused and anxious about the popularity of the Straussians in universities, wondering which "esoteric" and "exoteric" reasons are responsible for this. Meanwhile, most of Carl Schmitt's books have been translated into Chinese and have also led to heated debate. In this essay I will focus on Leo Strauss and Carl Schmitt, since both thinkers are particularly fashionable in present-day China and the main theoretical sources of much Chinese criticism of liberalism. Before accepting their ideas, every Chinese political philosopher, I believe, should ask himself or herself the following questions: Why should we Chinese read these scholars today? Does their conception of politics have any pertinence to Chinese circumstances? Is there anything we can learn from their theories?

By analyzing these philosophers' ideas and influences, I hope to answer two distinct but related questions: Why are they so popular, and whose ideas are relevant to the context and issues of Chinese political tradition and existing political practices?

THE "CHINA MODEL" DEBATE

Five years ago, Joshua Ramo, a journalist from *Time* magazine, coined the new term "Beijing Consensus" to summarize Chinese economic success: a combination of mixed ownership, basic property rights, heavy government intervention, and so on. In contrast to the "Beijing Consensus," terminology based in a Western perspective, people in China and elsewhere now prefer the similar term the "China Model" to analyze the achievements, if any, of political reform in China and to anticipate the potential contributions of Chinese political reform to world history.

Four essays have been labeled by some liberals as "Declarations of

Nationalism" since 2008: Gan Yang's "From the First Emancipation of Mind to the Second Emancipation of Mind," Zhu Suli's "The Comparative Study between Socialism's Rule of Law and Capitalism's Rule of Law," Jiang Shigong's "Presidency of the People's Republic of China: On the Building and Improvement of a Constitution of 'Trinity,'" and Wang Shaoguang's "The Possibilities of Political Study." Although the term "China Model" appears only once in these four essays, all refuse to invoke Western ideas and conceptual schemes to interpret the Chinese experience; the authors believe it is time to claim that China has succeeded in providing an alternative to Western modernity, not only in economy but also in politics. Specifically, the system of a one-party state is no longer regarded as a negative feature of the last sixty years, but as a positive one. For example, Zhu Suli points out that the main characteristic of Chinese socialism's rule of law is the leadership of the Communist Party; Jiang Shigong argues that the government characteristic of the Chinese Constitution can be labeled a trinity (composed of the Communist Party, politics, and the military), with one person holding the titles of general secretary of the Communist Party of China, president of the People's Republic of China, and chairman of the Central Military Commission.

Although many use the terms "China Model," "Chinese characteristics," and the "Chinese experience" interchangeably, there are some important differences among these terms. The "Chinese experience" is a neutral, descriptive term that does not have any further theoretical implication; by contrast, "Chinese characteristics" is a kind of theoretical term; it appears in the wake of almost every attempt to react against the Western model. Compared with this term's reactive character, "China Model" is rather an active theoretical construction that implies another kind of discourse of universalism, different from the Western discourse. Paradoxically, while "China Model" does have a universalist implication, some scholars who support it do not claim universalism explicitly but emphasize that they do not intend to provide a model for other states to mimic.

How to understand the apparent tension between universalism and particularism embodied in the discourse of the China Model? Is it theoretical confusion or political strategy? What are the substantive claims of the China Model? Before exploring these themes, I would like first to examine a general philosophical issue, that is, the contrast between universalism and particularism, which is the philosophical underpinning of debates over the China Model.

In general, there are two kinds of views on the nature of political philosophy. The first is that political philosophy is applied ethics. While political philosophy shares with political science its concern for accurately describing the realities of political life, the distinctive aspect of political philosophy is "its prescriptive or evaluative concern with justification, values, virtues, ideals, rights, obligations—in short, its concern with how political societies should be, how political policies and institutions can be justified, how we and our political officeholders ought to behave in our public lives."[1] In this sense, political philosophy can be aptly characterized as a branch or an application of moral philosophy. By contrast, the second view is that political philosophy is quite different from ethics; it is concerned with political actions and political strategies—with power, in other words, not with rights or justice. The former view has been shared by most political philosophers in Western intellectual history, from Plato to Aristotle, Locke, Kant, and John Rawls (although the later Rawls emphasizes the political dimension of justice, he never denies it has a moral dimension). The representatives of the second view also have a long tradition, the list including the ancient Greek sophists, Machiavelli, Hobbes, and more recently Raymond Geuss and Bernard Williams. However they differ, they share a core understanding of the pragmatic nature of political philosophy and could be labeled "realists." Roughly speaking, the contrast between these two understandings of political philosophy echoes the ancient dichotomy between nature (*physis*) and convention (*nomos*), or, to use Isaiah Berlin's terms, between *monism* and *relativism*.

According to Berlin, the underlying belief of monism is that to all true questions there must be one true answer and one only, all the other answers being false, for otherwise the questions cannot be genuine questions. There must exist a path that leads clear thinkers to the correct answers to these questions, as much in the moral, social, and political worlds as in the natural sciences; once all the correct answers to the deepest moral, social, and political questions that occupy (or should occupy) humankind are put together, the result will represent the final solution to all the problems of existence. While Berlin objects to monism, it doesn't follow that he embraces relativism. Rather, he regards himself as a "value pluralist."

What, then, is the difference between pluralism and relativism? According to Berlin, relativism maintains that different values are arbitrary and incommensurable; for example, my values are mine, yours are yours, and if we clash, too bad—neither of us can claim to be right. Hence, there is neither argument nor discussion among relativists. In some sense, pluralism shares two points with relativism: first, that there are different values that cannot be reduced to one; and second, that there might be no objective standard to assess different values. Nevertheless, what is distinctive about pluralism—what makes it different from relativism, according to Berlin—is that the multiple values are an objective part of the essence of humanity rather than arbitrary creations of men's subjective fancies. And more important, for Berlin, if I pursue one set of values I may detest another and think it is damaging to the only form of life I am able to tolerate, for myself and others; in this case I may attack it and even—in extreme cases—go to war against it.

It seems, however, that Berlin does not succeed in distinguishing pluralism from relativism. As long as he maintains that different values are objective and incommensurable, value pluralism is taking a big risk of being reduced to value relativism. It is wrong to address the conflicts between different values solely by making emotional claims of damage to one's form of life; such claims are too subjective and arbitrary to be standards.

As Habermas points out, overcoming both moral relativism and modern value skepticism is his and John Rawls's common task.[2] Their main method is to construct basic moral laws and political principles through public reason. I am not going to articulate their ideas; instead I will put forward some of my own conclusions in light of their thought. First, rejecting moral relativism is not the same as rejecting any kind of universalism. Furthermore, in order to overcome value skepticism and relativism, we need to argue for universalism in the sense of public reason. Second, universalism in the sense of public reason is not purely procedural but upholds some very basic values that guarantee the possibility of healthy political argument and public discussion. Third, the foundation of these basic values is not metaphysical but historical; that is to say, it is neither transcendental nor self-evident; the foundation itself could be examined and discussed through public reasoning. Finally, we must realize that it is impossible to defeat relativism once and for all on a theoretical level; we have to argue with it in every particular case, which is a tough and endless job.

Keeping these basic ideas in mind, I will show the force and bearing of this general debate between universalism and relativism on contemporary Chinese political issues. I agree with Ronald Dworkin's idea[3] that as long as people share common ground or very basic political principles, and debate which concrete policies better reflect these shared principles, real argument is possible. Until now, no matter how the Chinese government and some scholars highlighted the significance of the "China Model," they still used the basic ideas of the Enlightenment and modernity: the rule of law, democracy, human rights, and so on. That is a shared platform from which different parties may argue.

In the following I will focus on two special issues: the unique understanding of democracy in China and the discourse of political legitimacy in China. So far as I know, there are two typical approaches to interpreting democracy in China: redefining democracy by replacing it with the state's capability, and highlighting the merits of deliberative democracy over electoral democracy. Both of them tend to reject the conventional democracy paradigm of the West.

Recently, Wang Shaoguang has argued in many articles and interviews that Western democracy has failed and become a so-called electocracy. The key to Chinese political change (he prefers the word *change* to *reform*) is not to follow the West or to set up Western competitive electoral institutions, but to promote ordinary peoples' interests. In order to achieve that goal, China must strengthen the state's capabilities. Wang Shaoguang defines democracy as "a combination of responsibility, responsiveness, and accountability." He claims that only when political reform is no longer solely equated with competitive elections can the true nature of political change in China come to light.

The other approach is to replace conventional competitive democracy with deliberative democracy. Some scholars claim that this is what the Chinese government has been doing since 1949, for instance, through the institution of the Chinese People's Political Consultative Conference, Villagers' Self-Administration in rural China, and so on.

Clement Attlee said in 1957, "Democracy means government by discussion, but it is only effective if you can stop people from talking." This implies that the crux of the matter is figuring out how to stop people from talking, or how decisions can be made after talking in the process of democracy. This, then, is the most important criterion for judging whether or not a society is a democracy. Deliberation and discussion play a very important role in democracy, but they are not the only things that matter; the role of elections and ballots as the expression of the effectiveness of the process of public reasoning is also very important. In some sense, without monitored democratic elections, the idea of democracy is nonsense upon stilts.

Similarly, there is no doubt that responsibility, responsiveness, and accountability are very important aspects of democracy. But it does not follow that they are sufficient to define democracy. Abraham Lincoln expressed clearly what democracy means in his famous Gettysburg Address. He called it government of the people, by the people, and for the people. These three elements are correlative and inseparable parts of democracy, but only the second, "by the people," is distinctively democratic. Wang Shaoguang argues that real democracy comes when the people can express their will and the government can respond successfully. The implication is that the Chinese government is for the people, but not by the people. This might be a sort of enlightened absolutism or responsive authoritarianism. but it is not real democracy.

Now let us consider the issue of political legitimacy. As we all know, Marx and Engels label their theories "scientific socialism," declaring them to be in accordance with historical law; therefore this approach reflects the only truth about the nature of human society. Classical Marxism, then, belongs to monism, or to use Karl Popper's term, historical determinism. When Marxism was introduced into China at the beginning of the twentieth century, the Chinese Communist Party (CCP), in spite of the theory's transformation, never doubted that Marxism is the only truth; it provided the foundation of the legitimacy of the revolution and the People's Republic of China. However, this foundation shifted with the end of the Cultural Revolution; after this point, the CCP seldom claimed Marxism as timeless truth, instead maintaining that every state develops its own approach. From scientific socialism to "Chinese characteristics," it is a great leap from monism to relativism. Just as Yao Yang, a professor from Beijing University, said, "Since the Chinese Communist Party (CCP) lacks legitimacy in the classic democratic sense, it has been forced to seek performance-based legitimacy instead, by continuously improving the living standards of Chinese citizens." Yao Yang's conclusion is that "so far, this strategy has succeeded, but there are signs that it will not last because of the growing income inequality and the internal and external imbalances it has created."[4] In my opinion, the performance-based strategy is destined to lose not because of growing income inequality, but because it is not the right approach to legitimating the state.

Traditionally, there are two different approaches to justifying the state, an emergent approach and a teleological approach. In light of the ideas of Hannah Arendt, A. John Simmons, and David Schmitz, the former approach takes justification to be an emergent property of the process by which political powers arise, which can be labeled legitimacy; by contrast, the latter approach seeks to justify political powers in terms of what they accomplish, which cannot be labeled legitimacy but only justification. Thus, against the background of modernity, any government whose political power does not come from the people has no legitimacy, no matter how it is used to benefit the people. Unless we make a sharp distinction between legitimacy and justification, we won't realize why the performance-based strategy to legitimate the state is destined to fail.

On February 22, 2010, the *People's Daily,* one of the most important official media outlets of the CCP, published an article on the rule of law. The author maintained that China is totally different from the West, in terms of political institutions, the rule of law, economic institutions, ideologies, cultural traditions, and so on. He concluded that it is hopeless for China to copy Western institutions completely. No doubt only an extreme version of relativism rejects any discussion and evaluation of different values, and this topic has been no more than a platitude for every Chinese since childhood. However, more and more Chinese have begun to accept these ideas since 2008; they feel proud of their country, for China is the only ancient civilization in human history to have reemerged as a major force in the world. It is unwise to be insensitive to such reasonable national confidence. Generally, then, liberalism in China faces two challenges. First, theoretically, liberalism becomes virtually synonymous with the philosophical demeanor itself and has less ability to interpret Chinese experience. Second, practically, liberalism is losing its chance to acquire political power as a prejudiced and fighting creed (or set of creeds); on the contrary, it has been defined as an antistate framework.

There is still ongoing debate over the so-called China Model. Most liberals deny it and maintain that the Chinese experience is still a version of capitalism, even a worse one; by contrast, some New Leftists and conservatives are trying their best to figure out a coherent theory of the China Model, while hesitating to claim universalistic implications. "China Model" might be the most fashionable term in contemporary Chinese political thought; however, it is difficult to catch its exact meaning and specific content. In my view, no matter what it is, it should not provide an excuse to reject any influence from outside or to suppress any healthy discussion from inside.

GAN YANG'S "INTEGRATION OF THREE TRADITIONS"

A number of facets characterize the academic career of Gan Yang. He has changed his standpoints at least three times since the 1980s. First of all, according to his own words, he was a liberal. It was he who first introduced into China Isaiah Berlin's famous essay "Two Conceptions of Liberty." It had a wide impact on Chinese intellectuals but unexpectedly led to a rejection of democracy in the name of liberalism and of the French Revolution in favor of the English Revolution. Then, at the end of the 1990s, Gan wrote another essay, "A Critique of Chinese Conservatism" (the more impressive Chinese title is "Liberalism: For Autocrats or for the People?"). By that time he was already known as one of the most important leaders of the New Left, a label he never truly accepted, preferring the term liberal Left. And finally, in 2002, he wrote a very long introduction to the Chinese version of Leo Strauss's *Natural Right and History* and has since been regarded by most Chinese scholars as a conservative. Once again, I doubt that he would accept such a label.

Gan Yang's very complex and interesting academic background is not the reason for discussing him here. Despite their differences and similarities, the terms *liberal, liberal Left,* and *conservative* are not so unique. A more interesting idea recently developed by Gan is the so-called integration of three traditions, according to which, in order to show the strength of Chinese political power and maintain the accomplishments so far obtained by economical transformation, we should combine old Chinese traditions (Confucian ones in particular) with the traditions of Mao Zedong and Deng Xiaoping.

Gan first coined this unique phrase in a newspaper interview at the end of 2004. He came back to it in a public lecture at Tsinghua University in 2005. According to Gan, the main points of Deng's tradition are the market economy and the notions of liberty and rights; Mao's tradition is based on equality and social justice, whereas deep-rooted cultural values and ideals form the core of the Confucian tradition. Gan thereby concurs with the ideas of Daniel Bell, in that modern society is made up of different and contradictory factors, with no single factor ever having supremacy over the others. Consequently, for a better understanding of modern society, one should not use only one theory or model, but rather depend on a variety of different models. Bell said that he is economically socialist, politically liberal, and culturally conservative. Gan follows Bell's approach and ranks his own values in order: he is first socialist, second conservative, and then liberal. In other words, Gan suggests that only by insisting upon the tradition of socialism and classical culture can China develop liberalism.

Gan has recently written a new paper, "The Chinese Way: Thirty Years and Sixty Years" (2007), the core ideas of which are similar to the above-mentioned "integration of three traditions." In this essay he advances the new term "Confucian Socialist Republic" to interpret the meaning of the People's Republic of China. On the one hand, Gan claims that "China" refers to Chinese culture. Since the main components of Chinese culture are Confucianism and other factors such as Taoism and Buddhism, "China" is the equivalent of, and could be replaced by, "Confucian." On the other hand, "People's Republic" means that this is not a republic of capital interests but one of workers, peasants and, other laborers: a "Socialist Republic."[5] Gan claims that a "new consensus of reform" should be based upon acceptance of the legitimacy of the three traditions. First of all, China's official policy of "social harmony" is deeply rooted in Confucian tradition, which fundamentally differs from "class struggle." Second, the purpose of "social harmony" is to pursue "common wealth," which was the core aim of Mao's tradition. Third, this purpose cannot be attained without the market economy. Gan admits that there are continuing and essential tensions among these three traditions. However, in order to maintain the unique character of "the Chinese way," this "new consensus of reform" must necessarily comprise all three of these traditions.[6]

It is difficult to find any strong arguments to support Gan's views. For example, he quotes Susan Shirly's idea that Mao actually created better conditions for later transformation by destroying centralized control. However, there is a difference between doing so intentionally and mere random destruction. It is unacceptable to confuse causal and diachronic relations. Although Gan gives us an idealized model for a political legitimacy, he gives us no political program for achieving this.

Shadia B. Drury points out that Strauss believed that intellectuals have an important role to play in politics. It was not prudent for them to rule directly because the masses are inclined to distrust them; but they should certainly not pass up the opportunity to whisper in the ears of the powerful. In my opinion, the idea of "integrating three traditions" shows that Gan Yang is precisely trying to whisper in the ears of the powerful, although his exegesis looks as if it is "exoteric" and not "esoteric."

Zhao Tingyang's Idea of "All-Under-Heaven"

Zhao Tingyang has been widely acknowledged as one of the leading members of the new generation of Chinese philosophers, ever since the 1993 publication of his second book, *On Possible Life.* Since then he has published eight books, the latest three being *The World without a World-view, The System of All-Under-Heaven: A Philosophical Introduction to a World Institution,* and *Investigation of the Bad World: Political Philosophy as First Philosophy.*

Zhao has developed two main types of methodology over the last ten years: the so-called syn-text and non-stance analyses. According to him, "it should not be a surprise that the central focus of philosophical work nowadays is on political or ethical philosophy."[7] This is because "there are economic concerns behind contemporary political and ethical issues, and therefore political issues are structurally linked to economic ones. Since cultural issues are closely related to the historical stance of political problems, and perhaps to a deep structure of politics and economics, the historical structure of philosophy thus comes into being: a structure based on politics, economics and culture" (*World,* 1). Zhao subsequently concludes that contemporary philosophers should seek answers in such reciprocal knowledge structures. As a matter of fact, the concept of "reciprocal knowledge" has recently been developed in one European epistemological movement.

Without knowing the term beforehand, Zhao created a term similar to "reciprocal knowledge" almost at the same time. He names it "syn-text," which means that "given encyclopedic knowledge about any one thing, there needs to be mutual rewriting of various knowledge systems by some kind of method, so that we can, first of all, structurally change those knowledge systems and then, secondly, jointly create new knowledge and questions" (*World,* 2).

The other type of methodology is "non-stance" analysis. This requires the thinker "to suspend his own preferences or inclinations when making justifications, thereby seeing, hearing and understanding others" (*World,* 3). The approach of old philosophy is "from myself to others." Zhao's methodology of "non-stance" analysis, on the contrary, is "from others to myself." Zhao stresses that the principle of philosophical analysis should be "from others" or "from things." Just as Laozi summarized more than two thousand years ago: "A man can only be understood in terms of his interests, a village can only be understood in terms of its situation, a state can only be understood from the point of view of a state, and all-under-heaven can only be understood from the perspective of all-under-heaven" (4). Although one may doubt the possibility of such pure "non-stance" analysis, this "see X from X" principle could be very helpful for us to understand the world from its own perspective and for its own sake.

In my opinion, two of Zhao's ideas deserve to be highlighted: "all-under-heaven as a world institution" and the "Chinese representation of philosophy." Let us start with the latter. The phrase "Chinese representation of philosophy" should be understood in the light of two aspects: one "the representation of philosophy" in general and the other the "Chinese representation of philosophy" in particular. Zhao does not deal with the former ad hoc in his book, but we can ascertain his basic attitude to this question, that is, trying his best to use ordinary language instead of theoretical terms. I interpret this as meaning "let philosophy speak in ordinary language," an approach in which many will recognize the influence of Wittgenstein. For Zhao, the "Chinese representation of philosophy" could be interpreted as "letting philosophy speak in Chinese." This is in fact the main point that Zhao argues in his book.

Zhao says that for a long time Chinese-Western comparative cultural studies have used a unilateral approach based only on Western standards. In other words, Chinese culture has been only the interpreted, not the interpreter. Therefore, according to Zhao, every Chinese philosopher should ask the question of whether or not Chinese philosophy can be a part of world philosophy. To put it concretely, can Chinese philosophy be not only an object of study for Westerners but also living words contributing to world philosophy as a whole (*World*, 159–64)?

In order to answer this question positively, Zhao thinks that great efforts must be made in two fields: first, some traditional Chinese concepts should be made a part of the system of world thought; and second, some particular Chinese questions should be made a part of the system of world issues. He claims that only when some key traditional Chinese concepts become universalized will Chinese philosophy be a tool and basis of universal thought; only when philosophy is also voiced in Chinese can it, and the world itself, be represented differently. Furthermore, Zhao points out that there will be three key themes in the philosophy of the future: (1) the theory of communication and cooperation; (2) the philosophy of the mind; and (3) the relationship between rights and obligations. Chinese philosophy should contribute to resolving these problems (*World*, 178–79).

If Zhao's intention is to answer the question of how Chinese philosophy can contribute to world philosophy by means of the "Chinese representation of philosophy," then "all-under-heaven" as a world institution is his practical and direct response to this question.

All-under-heaven as a world institution has been the focus (and the title) of his presentations at two international conferences, "Universal Knowledge and Reciprocal Knowledge" (Goa, India, November 2002) and "Empire and Peace" (Paris, France, February 2003). Beginning with the amazing statement "Our supposed world is still a non-world," Zhao argues that "the world we have now is one of geographical oneness rather than political oneness . . . for there is no coherent world society under a universally accepted world institution" (*World*, 7). In order to organize the global reality into a "world," a world institution seems necessary. But according to Zhao, "in the Western political framework, the greatest political entity is found to be the state, which thus confines the Western understanding of political theory to the perspective of the state."

Consequently, "Western representations of world totality are nothing else but internationalism, the United Nations or globalization, with nothing going beyond the framework of nation-states. Such projects have essential difficulties to attain the oneness of the world, as a result of the limitations of the perspectives of nation-states" (*World*, 12). In accordance with the principle of non-stance analysis, it is obvious that seeing the world from the perspective of the world as a whole is not the same thing as seeing it from the angle of just one individual part. Western philosophy lacks a worldview from the angle of the world as a whole; its standpoint is that of state ideology. Furthermore, it lacks a global concept of the world, despite its scientific concepts. In contrast, argues Zhao, the traditional Chinese notion "all-under-heaven" provides just such a global concept of the world. In his opinion, the term "all-under-heaven" is essential for any possible comprehension of the Chinese perception of the world, society, institutions, and polity (9–10).

By analyzing such traditional Chinese concepts as "all-inclusiveness," or "nothing excluded," and "rite," Zhao argues that Chinese philosophy's main contribution to political theory could be the notion of "all-under-heaven." Zhao further developed this theory, publishing a revised version of it in 2005, under the title *The System of All-Under-Heaven: A Philosophical Introduction to a World Institution*. In my opinion, the central idea of this book is the notion of "all-under-heaven as an empire and a world institution"; the only difference is that Zhao replaces the methodology of "non-stance" analysis with two distinct but interrelated types of methodol-

ogy: "methodological holism" and "the principle of consistency and transference between different political systems." According to Zhao, the main
difference between Chinese philosophy and that of Western countries is
one of methodology when it comes to understanding political institutions.[8] These two types of methodology play different roles in the revised
version of "all-under-heaven." By introducing the idea of "methodological
holism," Zhao rejects liberal "methodological individualism" and claims
that in order to see the world from the perspective of the world as a whole,
it is necessary to start from the biggest political unit, the world itself, or
"all-under-heaven." He argues that instead of "justifying the state," the central project of political philosophy should be "justifying the world."

The world thus replaces the state as the legitimate starting point of
political philosophy (*System*, 135). This leads to an extremely judicious
analysis. However, although one may agree that "seeing the world from the
perspective of the world as a whole" and "methodological holism" are altogether desirable objectives, the question of whether or not they are feasible
remains.

In order to answer this question, "the principle of consistency and
transference between different political systems" needs to be introduced.
The meaning of this methodology is that "given any political institution
. . . it must be able to be generalized on all levels, that is, applied to any
political unit, and transferred across different levels in any political system.
Otherwise, it is theoretically incomplete" (*System*, 141). In terms of this
methodology, one should not only "see X from X" (e.g., a family from the
perspective of a family, a village from that of a village, a state from that of
a state, and all-under-heaven from that of all-under-heaven); the structure
of political institutions across family, village, state, and all-under-heaven
should also have a strict logical isomorphism and be easily transferable.
Thus, by introducing this methodology, starting from the family as a premise, one arrives at the most important of all institutions, "all-under-heaven."

There is no doubt that Zhao's methodology is totally different from
most modern approaches. *Gemeinschaft* and *Gesellschaft* are sociological
categories introduced by the German sociologist Ferdinand Tönnies for
two normal types of human association. However, according to Zhao, the
essence of the political sphere is not only to organize and arrange a *Gesellschaft* but also to live a good life in a *Gemeinschaft*. Since the family is the
most desirable basic ethical and political institution, it should serve as a
model for supreme political institutions as a whole.

It is unfair to assert that Zhao has completely neglected the acknowledged categorical distinction made by Tönnies, since he holds that the
idea "all-under-heaven," in contrast with the Western concept of empire,
is closely related to the supposedly universal *eidos* of an empire. In other
words, all-under-heaven is a concept that refers to the ideal of an empire: it
is more related to the *eidos* than to the historical status of empires. Basically
speaking, it is merely a utopia.[9]

Connected with the above-mentioned defect, another mistake Zhao
might make is that he confuses the aims of moral philosophy and political philosophy. For me, the former's concern is "How should I (we) lead a
good life?" while the latter's concern is "How should we live together?" It
is unacceptable to replace the latter with the former in a reasonable pluralistic modern society, for this would cause "the fact of oppression." While
the topics explored by Zhao are radical and fresh, as compared with the
concerns of "old" philosophy, I do not think that he has found adequate
conceptual schemes and methodology to deal with these topics. However,
their theoretical charm is still altogether fascinating.

Leo Strauss and Carl Schmitt in Mainland China

Stanley Rosen once said, "A very, very significant circle of Strauss admirers
has sprung up in, of all places, China." Fortunately or not, this observation
is absolutely correct. Leo Strauss was first introduced into China in 1985.[10]
Eight years later, his *History of Political Philosophy* was translated into Chinese. However, at that time few Chinese scholars noticed the significance
of his thought. This situation did not change until Liu Xiaofeng decided to
interpret and popularize Strauss's thought in the year 2000.

Liu is one of the most distinguished scholars in Mainland China. He
has written more than thirteen books since the end of the 1980s and has
translated and introduced the work of a number of Western philosophers,
sociologists, and theologians, including Max Scheler, Leo Strauss, Alexan-
dre Kojève, and Carl Schmitt.

In 2000, Liu launched the series "Hermes: Classics and Interpretation."
Since then, more than one hundred academic works have been translated
into Chinese as part of this series, most of them interpretations of Western
classical texts, especially Greek writings. Meanwhile, some of Leo Strauss's
books, such as *The Political Philosophy of Hobbes, On Tyranny,* and *Natural
Right and History,* have also been translated; some of his disciples' works,

like Allan Bloom's *The Closing of the American Mind* and *Giant and Dwarf,* and Stanley Rosen's *The Mask of Enlightenment* and *The Quarrel between Philosophy and Poetry,* have also been introduced into China.

Liu Xiaofeng and his followers take such a keen interest in Leo Strauss and seek to spread his ideas for very complex reasons. Two literal explanations for their interest are perhaps to be found in their essays. First, on a theoretical level, they agree with what Leo Strauss called going "back to the classics" and with his claim of being able to understand what classical writers such as Plato said, in just the same way as they understood themselves. This implies that most modern scholars have misinterpreted the classics, unable to abandon their own theoretical burdens and *Vorsicht.* Second, on a practical level, they are concerned about the consequences of skepticism and nihilism, attributing these to modernity and liberalism. Chinese Straussians seek to reconcile traditional values with the modern world.

As we already know, Straussianism became prominent and influential in U.S. academic circles as a result of the myth that it formed the theoretical backbone of the Bush administration's foreign policy and the war in Iraq. This exaggerated belief is precisely what some Chinese Straussians have accepted, since it leads them to believe that, as members of a chosen few who know the truth, they also will be entitled to rule the world someday. In present-day China, unlike in the United States, being a critic of liberalism or democracy, or both, is not at all dangerous. On the contrary, such a position gains the critic a reputation as being more thoughtful and profound than vulgar liberals. Liu has a particular aversion to liberalism and democracy, and his literary talent easily impresses eager young Chinese, attracted as they are by this scholar and his ideas opposing modernity.

Liu's interpretation of Leo Strauss flows directly from Heinrich Meier. This gives his approach a preference for political theology. In contrast with Liu, Gan Yang, who wrote a renowned introduction to the Chinese version of *Natural Right and History,* emphasizes the political implications of Straussian thought. Leo Strauss's ideas have strengthened Liu's resolve to seek an absolute standard for moral values and to criticize liberalism as being the cause of declining social mores and moral nihilism. On the other hand, Carl Schmitt's influence has helped him reject liberal democracy and pursue what he calls "great politics."

Liu argues that the political context of present-day China is similar to that of post-Bismarck Germany. As a result of radical transformations in society, cases of social inequality abound, leading to heated debates about the liberal economy and social justice. Here Weberian influences make themselves heard: Chinese scholars are politically immature and fail to recognize China's economic maturity. Political maturity remains, however, the main priority.[11]

Because he misunderstands the essence of politics, Liu agrees with Schmitt that liberalism considers social welfare and justice as political criteria, thereby confounding the political order and the legal order and failing to recognize that the former is a question of legitimacy, not legality. In order to justify this point, Liu argues (105–6) that the "state of warfare" induced Chinese scholar Yan Fu to abandon liberal democracy, while a "national crisis" led Max Weber to claim that a nation-state's interests and power were paramount. Liu's argument is not valid, since his conclusion does not respect the premises on which it rests. Moreover, his claim implies that whatever the circumstances, liberal democracy is impotent and that a nation-state's interests and power take precedence over any other consideration.

Carl Schmitt suggests that only the church can constitute the basis of political legitimacy. With the separation of church and state, then, political legitimacy was emptied of its essence. Liu concludes that the fundamental problem of modernity is the vacuity of legitimacy and that the only way to escape this predicament is to adopt Schmitt's distinction, in the political sphere, between "friend" and "enemy." For Liu and Schmitt, politics identifies the essence and existence of a community. Political sovereignty is an existential question, since it concerns the resolution of an existential conflict.

In my opinion, by advancing a theological position, this neoconservative school of thought intentionally depreciates philosophy. It discards history and experience by emphasizing a transcendental dimension. By adopting an "either/or" attitude, it seriously compromises itself between the two extremes of absolute legitimacy and absolute illegitimacy. This type of "existential politics" not only lacks the necessary "serenity of thought" but also includes dangerous connotations in terms of nihilism and political immaturity.

Liu's final words are that "the appropriate education of legislators is the primary premise of 'superior politics'" (270). This is obviously an echo of what Plato says in *The Republic* and what is stated in classical Confucian texts: that the core of politics is the self-cultivation, ethics, and statecraft of rulers (legislators and administrators). As Mark Lilla says, anyone who tries to learn from Carl Schmitt "should be scrupulous in distinguishing liberalism's genuinely philosophical critics from those who practice the politics of theoretical despair"; he or she will learn nothing at all if this elementary distinction is not made.[12] In my opinion, every Chinese scholar should keep Lilla's words in mind whenever he begins to read Carl Schmitt and Leo Strauss.

John Rawls specifies four roles for political philosophy.[13] Regarding the fourth role, he says: "We view political philosophy as realistically utopian: that is, as probing the limits of practicable political possibility." In my opinion, political philosophy is realistic because it should maintain its cultural acceptability and socioeconomic feasibility; it is also utopian, since its purpose should be morally desirable. Finding a balance between these two dimensions requires practical wisdom. As Aristotle writes, to avoid becoming impractical political thinkers, we should consider "what sort of government must be most in accordance with our aspirations, if there is no external impediment," but we must also consider "what kind of government is adapted to particular states" (*Politics* IV.1). In other words, although it is necessary "to know the form of government which is best suited to states in general," it is also essential "to say how a state may be constituted in any given conditions." Most important of all, it is necessary to know "not only what form of government is best, but also what is possible." Since "the best is often unattainable," the true legislator "ought to be acquainted also with what is best relative to circumstances" (V.1–2).

The most important thing is to identify conditions in present-day China, providing that we begin by studying Chinese political philosophy. No progress can be expected until most Chinese scholars reach some kind of consensus on this point. Besides a failure to reach consensus, in the current context, the second worst thing would be to regard what is most fashionable as also most desirable; the worst would be to equate what is most fashionable with what is most relevant.

NOTES

1. A. John Simmons, *Political Philosophy* (New York: Oxford University Press, 2008), 2.

2. Jürgen Habermas, *The Inclusion of the Other: Studies in Political Theory*, ed. Ciaran Cronin and Pablo DeGrief (Cambridge, MA: MIT Press, 1998), 79.

3. Ronald Dworkin, *Is Democracy Possible Here? Principles for a New Political Debate* (Princeton, NJ: Princeton University Press, 2006), 4–5.

4. Yao Yang, "The End of the Beijing Consensus," *Foreign Affairs* 89 (2010): 24–26.

5. Gan Yang, "The Road to China: Thirty Years and Sixty Years," *Dushu* 6 (2004): 5.

6. Ibid.

7. Zhao Tingyang, *The World without a World-view* (in Chinese) (Beijing: Renmin University Press, 2003), 1 (hereafter cited in the text).

8. Zhao Tingyang, *The System of All-Under-Heaven: A Philosophical Introduction to a World Institution* (in Chinese) (Beijing: Jiang Su Educational Press, 2005), 23 (hereafter cited in the text).

9. Ibid., 40.

10. See Jeet Heer, "The Philosopher," *Boston Globe,* May 11, 2003, http://www.boston.com/news/globe/ideas/articles/2003/05/11/The_philosopher/.

11. Liu Xiaofeng, *The Modernists and Their Enemy: An Introduction to Carl Schmitt* (in Chinese) (Beijing: Hua Xia Press, 2006), 123 (hereafter cited in the text).

12. Mark Lilla, *The Reckless Mind: Intellectuals in Politics* (New York: New York Review of Books, 2001), 76.

13. John Rawls, *Justice as Fairness: A Restatement* (Cambridge, MA: Harvard University Press, 2001), 4.

3

All-Under-Heaven and Methodological Relationism

An Old Story and New World Peace

Zhao Tingyang

About twenty-five hundred years ago, a Chinese duke, lord of a sub-state in the all-under-heaven system, asked Confucius about "the most important thing" in the world. Confucius answered: "It must be politics."[1] The Chinese word for politics means "justified order," indicating the civilized order that determines the common fortune of all peoples. It defines a political concept not opposite but alternative to politics as the public life of the Greek polis. Earlier than Confucius, in the minds of the kings of the all-under-heaven system, the greatest and ultimate political goal was "to create harmony of all nations and all peoples,"[2] the earliest words on harmony, pointing to world politics rather than to the states and international politics. Greek and ancient China began politics with different political starting points, orientations, and pursuits. Polis developed state politics, while all-under-heaven invented world politics, both of which open the most important political spheres. It seems the creation of polis was more natural as a development from earlier communities, whereas the creation of all-under-heaven was something unusual and quite avant-garde in thinking and doing politics with world problems in the early days of civilization. I would like to renew the concept of all-under-heaven, since globalization is now inviting world politics to come again, or to come in the future.

KNOWLEDGE OF FORTUNE AND
METHODOLOGICAL RELATIONISM

The knowledge of human actions and behaviors is that of fortune, that is, knowledge of the feasible or appropriate ways (*Taos*) of making better fortune for human beings instead of discovering the universal and necessary laws of nature. It is an approach essential to understanding Chinese philosophy. Roughly, China's spirit has a *Confucian heart* that decides basic values and a *Taoist mind* that chooses strategies. Both Confucianism and Taoism, as well as most other influential schools, are creative reinterpretations of a series of China's earliest and most respected classic works, such as *The Changes* (Yijing), *The Book of Political Documents* (Shangshu), *The Institutional Norms of Zhou* (Zhouli), *Discourses of the States* (Guoyu), *Interpretations of Norms* (Liji), and so on. In all these classic works we see some very important, influential, and enduring general ideas: the metaphysics of changes and ways, methodological relationism, historical-political views of order-and-disorder, and the political ideal of all-under-heaven. They explain the central place for knowledge of fortune, especially for political philosophy, in Chinese minds. I think Confucius would consider political philosophy to be the first philosophy, while Lao-tzu might agree with Aristotle that metaphysics should be taken as the first philosophy. But both of them would be very hesitant to agree with Descartes's *cogito*.

The metaphysics of changes or ways understands all things, including natural occurrences and social events, as a continuum of endless changes that make every next step uncertain and unpredictable. But this does not mean that all our actions are blind leaps into the dark. The knowledge of fortune can do something to lead us. Yet it is far from foretelling the future or foreseeing determined fate or destiny; it means instead humans' creative rewriting of their own fortunes, a challenging engagement that is no end in itself, so that knowledge of fortune becomes part of our fortune itself. In other words, we are unable to change the world, but we can instead change what we do to the world. As Confucians say, human beings have been given the chance of "negotiating and cooperating with the heaven and the world," so as to be able to remake their fortune with each feasible step.[3]

A good comprehension of changes teaches the ways of doing things with flexibility, resilience, and compatibility, characterized by Lao-tzu as the *methodology of water*. He says: "Nothing does better than water."[4] The metaphor of water indicates that the best feasible strategy to deal with changes of great complexity is to go as naturally as water does, in immediate conformity to fast-changing situations, aware of the limits of any power and thus always conservative, leaving room for unknown possibilities or letting things be done a little bit less than perfectly so as to be ready for unknown changes. This methodology of water seems to be working well in Chinese politics in pursuit of harmony rather than war.

Neither war nor peace is the best solution to the problem of conflicts. We all know that war is notorious for its destruction and also, unfortunately, its self-destruction. Beyond the concepts of war and peace, "harmony" seeks reasonable resolutions of conflicts and stable security by building truly reliable correlations of mutual benefit in the long run, as well as reciprocal acceptance of the other's values. It is obvious that harmony is a higher goal than peace, since peace is only a by-product of harmony.

With the consciousness of endless changes, the world is understood as an always open story of unpredictable changes in forms of order and disorder, a story of neither linear progress to the end of history nor the determined cycle of fatalism. In other words, the world exists as a process of uncertain possibilities, something like irrational numbers. This Chinese view of history might be better called historical naturalism, though it is sometimes confused with a sort of historicism or a circulation theory of history.[5] The point is that historical naturalism does not suggest any mysticism or superstition. On the contrary, it encourages a positive consideration of human deeds as the power to partly determine situations. The best way for human action is to do things in harmony with nature, with the world, and, most important, with other peoples.

The concepts of order and disorder are employed in political analysis in terms of a holistic explanation that the human world is, after all, part of the natural world. It is therefore believed that nature has set up a best example of integration of all, a great order to control disorders; the Way of Nature (natural *Tao*) implies the Way of Humanity (human *Tao*). Following this logic, the great order of a society, the social situation of all-in-order (*Dazhi*), in which all people are well positioned and suited by their favorable correlations, is regarded as the necessary condition for social cooperation.

Confucius criticized the "collapse of normative and cultural orders" in his time, for fear of the destruction of values and the loss of virtues. It is true that all-in-order is a necessary condition for social cooperation, whereas a situation of all-in-disorder (*Dalun*) brings about all dangers. But all-in-order is still not sufficient for a decent society, since an all-in-order society could be one with suppressive discipline, harsh rules, and excessive routine. The Confucian solution is to let the social order always reflect the best virtues of humanity, which can be explained in terms of harmonious relations based on "familyship." The most important idea developed by Confucianism is its philosophy of relations, better termed *relationology*, which implies *methodological relationism*, a universal approach to understanding, analyzing, and explaining human actions and values in terms of *relations* rather than *individuals* (independent agents, subjects, or monads). I take a renewed methodological relationism as a better horizon to discover solutions to the problems of conflicts, as well as a more reasonable and feasible approach to deal with the problematic situations of the multiversal world and/or the multicultural society with peoples of different hearts. Yet this does not mean replacing *methodological individualism*, but erasing the mistakes or reducing the dangers caused by modern methodological individualism.[6]

From a relational point of view, an independent individual is not a proper object of inquiry, since it does not make any problem by itself. A question about an individual is neither meaningful nor answerable unless it is a question clearly defined in terms of relations with others. In other words, the meaning of a thing consists not in itself but in its relations with others. When we say that a man is selfish, this is a description rather than a question. We question only problematic relations. Therefore, relations matter more than individuals. For instance, a man acts rather than simply is. No one is good by himself; one's presence as such is decided by one's relations with others; that is, a man is good only in so far as he acts to someone with goodness.[7] All the things that matter to our life, fate and fortune, success and failure, love and hate, goodness and evil, freedom and bondage, happiness and misery, to be or not to be, are made meaningful and problematic by human relations.

In a worldview constituted by and defined in terms of relations, other people stand out as paramount. Everyone is culturally, socially, and politically nobody in the absence of others. The existence of others sets the boundary of my existence, and the freedom of others limits and defines my freedom, so that instead of individuals it is relations that define and explain values and available choices. Different from the modern concern with the maximization of individual interests and rights, the primary inquiry in Confucianism instead centers on: "What is the expectable best relationship?" This question has driven Confucianism to investigate the available and accessible possibilities of human relations. Philosophically speaking, Confucianism pursues what I call an *ontology of coexistence,* instead of a *philosophy of existence.* It is based upon the truth that my existence is made possible and meaningful if and only if I am in coexistence with others. Moreover, all problems of existence, such as conflict and cooperation, war and peace, happiness and misery, have to be resolved by virtue of coexistence. Therefore, *coexistence is prior to existence.*[8]

It seems reasonable that better possible worlds of life could be made accessible by virtue of coexistence aiming at the maximization of cooperation and the minimization of conflict. Based on the ontology of coexistence, methodological relationism focuses on reliable interests by means of *relational rationality,* or relational calculation, considering that relations are the limits of accessible interests, instead of the aggressive pursuit of the maximization of self-interests, as *individual rationality* encourages. The basic consideration of relational rationality is this: never demanding too much; always leaving room for the unknown; and, most important, always taking others into consideration, briefly, never maximizing self-interest. Lao-tzu advises: "The best is less than perfection."[9] According to the ontology of coexistence and relational rationality, the so-called individual rationality to maximize self-interest is unreasonable and actually irrational. To think in terms of relations or in terms of individuals: that is the question. I believe methodological relationism is the better choice, since it is more likely to lead to peace and cooperation. I will use it to analyze the theory of world politics.

The most important principle of coexistence is the *priority of human obligations (Renyi).* In Confucian belief, humanity is created by humanization, that is, by doing to others as a human being ought to do; it is thus better identified as *human culture* rather than as *human nature.* It is taken for granted that human obligations—like mutual assistance to each other in difficult situations, repaying obligations, and gratitude to those who once offered unselfish help—are considered the qualifications for a human being to be as such. The reciprocity of human obligations creates the available, accessible, and reliable solution well within reach, instead of the uncertain and unreliable salvation of God so far away.

In the logic of relationology, human obligations come first in the ranking of values. Yet this does not imply that Confucianism would refuse human rights. I believe that Confucius would have taken great interest in the concept of human rights if he had learned it. In the contemporary context, human obligations could well balance human rights. Human obligations and human rights are equally necessary to any better possible life, in that human rights are a *negative security,* while human obligations provide *positive insurance* for human beings. Without the insurance of human obligations, human rights are *practically* impossible and unprotected, because human obligations are exactly the final guarantee of human rights. The point is that human rights as the protection of our freedom are unable to protect themselves, so they have to be protected by human obligations. Simply put, human rights depend on human obligations.

In the framework of relationism and coexistence, Chinese political philosophy defines and develops a political system of structures that are very different from Western ones. This is interesting because of differences in theoretical horizons rather than so-called cultural diversity. In my understanding, the structure of the modern Western political system could be described as consisting of *individuals, communities,* and *nation-states,* whereas the Chinese system is structured in terms of *families, states,* and *all-under-heaven (Jia Guo Tianxia).* It is obvious that the different choices of political structures are related to methodologies of political thinking,

The system of individuals-communities-nations has structurally inaugurated the games of competition and the trial of conflicts for all political entities from individual persons to nation-states, designed to maximize self-interest and never make a concession unless defeated. In this regard, a system of individuals-communities-nations encourages zero-sum games and wars in a loose sense, essentially reluctant to develop peace or to reduce conflicts. As a matter of fact, true peace and reliable cooperation are possible and made accessible only in nonconfrontational games defined and created by means of good relations. This is the reason for Confucianism to take *Ren,* which literally means "of-two-persons" and philosophically means "the best of mutual relations," to be the first virtue of humanity as human culture. The recognized best place to develop *Ren* is the family, the smallest unit of best mutuality, thus regarded as the foundation for the ethical and the political. Based upon the conception of familyship, a system of families, states, and all-under-heaven tries to develop games of harmony.

According to the ideal of all-under-heaven, the world should be reorganized or reconstructed into a universal political system of familyship so as to minimize conflicts in economics and cultures. The universal system of all-under-heaven is not only a conceptual ideal but also a political order that existed at one time, of equal importance in history as the Greek *polis*. I will argue that today's chaotic world is in need of a new all-under-heaven to establish true perpetual peace.

The Need for All-Under-Heaven

Our supposed world is actually a non-world. Our globe has not yet become a world of political oneness, but remains a Hobbesian chaotic anarchy of conflicts and noncooperation, since it has not been made a coherent world society under a universally accepted political system. The world in which we live is nothing more than a geographical physics, where the political identity of the world is still missing. A world of perpetual peace will depend on a worldwide institutional system. The first step to a new world should be a new worldview, a philosophy of world politics in place of international politics.

People have tried in vain to make a world by means of either traditional empires or the modern imperialism of interest groups or dominating powers. These attempts have been frustrated by the never-solved problems of lasting conflicts and always unstable cooperation. Our minds have been inclined to be fixed on a view of selfness, seeing the world as the hostile and negative externality, thinking nationally or regionally. Simply put, the *worldness* of the world is absent in the modern horizon of world.

The notion of "nation" is familiar to all. We all know what needs to be done for the nation. However, this is not the case for the notion of "world," since people are unaware of what should be done for the latter. The key problem today may be better described as a *failed world* instead of so-called *failed states*. In the age of globalization, no country would be really safe and immune from global disorder and dangers in a failed world. In order to understand the truth of the world, our view has to be extended to world size and reformulated in terms of "worldness." This question could be better understood in the modern situation.

The Kantian *perpetual peace*, or the "Kantian culture," in Alexander Wendt's terms,[10] has been proven a most important idea by its political products, such as United Nations and the European Union, as well as the inspiration for the very popular "democratic peace theory." But the much-loved Kantian politics meets a theoretical limitation that prevents it from the universal success of perpetual peace, mainly due to its inability to deal with Huntington's widely quoted theme of the "clash of civilizations," which

was not yet a clear and urgent problem in Kant's time. Now we should recognize that we have been living in a world of incompatible worlds, a world
of multiversality, far from universality. And we do need a much wider horizon so as to take into account Huntington's problem made of culturally or
spiritually irreducible differences and conflicts.

An interesting question put forward by Martin Wight in 1966 was:
"Why is there no international theory?"[11] Although many years have
passed, this question still seems relevant to the issue discussed here. Wight
argued that we did not prepare qualified international theories but instead
so-called political theories based on the domestic politics of states and
embellished with some poor parerga concerning an international "balance
of power." It is implied that people did not really know what internationality was. I think Wight would have changed his mind had he known of the
Chinese philosophy of world politics in terms of all-under-heaven, focusing more on *worldness* than on *internationality.* Wight's question might
better be rewritten as "Why is there no world theory?" so as to fit in with
the new context and changes of globalization. The more and more complicated world needs to be reconsidered within an overall political viewpoint
of worldness, an "all-in-one" framework,[12] which is absent from international theories. One thing that should be noted is that world politics will be
impossible until the universal well-being of the world overrides the exclu-
sive interests of nation-states.

What is called the modern *world system* is far from a just *universal system of the world.* A world system is always an imperialistic dominance, as
Wallerstein points out in *The Modern World System;* in other words, in a
world system, one powerful nation-state, or a group of powerful nation-
states, wields its political, economic, and cultural dominance over the less
powerful ones. As a matter of fact, a world system is essentially a denial
of worldness, nothing more than an imperialistic system in terms of *dominance* by hard and soft powers. Now the imperialistic system has been
proved to be an ineffective solution to the conflicts in the world, since it is
something imposed on the world, rather than being *of* and *for the world,*
not to mention *by the world.* What the world needs is a politically justified
universal system of world, to improve universal well-being, public interests, and common goods. This is what we expect.

Unfortunately, the story of imperialistic systems continues. Hardt and
Negri impressively argue that the emerging new empire is a sort of global
empire that is rehashing, by means of globalization, the ancient empire

that accepted no limited boundaries, a Roman empire in a new form.[13] We could add that the complicated composition of the new empire inherits not simply the ancient ideal of empire but also both modern imperialism and the Christian ideology of cultural universalism, a "decent" combination of hard and soft power, as Joseph Nye advocates. The American empire has been trying to reshape the concept in all these dangerous possibilities, creating the paradox of launching wars in the name of making peace and destroying liberty in the name of defending human rights.

The American empire seems to be declining dramatically in recent decades because of its self-defeating use of hard and soft powers. There are indications that these imperialistic efforts are very likely guilty of the world's current disorder. Just as Joshua Cooper Ramo argues, it is a tragic paradox in which "best intentions" and terrible results coexist in a horrific mirror-image dance: "Policies designed to make us safer instead make the world more perilous. History's grandest war against terrorism, for instance, not only fails to eliminate terrorism, it creates more dangerous terrorists. Attempts to stop the spread of nuclear weapons instead encourage countries to accelerate their quest for an atom bomb. . . . Decisions taken to stem a financial crisis appear, in the end, to guarantee its arrival. Environmental techniques engineered to protect species lead to their extinction. Middle East peace plans produce less peace."[14] Behind these phenomena, it is the philosophical failure, rather than strategic mistakes, that is fundamentally guilty for this paradox.

Even if an empire rules everywhere, it makes no world. Ruling the earth does not mean possessing a world of worldness, as argued in Confucian theory, since having hold of the land, in a geographical sense, instead of the "hearts" of all peoples, would lose the world in a spiritual sense. The world exists where and when peoples want it to be. In other words, the world is if and only if it is justified, and it is justified when a political system of universal "harmony" makes the worldness. This is exactly today's problem: the world is virtually a non-world for lack of the *eidos* of world, a conceptual form of worldness.

Globalization is blindly leading to an uncertain new age without a well-prepared new concept. If misled to increase international conflicts rather than universal cooperation, globalization will be more likely to make a failed world, which is much worse than failed states. The future could be derailed by unpredictable events, thus defeating our intentions. And the absence of a new philosophy that fits the world, or worse, the domination of a wrong-minded philosophy, would be a disaster in making history. Now the ideologies of modernity, in terms of subjectivity, individual rationality, and linear progress, linked with the modern political products of individuals, nation-states, international treaties, and organizations, are all outstripped by the sweeping changes of globalization. The confused or misled actions in response to globalization are mainly due to the political ignorance of the *mundus qua mundus,* to the lack of a new political philosophy from the viewpoint of "worldness," a worldview for the sake of the world above nations. Unfortunately, popular ideologies nowadays rarely care about worldness. They remain either unilateral universalism, actually aggressive imperialism serving the national interests of the most developed countries, or noncooperative pluralism, essentially resistant nationalism to protect the local interests of less developed nations. Such a situation of unilateral universalism versus noncooperative pluralism leads to a sort of prisoner's dilemma, preventing any possible improvement in world peace and mutual development.

In order to remake the world order, we need the creation of a universal system of the world, based upon a new philosophy that speaks for the world. The question is, in turn, how to take care of the world for the world. We need an idea more than a voice of appeal. This practical question leads us back to the claim in the Documents of King Yao, who is regarded the best king in history: the ultimate political task is "to create universal harmony of all peoples."[15] This is my reason for introducing and renewing the Chinese philosophy of world politics in terms of *all-under-heaven* (*Tianxia*), a notion that originated about three thousand years ago. I argue that a renewed theory of all-under-heaven might be helpful in finding a better solution to the chaotic situation of the world.

THE STORY OF CREATING AN ALL-UNDER-HEAVEN

An old story tells of the creation of an all-under-heaven system. Approximately three thousand years ago, many tribes of different cultures and ethnicities, perhaps over one thousand, lived in China. By means of a successful military adventure, the tribe Zhou defeated the dominating tribe, Shang, then the leader of the political alliance of tribes, and started the eight-hundred-year Zhou Dynasty. This was a political institutional revolution, establishing an all-under-heaven system, a very different political existence compared to the Greek *polis.* In much the same way as in Europe prior to the Greek city-states, there was no conceptually defined politics (literally "justified order") in China before the Zhou, only rule by force. Thanks to the Zhou invention of all-under-heaven, China began its politics with a world perspective and the task of making, serving, and managing the world, whereas Athens and other Greek city-states started their politics with *polis,* a task of making, serving, and managing a state. It seems quite unusual for the political to begin with world problems in such an early period of civilization: world politics would seem too avant-garde and unrealistic at a time when ancient minds did not have true geographical knowledge about the world. However, this indeed happened. And the creation of a world as the starting point of politics, as well as its greatest pursuit, has set the ever-lasting orientation for Chinese political thinking.

The brilliant first-generation leaders of the Zhou Dynasty, especially its first Zhou-Gong, or Duke Zhou, in response to the challenging demand of managing so many tribes, came up with some original political ideas: (1) successful solutions to the problems of world politics should resort to a universally acceptable world system instead of force; (2) a universal world system is politically justified if its institutional arrangements benefit all peoples of all nations and maximize the common goods of the world, sharable and accessible by all peoples; (3) a universal world system works if it creates harmony of all nations and all cultures. The general spirit of all these principles is that politics should make an effort to gain the ardent support of all by creating correlations accepted by all, rather than by making individual boundaries accepted by each. Upon these principles, Zhou created a universal system of all-under-heaven, an all-inclusive network of autonomous substates with a central supervisory government.

Theoretically speaking, all-under-heaven is an ideal concept open to possibilities for different original designs of a universal system of the world. Zhou's design of all-under-heaven was the first and only example put into practice in history. That does not mean that this ancient Chinese design is applicable at any time, for it is too simple to fit the complicated world of our age. Yet it is a meaningful example worthy of being rethought and is probably helpful for our future. Zhou's interesting design of all-under-heaven can be briefly described as follows:[16]

1. It is a mixed political system of monarch and aristocracy.
2. It is an open network with no boundary, consisting of a general world government and substates. The number of substates depends

on the diversity of cultures, nations, or geographical conditions. The substates pertain to the general political system, in the same way that subsets pertain to a greater set. The system of all-under-heaven, designed to be worldwide as a world-home for all peoples, is surely open to all nations in the world. Each nation is welcome to participate whenever it is willing to join or instead to remain independent if it is at peace with the nations included in the system.

3. The world government is in charge of universal institutions, laws, and the world order. It is responsible for universal well-being and the common good of the world, upholding world justice and peace; arbitrating international conflicts among substates; and controlling common or shared resources such as great rivers, large lakes, important minerals, and materials. It has the authority to examine and recognize the political legitimacy of substates, to supervise substates' social situations and political order, and to lead a punitive expedition if a substate breaks the universal law or order. On the other hand, the world government loses its legitimacy if it betrays justice or abuses its responsibilities. In this case a change of regime is justified.

4. Substates may be autonomous in their domestic affairs, such as economics, culture and the arts, and social norms and values; that is, substates are autonomous in almost all forms of life except their political legitimacy and obligations. Substates are legitimated only when politically recognized by the world government and are obliged to make certain reasonable contributions, in proportion to their products and natural resources, to the common wealth of the world and to render possible aid to other states in the event of disaster, water control, and so on.

5. A proportional institution plays a key role in maintaining long-term cooperation in the system of all-under-heaven. The world government directly rules a land called king-land, about twice the size of a large substate, about four times that of a medium-sized substate, and so on. The military force controlled by the world government is greater than those of large, medium, and small substates, by ratios of six to three, six to two, and six to one.[17] This proportional design limits the world government's king-land in its advantages over the substates in either resources or military power and limits the advantages of a larger substate over a smaller, so that a dominating super-

power is conceptually impossible, while revolution is a potential but real threat preventing the world government from becoming oppressive.

6. Another policy of top importance is that people enjoy the freedom of migration, either emigration or immigration, so that they could move to and work in any state they like. It implies worldism instead of nationalism. As an interesting result, most of the state's famous ministers, generals, and thinkers in the later period of Zhou Dynasty, for instance, were foreigners from other states, never accused as traitors. Traveling far and wide, Confucius was one of those who tried their fortunes in other states.

Zhou's institutional design of all-under-heaven, characterized by its worldism, its primary consideration of universal and common goods, and its principles of harmony of all nations and the least discrimination, created peace lasting for centuries in China. The spirit of all-under-heaven has such a great influence on Chinese political thinking that even contemporary Chinese politics cannot be properly understood without a good knowledge of this system. The system of all-under-heaven, which Confucius appreciated as the best political system for the world, cannot find its counterpart in Western concepts. It is neither a huge nation-state nor a great empire, although it looks a little bit like these in some aspects, for instance, worldwide ambition. It would be better interpreted, however, as an *anti-empire,* in that it is first concerned with the universally beneficial order of the world, based upon the philosophy of *coexistence,* rather than the unilaterally imposed order of the world, based upon the philosophy of *existence.* Confucianism calls this the "kingly way" (*Wangdao*), against the "overlord's way" (*Badao*)—in modern terms, harmonious order versus the hegemonic rule.

One of the contributions of all-under-heaven that should not be ignored is its political thinking beyond antagonism or confrontation, so that it is free from the anxious and nervous consciousness of enemies and fundamentally opposed to Hobbes's statism or Carl Schmitt's friend-enemy idea,[18] which reflects an unreasonable hostility toward others in their irreducible otherness. From the Confucian point of view, a mature and decent politics should be based upon the philosophy of harmony instead of restless hostility and immature tension, so as to be able to create universal *familyship* by virtue of mutual support, to change hostility into hospitality by mutual acceptance, and to allow benefits to all peoples. Simply put, the best politics needs a peaceful mind free from the trap of thinking in terms of war, enemy, winner, and loser. This is a political mind very different from Machiavelli, Hobbes, Marx, Freud, Schmitt, and Morgenthau and also different from the Kantian peace and Christian cosmopolitanism.

The story of Zhou's all-under-heaven ended in 221 B.C., when the first emperor of China annexed all other states and established the Qin Empire, with a new system of imperial centralization of authority, thereby distorting the concept of all-under-heaven. The decline of Zhou's all-under-heaven is also illustrative. Absurdly, it waned because it was too good to exist. One interpretation of its decline might conclude that the very limited power and force of the world government of all-under-heaven proved incapable of coping with the avaricious and ambitious challenges from substates as they grew stronger. This lesson was the main argument for Qin's political revolution.[19] This paradoxical problem of institutional design foretold the stubborn difficulties of world cooperation and peace, still challenging our minds to renew the concept of all-under-heaven, which is nevertheless a most important and inspiring approach for a possible world politics in the future.

Toward a Philosophical Renewal of All-Under-Heaven

The term *all-under-heaven* (*Tianxia*) means more than the "world." It can be used to refer to the world in the usual literature or in ordinary language, but essentially speaking, it is a philosophically dense concept of "world" consisting of a trinity of meanings: (1) the earth or all lands under the sky (ordinary usage); (2) a common or public choice made by all peoples in the world, truly representing the general will (in Chinese, a universal agreement in the "hearts" of all peoples [Confucianism's interpretation]); and (3) a universal political system for the world, with a world institution responsible for universal order and justice (Zhou's idea and also the Confucian ideal).

It is implied that the physical world, or the earth, is far less than the humanized world as all-under-heaven. A humanized world *is* only when the world is otherwise *made to be* a political world by means of a worldwide institutional system reflecting universal agreement and acceptance in the hearts of all peoples.[20] In other words, the natural world will not be *our world* unless it is constituted as *all-under-heaven*, the synthesis of the physical world (land), the psychological world (the general will of all peoples), and the political world (a worldwide institutional system). In this sense, the earth is thus still a non-world, not yet in the order of a world institution representing all peoples and fully accomplishing the universal *eidos* of worldness.

Chinese philosophy engages itself so much in the problems of relations that its metaphysics of facts or ontology of coexistence could also be identified as *relationology*. In the relationological perspective, the philosophical landscape of the world of facts is made of relations rather than individuals, so everything should be analyzed and measured in terms of relations rather than individuals. The truths of facts, for instance, depend on certain relations. Nothing could be properly described as a *thing so and so* unless in terms of relations; for example, we find someone a *friendly person* when we treat him in a friendly way, and in other cases we might have an opposite knowledge of him if we treat him wrongly. This fact speaks the truth that it is relations that define and decide what something actually is. Likewise, values are founded on relations, not on any individual. No relations, no values.

The first of the most important principles of all-under-heaven is "exclusion of nothing and nobody" or "inclusion of all peoples and all lands."[21] According to this principle, nobody can be excluded or pushed aside. It refuses any discriminatory identification or resistant recognition of others as essentially incompatible, say, as pagan or evil. It could be called the principle of the minimization of discrimination.

The idea of nobody being an outsider logically implies that nobody is a pagan or a cultural enemy. This principle is a negation of any cultural, religious, or ideological hostile attempt to discriminate against some groups of people as incompatible. An interesting ancient argument declares that heaven is born to be universal and impartial. Symmetrically, all-under-heaven should be so created to be universally fair and impartial to all peoples. The words are firm and strong: "All-under-heaven is meant to be of all and for all, and never of and for anybody in particular."[22] This explains the Chinese rejection of the domination of any religion and any notion of a chosen people. It is considered unjustified in any sense to identify some people as pagan or outsiders, because everyone is born to share all-under-heaven.

A Political-Ethical Circle

The most interesting principle implied in the theory of all-under-heaven is the political-ethical circle, which suggests a coherent circuit between ethical justification and political legitimacy, or between ethical values and political power, to create the best universal political system. This principle represents much of the Confucian mind. The second famous Confucian, Mencius, calls it an approach of "transposition" (*Tui*), supposed to be an approach to make coherent transitive changes from the ethical to the political, then back to the ethical, so as to make the ethical-political reciprocal justification. The way of families-states-all-under-heaven indicates the transformation from ethical relations to political institutions, and in reverse, all-under-heaven-states-families explains the political responsibility to protect ethical relations and defend basic values. This two-way formula makes a perfect circuit, providing a reasonable justification of a political system. From this point of view, I suppose, Confucians would not accept the Western modern political justification, since it is a self-referential justification of a political system by its own political ideologies. For instance, democracy has to resort to the ideology of democracy, for nothing can justify or guarantee the truth, goodness, or rightness of the majority's choices.

Relationology, or the ontology of coexistence, establishes the universal foundation for ethical values, that is, relational values defined in terms of universally acceptable and consensual relations instead of individuals. Relational values are universal because they always coincide with the conditions of mutual benefit and reciprocal acceptance. Confucianism takes family for granted as the basic unit of human relations, inclusive of the best of all possible relations, such as love, harmony, mutual aid, and reciprocal obligations—briefly, the relations of hearts more than of interests; family can therefore serve as the model of "the true humanity."[23] It is thus a qualified archetype for social systems. Confucianism insists that states and all-under-heaven would be better developed by adopting the model of family, inheriting the harmonious gene of familyship, constituted to maximize the possibilities of universal cooperation and peace. Running a state and even all-under-heaven, so to speak, should follow the spirit of running a family.[24] This is the relationological ethical justification of the political system of families-states-all-under-heaven.

As we have seen, the way of families-states-all-under-heaven transforms ethics into politics in that human obligations are transformed into political responsibilities. On the other hand, political power comes in turn to carry out its political responsibilities in terms of human obligations along the way of all-under-heaven-states-families. To put it more clearly, political power should carry out its political responsibilities, and reconfirm its ethical justification, by creating universal order, improving universal well-being, and protecting universally beneficial relations and values. Consisting of the ascending ethical way from families to states to all-under-heaven, and the descending political order from all-under-heaven to states to families, the ethical-political circle makes a circuit of the political from and to the ethical. Confucianism and most other Chinese schools, except Legalism, always highlight the reciprocal justifications between the political and the ethical. This is often misunderstood as Confucian denial of the rule of law. I think the truth is that Confucius finds law of secondary importance and that the best politics is to make a society of "no lawsuits."[25] This seems an overstatement and may mean "few lawsuits."

Two Universalisms, Three Politics, and Four Cultures

Whether successful or not, Confucianism has developed a compatible or relational universalism instead of uniform universalism. All universalisms mean the same in "applying to all" but differ in "all what." Modern uniform universalism means "applying to all individuals," trying to make a civilization of uniformity in place of cultures of differences. It is considered a universal civilization that could be numerically and commensurably explained and estimated by linear progress, individuals, statistics, and calculations, whereas compatible universalism means instead "applying to all relations," trying to make a multiverse of compatibility.

Uniform universalism easily falls into a unilateralism that imposes on others the values they do not want, creating rivalrous games or hostile competitions and fomenting nervous sensitivity in search of enemies. In addition, modern individualism defines absolute political "borders" for everything, from individuals to nation-states, legitimating self-interestedness in all cases and encouraging overheated or overacted self-defense of individual rights and interests, which leads unilateral universalism to be more nervous and aggressive.

The very advantage of compatible universalism comes from its relational rationality, by which people would discover better universal values in terms of relationship instead of individuality and would pursue more reasonable maximization of accessible interests in terms of relational interests. To clarify, compatible universalism always recognizes: (1) toleration of different forms of life for others; (2) the priority of universal values in terms of relationship over the values of individuality; (3) the primacy of relational interests over unilateral self-interests. Generally speaking, compatible universalism is meant to foster a compatible multiverse united by universal relationship. For instance, compatible cooperation, it is hoped, would be established between the East and the West, Confucianism and liberalism, Islamic and Christian beliefs, and so on, only if relational rationality could replace individual rationality in our minds. I would like to stress that relational rationality is a realistic approach and not merely an ideal, given the simple truth that unilateralism does not work well because of its destructive results.

Another important change is that the concept of politics should be extended from the domestic and international to the world. More and more evidence shows clearly the impossibility of solving international problems in the framework of internationality. In other words, international politics is a smaller space and a weaker approach than is demanded by worldwide political and cultural problems. The absence of the dimension of world politics can be blamed for the incompleteness of political thinking, as well as many mistakes in dealing with global challenges. In order to improve the capacity of political thinking, we need, practically, three different but related political horizons: *national, international,* and *world*.

From an international political view, Alexander Wendt identifies three cultures: Hobbesian culture, which sees conflicts or war; Lockean culture, which substitutes competition for war; and Kantian culture, which advocates collaborative alliances.[26] Wendt strongly supports Kantian culture as the solution to international conflicts. Maybe Kantian culture could relax the tension of the international situation and reduce hostility, but it still seems far from fostering worldwide perpetual peace and cooperation. I am afraid that Wendt has not learned about the Chinese idea of all-under-heaven, which suggests more than a Kantian project. Considering the changes brought about by globalization, as well as the world politics to come, I would rather think alternatively about four relevant cultures: that of Rome, Christian universalism, Kantian peace, and all-under-heaven.

My suggestion for the revival of all-under-heaven may seem too beautiful to be true; some Western scholars might be suspicious, reading it as a Chinese challenge to Western power. For example, William Callahan worries about the Pax Sinica, a new Chinese imperial system in the name of all-under-heaven.[27] I would try to remove such misunderstandings by asserting that all-under-heaven is an open concept to be renewed or updated by better ideas, instead of a return to an old pattern that is no longer suitable in the contemporary context. More important, a future all-under-heaven does not necessarily mean "a Chinese system," but instead suggests a universal system of and for all peoples. It is not my place to worry about misunderstandings caused by war-oriented thinking, a typical complex in Western political consciousness or subconsciousness, leading to much unnecessary fear of nonexistent enemies. I am rather troubled by a larger problem: the war-oriented thinking has actually encouraged wars to happen and the wars themselves, which have proved more self-defeating than successful.

An Imagination of a New All-Under-Heaven

Globalization has deeply involved all nations, societies, and cultures; nothing is left alone. It seems to me that a new all-under-heaven as an institutional commonwealth holds the most promise for perpetual peace and world order. Allow me to introduce my tentative imagination of a new all-under-heaven system, based upon the philosophy of coexistence with methodological relationalism that I have developed. It consists of approximately at least three aspects. First, a new all-under-heaven needs, of course, a world constitution. The political existence of the world should not be an enlarged nation. It must instead be a compatible all-inclusive system. Compatible universalism may be the only hopeful way to deal with the problem of different hearts. It is my belief that the world constitution of a new all-under-heaven should be founded on universal values redefined in terms of relational values instead of individual values. As argued, relational values concern only relations for possible cooperation, mutual aid, and human obligations; in other words, they should never impose anything on others, so that they are the most prudent, most reliable, and safest universal values, unlikely to involve troubles and logically impossible to be self-defeating. Only relational values could be universalized in a way that would not harm others, since they are meant to minimize mutual hostility instead of maximizing respectively conflicting self-interests. It is not definite that relational values are perfect, but it is definite that relational values are nevertheless better than individual values as the foundation of a world constitution.

On the basis of universal values renewed by methodological relationalism, a *law of peoples and relations* must be established, a combination of the Western tradition of the law of peoples (from Rome to Rawls), focusing on *human rights,* and the Confucian principle of relational harmony, based on *human obligations.* Generally speaking, human rights and human obligations are parallel, of equal importance. However, we must see the danger that the notion of human rights could be misused or abused in some cases, led astray by the concept of the self-centered individual, leading to practical threats to the human rights of others. A reasonable solution could resort to metarules: (1) human rights and human obligations are mutually conditioned; (2) human obligations are above human rights, if there is no room for compromise in some extreme cases between the two.

Notes

1. *Liji* [Interpretations of norms], chap. 27.
2. *Shangshu* [The book of political documents], chap. 1.
3. *Zhongyong,* in *Li-ji (Liji),* chap. 31.
4. Lao-tzu, *Tao Te Ching,* chap. 8.
5. There was a Chinese school, the Yin-yang school, which developed a circulation theory of history that was popular in mass culture and often used to support superstitious interpretations of events. But it is of less philosophical importance or scientific meaning, not taken seriously by Confucianism.
6. This is related to the strict methodological individualism of Max Weber, Joseph Schumpeter, Friedrich Hayek, James Buchanan, and Gordon Tullock, as well as almost all modern economists and game theorists; it is also related to individualistic thinking from Hobbes, Locke, and Rawls, to most liberalists.
7. Cf. Confucius, *The Analects,* chap. 19.
8. See Zhao Tingyang, "Ontology of Coexistence: Relations and Hearts" (in Chinese), in *Yanjiu* (Beijing: Philosophical Research, 2009).
9. Lao-tzu, *Tao Te Ching,* chap. 9.
10. Alexander Wendt, *Social Theory of International Politics* (Cambridge: Cambridge University Press, 1999), chap. 6.
11. Martin Wight, "Why Is There No International Theory," in *Diplomatic Investigation,* ed. Herbert Butterfield and Martin Wight (London: George Allen and Unwin, 1966), 17.
12. I discuss the all-in-one methodology in my book *One and All Problems* (in Chinese) (Beijing: Jianxi Education Press, 1998).
13. Michael Hardt and Antonio Negri, *Empire* (Cambridge, MA: Harvard University Press, 2000), preface.
14. Joshua Cooper Ramo, *The Age of the Unthinkable* (Boston: Little, Brown and Company, 2009), 9.
15. *Shang-shu,* chap. 1.

16. Cf. *Shangshu, Zhouli* [The institutions of Zhou], and *Liji.*

17. *Zhouli,* chap. 4; *Zuozhuan* [History of the states]: "The 14 Years of Duke Xian" (in Chinese). See also Chen Fuliang (1137–1203), "The Military Systems in Dynasties" (in Chinese).

18. Carl Schmitt, *The Concept of the Political* (Chicago: University of Chicago Press, 1996), 26.

19. The argument was made by Li Si, the premier of the Qin Empire. See Sima Qian (145–86 B.C.), *Shiji* [The history], vol. 8, "The Story of the First Emperor of Han" (in Chinese).

20. As Xun-tzu (313–238 B.C.) pointed out: "The world as *all-under-heaven* does not imply people giving up their land by force, but having an institution that is universally accepted by all people." See *Works of Xun-tzu* (in Chinese), chap. 11.

21. This principle finds its earliest presentation in *Shijing* [The book of songs], in the chapter entitled "Xiaoya-Beishan," which is more than three thousand years old. See also Sima Qian, "Story of the First Emperor of Han"; Sima Guang, *Zizhitongjian* [The history of politics], vol. 27, chap. 19.

22. Lu Buwei, *Lu's History* (in Chinese), vol. 1, chapter on the priority of the common.

23. See *Liji,* the chapter entitled "Dazhuan."

24. *Daxue* [The great learning]. See also *The Works of Mo-tzu,* vol. 3.

25. Confucius, *The Analects,* chap. 12.

26. Wendt, *Social Theory of International Politics,* chap. 6.

27. William A. Callahan, "Chinese Visions of World Order: Post-Hegemonic or a New Hegemony," *International Studies Review* 10, no. 4 (2008): 749–61.

4

Debating the "Chinese Theory of International Relations"

Toward a New Stage in China's International Studies

Zhang Feng

China's international relations (IR) discipline is largely a creation of the past thirty years. Despite its short history, there have been some exciting developments—major achievements recognized by scholars as signifying progress, as well as sustained controversies and debates—over the past three decades. This chapter aims to review the recent history of Chinese IR and to assess one of its most important developments: the project of the "Chinese theory of IR" since the late 1980s and all the controversies and debates it has provoked.

Recent scholarly attention to Chinese IR seems to be primarily focused on the discourse of the "Chinese School," and the relationship between the "Chinese School" and the project of the "Chinese theory of IR" may thus appear baffling. I argue, however, that the "Chinese School" project, despite its recent prominence, is better seen as a subproject, alongside other subprojects, such as the longstanding proposal for building an "IR theory with Chinese characteristics," within the overall project of the "Chinese theory of IR." This larger "Chinese theory" project signifies a key trend in the Chinese IR field in the past two decades and should be explainable by the same factors explaining the development of the field as a whole.

The chapter proceeds as follows. The first section develops an explanatory model for the development of Chinese IR. The second section then applies the model to explain the evolution of the field, while also preparing essential background for the main discussion of the "Chinese theory of IR" project. The discussion distinguishes the "Chinese characteristics" subproject from the "Chinese School" subproject and describes their main features and the varied criticisms they have provoked. The fourth section offers my own assessment of the "Chinese theory" project, identifying its problems and suggesting some preliminary thoughts for its theoretical development. In the conclusion I look for threads leading to the possible future evolution of Chinese IR by revisiting the explanatory model developed in the first section.

An Explanatory Model for the Development of Chinese IR

Although several leading Chinese scholars have proposed periodizations of the history of Chinese IR and analyzed the features of different phases, none has provided a general analysis from the perspective of the sociology of science.[1] Yet there is now an adequate empirical base for attempting such an analysis; the sociology of science approach has also been effectively exploited by recent scholarship.[2] This section develops an explanatory model for the development of Chinese IR by building on the work of Ole Wæver.

Drawing on the sociology of science, Wæver has proposed an explanatory model for the development of IR in the West. His model consists of three layers: society and polity (including four dimensions: cultural-linguistic, political ideology, political institutions, and foreign policy); the general conditions and definitions of social science, as well as disciplinary patterning; and intellectual activities in IR, such as the social and intellectual structure of the discipline. Regarding the cultural-linguistic dimension in the first layer, a country's intellectual style—deriving, for example, from its historical, cultural, and philosophical traditions—can influence the style of its IR theorizing and analysis. In terms of political ideology and institutions, state-society relations are central in structuring the roles social sciences can play. With respect to foreign policy, it is argued that a country's foreign policy situation can influence its development of IR theory.[3]

Modifying and simplifying the model, I propose four explanatory factors for the development of Chinese IR: China's political, ideological, and social environment (largely what Wæver calls "state-society relations"); its international position and foreign policy; its historical and intellectual tradition; and the intellectual structure of the Chinese IR discipline. All these factors, with the partial exception of the third one, have undergone dramatic changes in the sixty-year history of the People's Republic of China (PRC). These changes indicate and to a great extent determine the developmental trajectory of Chinese IR.

Applying this model, we can now analyze the development of Chinese IR in the last sixty years. This approach will also enable us to place the dimension of the theoretical development of Chinese IR within the larger process of disciplinary development as a whole, both grounded in the methodology of the sociology of social science.

The Historical Evolution

The history of Chinese IR can be roughly divided into five phases.[4] During the first phase, 1949–1963, China did not have an academic discipline of international relations as such. The field, if there was one, was commonly referred to as "international studies," and research consisted solely of internal reference materials and research reports prepared for the government. There were few publicly available academic publications, and independent scholarly research was simply forbidden. This feature was determined by China's foreign policy requirements, as well as by the domestic political and ideological framework at the time. The founding of the PRC and the accompanying diplomatic challenge required research and teaching on foreign policy and international politics. The characteristic example was the creation of the Foreign Affairs College (now China Foreign Affairs University) in 1955 as a specialized institution for international studies and as a camp for training diplomatic talents. But China's international study, in line with the political and foreign policy principle of "leaning to one side," was heavily influenced in all areas by the Soviet model, from institutional setup and research focus to modes of thinking. International study was largely synonymous with policy analysis, in the form of annotated policy reports or advice.

The second phase, running from 1963 to 1978, was defined by two epochal events in the history of the revolutionary PRC: the Cultural Revolution on the domestic scene and the Sino-Soviet split on the international front. The Sino-Soviet split presented China with its gravest security threat since the Korean War, and it was the major stimulus behind the government's decision to enhance China's international research and teaching. In this context and under the direct guidance of top leaders Mao Zedong and Zhou Enlai, after 1963 China began to allocate resources and establish international studies departments in three major universities, as well as a number of research institutes under government ministries and the social science division of the Chinese Academy of Science (now the Chinese Academy of Social Science). The significance of this period consists of the institutional foundation it laid for the later development of Chinese IR: now China had, for the first time in its history, a set of quasi-academic institutions for the study of international relations. But in terms of research methods, focus, and style, this phase differed little from the first one. Indeed, it had become even more ideological as a result of the Cultural Revolution.

IR as an independent academic discipline in China began with the third phase, between 1978 and 1990. The fundamental factors behind this change were the "reform and opening up" process initiated by Deng Xiaoping and the relatively relaxed international environment in China in the 1980s. This was when China, lacking a disciplinary foundation, began a historically unprecedented process of studying and importing Western (predominately U.S.) IR. This was also when Chinese scholars, in the final years of the decade, began to ponder the Western and especially the U.S. dominance of IR study in China and to wonder whether China needed to develop its own sorts of IR theories. The first musings about a Chinese theory of IR occurred in 1987, when it was proposed during China's first major IR theory conference in Shanghai that China needed an "IR theory with Chinese characteristics."[5] Since then, the questions of whether China needs its own IR theories, what such theories would look like, and how to go about creating them have become staples of Chinese IR research. Viewed as a whole, however, Chinese IR in the 1980s was still in a crude stage, and in many respects academic research was no more sophisticated than in-depth journalistic reporting on international affairs. This sorry state was attributable to both the lack of theoretical consciousness and the near nonexistence of methodological awareness among scholars.

The fourth phase, between 1990 and 2000, was marked by a further awakening of the consciousness of social scientific theory and of IR as an independent academic discipline distinct from policy advocacy and interpretation. This period saw acceleration of the importation of Western IR, measured by the number of translations of Western works; multiplication of the use of Western theoretical approaches; and the rise of critical and independent perspectives among Chinese scholars. Begun in the 1980s, Chinese translation of Western scholarship has flourished since the mid- to late 1990s. By 2007, at least eighty-five Western IR theoretical works had been translated into Chinese.[6] Major Western theoretical approaches— realism, liberalism, and constructivism—had all begun to be introduced and adopted by various Chinese scholars in their research, though their focus was more on introduction than on application.

An Analytical Account

We can now recapitulate this account in a more analytical form on the basis of the explanatory model proposed in the preceding section. Both of the first two factors—state-society relations and foreign policy—have undergone profound changes, which can be divided between the revolutionary period (1949–1978) and the reform period (1978–present). During the revolutionary period, state control over society was tight and in some cases ubiquitous, and the communist and revolutionary ideology was pervasive not only in politics and government but also in academia and even daily life. This placed a severe and insurmountable constraint on what academic research could achieve. It is therefore not surprising that the reform process would release the pent-up energies of Chinese scholars and lead to the great flourishing of IR study in the following three decades. Although Chinese IR is still bound by a peculiar kind of authoritarianism, with all its ensuing ideological and bureaucratic pathologies, scholars now possess considerable space and latitude to conduct independent research.

The influence of China's international position and foreign policy on its IR development cannot be overemphasized. Indeed, Chinese IR had its origins and institutional foundation in the foreign policy needs of the revolutionary regime; its research focus and style were also determined by state needs. In recent years, however, in conjunction with the rise of theoretical self-consciousness, the influence of foreign policy on IR has turned in a new direction. In an important sense it is defining the shape and outlook of Chinese IR in that the rise of China has provided both the occasion to develop the "Chinese School of IR" and the perceived urgency of doing so.

The intellectual structure of Chinese IR is crucially shaped by the intellectual makeup of Chinese scholars themselves. The generation currently leading the field grew up during the Maoist period, but their intellectual development benefited from Deng's reform policy in that many of them had academic experiences in the West in the 1980s and 1990s. They thus have a somewhat complicated intellectual background, familiar with both Chinese political discourse and Western IR theory. They are weak, however, in their training in and understanding of China's historical and cultural traditions.[7] The effect of this constellation of intellectual and disciplinary factors is that Chinese IR in the past two decades has been predominately Western oriented, becoming increasingly critical of such an orientation yet unable to break away from it. This generation has made foundational contributions to the development of Chinese IR, but they are best viewed as representing a transitional phase; it remains to be seen how the next generation—raised and trained under very different political and academic environments—will take Chinese IR to new directions.

Despite China's long history and rich traditions, these apparently had no influence over Chinese IR until the 1990s. A moment's reflection, however, reveals that this is not so surprising. During the Maoist era— the beginning stage of Chinese IR—Chinese IR was not just un-Western (apart from its Marxist and Soviet tinge) but also profoundly un-Chinese. Modern China has at various times renounced the value of China's traditions, and the period of the revolutionary PRC was particularly notable in its urge to break with China's past. With its own past still in the historical dustbin, to be recovered, China turned to the West for IR development, thus creating Western orthodoxy and dominance.[8] Only in the past two decades or so, in conjunction with the rise of China, have scholars begun to reevaluate and rediscover China's traditions for contemporary use. Given the resilience and growing appeal of China's traditions, and with the further rise of China as a world power, which is likely to stimulate more interest in and reinforce the appeal of China's traditional resources, we should expect this "Chinese aspect" of Chinese IR to become more prominent in the future, as it has in the past decade.

DEBATING THE "CHINESE THEORY OF IR"

The "Chinese theory of IR" (*Zhongguo Guoji Guanxi Lilun*) is a generic term that has been used to describe a variety of perspectives calling for the infusion of some vaguely specified Chinese elements into Western-centric

IR theories.[9] These include an array of terms, such as "Chinese character-istics" (*Zhongguo Tese*), "Chinese perspectives" (*Zhongguo Shijiao*), "Sini-cization" (*Zhongguohua*), "indigenization" (*Bentuhua*), and most recently the "Chinese School" (*Zhongguo Xuepai*), with overlapping but also differ-ent meanings as to what Chinese theories of IR would look like and how to go about creating them. The "Chinese theory of IR" is therefore best seen as an ongoing intellectual and discursive project without a precise mean-ing or clear boundaries, containing within itself subprojects such as an "IR theory with Chinese characteristics" and the "Chinese School" that com-pete to shape the larger project of developing Chinese IR theories. While the "Chinese School" has been the most prominent subproject within this discourse in the past decade, this should not obscure the fact that the call for Chinese brands of IR theory has been heard at least since the late 1980s and that the "Chinese School" subproject is a partial outgrowth of earlier debates and controversies surrounding the larger topic of the "Chinese the-ory of IR."

Perusing the diverse, somewhat vague, and at times confusing debates about the "Chinese theory of IR," one can identify four main per-spectives competing for allegiance among Chinese scholars. The first and earliest is the proposal for the construction of "IR theory with Chinese characteristics." Such advocacy has encountered criticism from the start. The first two groups of critics are those who reject the validity of the project and those who endorse it in principle but with reservations.[10] A third group of critics, though small and less visible, often include promi-nent scholars unwilling to be drawn into explicit debate. They tend to prefer scholarly reticence regarding "Chinese theory" at its current stage to explicit promotion of "Chinese characteristics." The fourth view is that of the "Chinese School," developed since 2000, which is in many respects more sophisticated than that of "IR theory with Chinese characteris-tics." This view has in turn generated heated debates and provoked two types of criticism that partially resemble earlier responses to "IR theory with Chinese characteristics": outright rejection and implicit or explicit criticism that falls short of rejection. These debates reflect the funda-mental dilemma of "Sinicization": how to reconcile indigenous Chinese ideas with foreign (Western) and more academically useful and influen-tial ones? I shall first outline the earlier debate on "IR theory with Chi-nese characteristics" before detailing the "Chinese School" project and its controversies.

"IR Theory with Chinese Characteristics" and Its Critics

As noted above, the first call for "IR theory with Chinese characteristics" was made during a 1987 conference in Shanghai. The idea was also a major subject of controversy during two subsequent conferences in Beijing, in 1991 and 1994.[11] Indeed, it has been a running theme of Chinese IR since the late 1980s, though its prominence has been displaced by the "Chinese School" in recent years.

An early and leading advocate of "IR theory with Chinese characteristics" is Liang Shoude at Peking University, one of China's most distinguished IR scholars at the time. According to his latest thinking, "Chinese characteristics" refer to theories that are developed under the guidance of Marxism, that are based on the paradigms of the international political theory of Chinese statesmen, that draw on both China's cultural tradition and Western IR theory, and that fit the realities of both the world situation and China's national circumstances by seeking the best convergence of the two.[12] The current leading promoter of this school is Zhu Feng, also at Peking University. He argues that China's rise and its growing influence in the world have created a need to develop IR and foreign policy theories with Chinese characteristics, in order to provide theoretical support for China's foreign policy, represent China's national interests and strategic objectives, and realize Chinese theoretical innovation as a result.[13]

From the start some scholars rejected the validity of "IR theory with Chinese characteristics." The objections vary. First, it is never entirely clear what "Chinese characteristics" refers to. Second, IR theory, being propositions about the regularities of international politics, is universal; hence it makes no sense to speak of "Chinese characteristics." Third, China should try to make Chinese IR more "scientific," and the proposal about "Chinese characteristics" is "unscientific." Fourth, the proposal is political and ideological, as "IR theory with Chinese characteristics" seems to be an academic variant of the political slogan "socialism with Chinese characteristics." Fifth, "characteristics" are not predesigned; they depend on the theory-development process itself. Sixth, the explanatory power of theories is more important than their having some "characteristics." Influential theories developed in non-Western countries have not been named after their countries. Besides, Western theories can also explain some Chinese problems, so proposing "Chinese characteristics" is itself "unscientific." Seventh, there is no need to raise "Chinese characteristics" explicitly, because research by Chinese scholars contains inherent Chinese characteristics. Eighth, emphasizing "Chinese characteristics" will expose the utilitarian nature of the theory, thus reducing its scholarly value.[14] Finally, the ambiguities of the goal of building "IR theory with Chinese characteristics" create limitations. Is such theory a single and uniform theoretical system, or is it an aggregation of a grand theoretical system subsuming different schools of thought? "Chinese characteristics" can be misleading in the sense that the project may be seen to explain international politics with reference only to China's international experiences. Moreover, how can "Chinese characteristics" be reconciled with new international realities such as globalization and the "common interests of humankind"?[15]

The second type of response is to endorse the project in principle, as scholars of this view agree that IR theories need to become less Western and more Chinese. But they are troubled by terminology such as "Chinese characteristics" or "Chinese systems." Other terms, such as "Chinese perspectives," "Sinicization," or "indigenization," are more palatable to their taste, as these seem less political and ideological. This group of scholars does not raise fundamental objections to building Chinese theories. One scholar of the "indigenization" view holds that the key to the indigenization of IR theory is to propose systematic explanations for international relations that accord with China's national interests. Such theories should first of all serve the goal of the reemergence of the Chinese nation, by demonstrating to the world that China's rise and development is a necessary requirement for world peace and stability.[16]

The third, more substantive view holds that the current task of Chinese scholars is not to discuss "Chinese characteristics," but to further enhance understanding of Western IR so as to be able to put forth original Chinese views of international relations. This group of scholars does not reject the premise that IR theory may have "national characteristics," but they think it is a mistake to emphasize this point. They stress that there is as yet no Chinese contribution to IR to speak of. Western IR is still much more "advanced" than Chinese IR; learning Western IR is therefore still a necessary and basic task for Chinese scholars. It is impossible to announce "Chinese characteristics" unless Chinese scholars command a sophisticated and comprehensive understanding of the state of the art in Western IR. Prominent scholars such as Zi Zhongyun (a former director of the Institute for American Studies at the Chinese Academy of Social Science) and Wang

Yizhou (formerly at the Chinese Academy of Social Science, now at Peking University) are leading voices of this view.

The result of this debate by the end of the 1990s, according to some observers, was widespread dissatisfaction with the Western dominance of Chinese IR and general consensus on the need to develop IR theories with Chinese perspectives, that is, the "Sinicization" of Western IR. The main controversy surrounds the term "Chinese characteristics." But if the obsession with labels is cast aside and the focus shifts to what has been substantively argued, the differences and disputes are not as wide as they first appeared, and the stage is set for the development of Chinese theories.[17]

The Rise of the "Chinese School"

Since the term's invention in 2000, the "Chinese School" has gained increasing currency at the expense of other projects on Chinese theories of IR. The theme of the 2004 IR theory conference in Shanghai, for example, was "creating Chinese theories, constructing the Chinese School."[18] The leading advocates of this project are Qin Yaqing at China Foreign Affairs University and Ren Xiao at Fudan University. It is more influential than the "Chinese characteristics" project—indeed, it is one of most notable and widely recognized theoretical projects in Chinese IR today—largely because its proponents are able to elevate their arguments to the level of the philosophy of science and have a more sophisticated understanding of the nature of theory. Its influence is also helped by the fact that its leading advocate, Qin Yaqing, is regarded as one of China's foremost IR theorists and the champion of constructivism in China, with a large number of followers.

What then do proponents of the "Chinese School" say? The curious observer new to the debate may be struck by the fact that despite its discursive prominence, such a school does not yet exist. It is therefore not able to say much substantive about what the theories it generates might look like. The discourse about the "Chinese School" is a discourse about the future, about the motivations for such a project, the principal sources for its construction, and its purpose and significance. To Ren Xiao, the project signifies Chinese scholars' confidence, ambition, and self-consciousness about theoretical innovation. The purpose is not to seek intentional opposition against Western theories but to demonstrate Chinese scholars' independent thinking and their courage to make theoretical contributions. As to why we need the "Chinese School," he suggests the simple answer that

Chinese scholars are dissatisfied with the status quo and want to become "knowledge producers."[19]

So far the most sophisticated argument for the "Chinese School" comes from Qin Yaqing, whose 2005 and 2006 articles have defined the tone and terms of the debate.[20] According to him, the "Chinese School" will originate from local (Chinese) culture, historical tradition, and practical experience, but it should eventually be able to transcend local traditions and experience in being universally valid. It seeks to create an IR theoretical system with both Chinese substance and universal significance by discovering China's traditional thought and practice, as well as by drawing on Western IR theories. Its purpose, and the purpose of Chinese IR theoretical paradigms in general, is not to displace existing IR theories, much less to promote academic nationalism or establish China's discourse hegemony, but to enrich IR theory and the knowledge structure of humankind.[21]

Qin gives three reasons why such a school has not yet emerged: lack of theoretical self-consciousness, the dominance of Western theoretical discourse, and lack of a vibrant theoretical hardcore. He particularly laments the absence of a core theoretical problematic in Chinese IR, believing that the developments of U.S. and British IR are results of their respective problematics. Hence, in advising how to construct Chinese theories, he places extraordinary emphasis on the importance of finding a distinct theoretical problematic. He proposes that one candidate for such a problematic is China's peaceful integration into international society. He further identifies three sources for the "Chinese School": traditional China's *Tianxia* worldview and the tribute system, the modernization philosophy and the Chinese revolutions, and contemporary China's reformist thinking and integration into the international system. He claims with great confidence that a "Chinese School" is not only possible but also inevitable.

Critiques of the "Chinese School"

Like the "Chinese characteristics" project, the "Chinese School" has also provoked varied critical responses, in some cases much more severe than the former has encountered. The criticisms are largely of two types: implicit or explicit criticism short of rejection and outright objection and rejection. The following identifies seven specific (though not always explicit) responses to the "Chinese School" project.

The first response cautions that it is not yet time to promote Chinese uniqueness in IR, because Chinese IR still lags far behind Western IR. The more urgent task is to realize and rectify the inherent weaknesses in Chinese IR by taking a self-critical view. Scholars also question how well and in what ways China's traditions can be successfully applied in contemporary theorizing.[22]

The second response is more specific regarding what Chinese scholars should do, and it emphasizes the need to conduct cross-cultural comparative research. As Wang Jisi, another leading scholar in Chinese IR, puts it, Chinese scholars' personal experiences of Chinese culture cannot substitute for the theoretical study of Chinese and other cultures. Only by understanding other cultures through comparative research can one gain a deep understanding of what Chinese national characteristics are. A narrow and parochial view of what Chinese or other cultures are does not qualify one to talk about Chinese characteristics.[23] These scholars do not reject proposals about "Chinese theory," but their comments (often made in passing) contain an implicit criticism of a serious flaw in these projects.

A few scholars have also advanced explicit criticisms without going to the point of rejection. One scholar focuses on a number of contradictions in the "Chinese theory" project: those between "Chinese problems" and "global consciousness," between "policy orientation" and "scientific spirit," and between macro- and microlevel research. Regarding the first, a key characteristic of the project is that it overemphasizes Chinese problems or characteristics at the expense of serious thinking about global developments. But China's problems must be related to global ones in some intimate and useful way. China now being in the world and Chinese civilization part of human civilization, there is little need or justification to continue to be suspicious of the outside world. Yet the project seems to contain an inveterate if largely implicit cultural self-centeredness, if not yet manifested in narrow nationalism and local sentiments. What is lacking therefore is a more universalist spirit. Regarding the second contradiction, China's IR research has a strong policy orientation. Reflected in discussions of "Chinese theory," more attention is paid to how such theories might serve some practical policy needs than to substantive issues of scholarship such as the independence and objectivity of research, which should really be at the heart of the discussion.

Regarding the third contradiction, Chinese scholars seem to be obsessed with building some sort of "grand theory" but are shallow and weak in methodology and empirical research. The main task at the moment, however, is not to construct grand theoretical systems, but to develop and apply midrange and microlevel theories. The development of Chinese theories of IR is a natural process dependent upon the pluralization of the field, the distinctive contributions of each individual scholar or research community, and mutual exchange and debate between these subnational-level "schools." A unified and uniform academic structure and research mode are unlikely to produce a "Chinese school."[24]

Using China's traditional resources to construct Chinese theories seems to be the least controversial part of the "Chinese School" project. Yet prominent scholars have also challenged this apparently solid method. For instance, while concepts like *He* are characteristically Chinese and are absent from Western discourse, it is not clear whether they could support a theoretical system or the "Chinese School." According to one distinguished scholar, key concepts of IR theory should be neutral, such as "interest" and "power" in realism, but Chinese concepts proposed so far contain strong ethical connotations, making them unfit for theory building.[25]

The most unrelenting critique of the "Chinese School" project comes from Yan Xuetong at Tsinghua University, another distinguished theorist and a champion of the "scientific method" in China.[26] Yan forcefully rejects the legitimacy and validity of the "Chinese School" label for three reasons. First, all well-known IR theories are labeled by people other than the creators of those theories themselves. Second, theories are rarely named after countries; it is more common to see a theory named after its core arguments, its creator, or the institution where it was developed. Theorizing attempts developed at his Institute of International Studies might be named the "Tsinghua School," but it is impossible to broaden this into the "Beijing School" or beyond because the diversity of IR approaches in Beijing would render such a name meaningless. Third, the term *Chinese* is too broad to designate any theory developed within China. No theory or school of thought can represent the diversity and complexity of China's history and tradition.

However, while such arguments suggest Yan's irreconcilability with the "Chinese School" project, he shares with the latter important similarities regarding how to develop IR theories in China. Although he seldom uses terms like "Chinese theory of IR," he also, like Qin Yaqing, emphasizes the importance of rediscovering traditional Chinese thought with the final goal of developing a new research program with a distinctive hardcore. The real division between them seems to be the label "Chinese School" itself, which is indeed an obsession for many scholars but may be less consequential for the substantive theory-building process. Yan emphasizes that the nature of the "Tsinghua School" is not to displace existing IR theories, but to enrich them with traditional Chinese thought based on modern methodology. Although he has given more emphasis to the "enrich" aspect of his project, this is also one of Qin's stated aims. Indeed, given Yan's emphasis and his substantive work on pre-Qin thought, Qin has put him and the "Tsinghua School" within his scheme of the "Chinese paradigm of IR theory."[27]

Another scholar who seems to have rejected the possibility of an entirely new "Chinese School" is Shi Yinhong at Renmin University. Shi bluntly asserts that across-the-board innovation is the illusion of "revolutionaries." There can never be an entirely new Chinese IR theoretical system (or, for that matter, such a system from any other country). He endorses the effort to Sinicize IR theory but believes this can only be done by taking into account all three elements: Chinese problems and value orientation; all basic developmental trends in the world, as well as China's own development; and comprehensive study and judicious use of Western IR theory.[28] In unpublished remarks he has also argued that a Chinese theory or school is not something to be consciously sought by Chinese scholars; rather, it is to be discovered by foreign observers. When their interest in China grows and when they begin to read Chinese works, they will automatically discover Chinese theories such as those scattered around in the thoughts of Mao Zedong and Deng Xiaoping and in a great many other areas of China's copious historical and intellectual literature.

ASSESSING THE "CHINESE THEORY" PROJECT

The preceding section has taken the discourse about the "Chinese theory of IR" over the past two decades as a large intellectual project seeking to shape the content and direction of the Chinese IR discipline. "IR theory with Chinese characteristics," the "Chinese School of IR," and their various critics are best seen as subprojects and intellectual currents seeking to influence and lead the overall project of "Chinese theory of IR." The development and change of this larger project and its components are among the most important and consequential developments in Chinese IR since the late 1980s, explainable by the analytical model posited in the first section. The diverse internal debates show a general consensus among Chinese scholars about the need for the Sinicization of Western IR theory, that is, for building some kind of Chinese theories of IR. But there is only partial agreement on how this can be done and no agreement on the seemingly basic question of what to call it in a more specific way, other than the catch-all term "Sinicization." I shall now offer additional observations and critiques regarding the weaknesses and merits of the "Chinese theory" project, before suggesting an overall assessment of the Sinicization effort.

The first observation concerns the nature of such projects. Are they serious scholarly and intellectual efforts or thinly and fashionably disguised political and ideological ones to serve some practical and utilitarian purposes? While Robert Cox's famous adage that "theory is always for someone and for some purpose" should be kept in mind,[29] it is nevertheless extremely important to get the motive straight. No doubt most scholars will vehemently object to the characterization of their projects as anything less than serious scholarship. But reading some of their writings, especially the recent work by Zhu Feng on the need to build theories of IR and foreign policy with Chinese characteristics, one indeed gets the impression that more is going on than theoretical ambition. Zhu sees the Sinicization of IR as part of the larger process of China's rise. The stated aim of his project is to provide theoretical support for China's foreign policy and national interests. An important objective is to "prove" China's peaceful rise, even though the process has not been completed. Another curiosity arises when Zhu writes that theories of Chinese characteristics should be developed to help maintain the Chinese characteristics of China's foreign policy under new circumstances. Are such theories then meant to justify "Chinese characteristics" or to explain them, as well as the realities of Chinese foreign policy and international politics? One gets a confusing mixture of "action-oriented" and "knowledge-oriented" theory (to adopt Qin Yaqing's distinction) in Zhu's project.

Even more seriously, Zhu writes that his project is to theorize the idea and practice of the "harmonious world," a political slogan that has become fashionable among scholars looking for clues to Chinese theory.[30] Without dismissing its scholarly aspect, it is hard to miss this approach's political nature. More generally, the belief that a necessary starting point for developing Chinese theories has to be the promotion of China's national interests is prevalent among many scholars. A recent textbook entitled *China's International Relations Theory Research* holds the same basic premise in suggesting an outline of Chinese theories.[31] One may note that such a

premise inhibits theoretical innovation by automatically suppressing critical reflections on theory, especially when scholars simply follow what the
government has defined as China's national interest (such as "peaceful
rise").

Second, behind the urge to build Chinese theories is a very problematic premise that Western IR theories are somehow unable to explain Chinese phenomena, as if they are only useful in the Western context. The
claim that Western theories are inapplicable in the Chinese context is based
more on assertion and a superficial understanding of these theories than
on substantive arguments about where exactly Western theories err on the
basis of an in-depth review of the state of the art in Western IR. What
is it in the Chinese and Asian experiences that Western theories cannot
explain? Questions like this can only be answered by substantive theoretical and empirical work. Other important questions surface as well. What
is the value-added of Chinese theories? What are the distinctive Chinese
concepts and theories that can explain not only the Chinese but also the
Western experience? These are also questions the "Chinese theory" project purports to tackle. Before serious answers to these questions are given,
however, one should not hasten to declare the inapplicability of Western
theories, but should rather focus on finding out their weaknesses, thinking about ways to rectify them, or taking lessons from them in one's own
theory-building efforts.

Third, and related to the preceding, scholars of the "Chinese theory"
project invariably claim that China's historical experiences, traditional culture, and philosophy are essential sources for theory construction. But
except for a very few,[32] no serious scholarly effort has been undertaken to
examine and discover the value and applicability of traditional resources
for contemporary theorizing. Many scholars, with only a weak background
in traditional Chinese studies, are more interested and better trained in
Western IR than in rediscovering traditional Chinese resources.[33] In a
sense, the "Chinese theory" project is being undermined by the poverty of
empirical research among its advocates.

More problematic still, many seem to take an uncritical view of what
China's traditions are, relying chiefly on a selective set of works produced
in other fields (mainly history, culture, and philosophy) that fit their needs
but will have to reexamined in light of the latest research. A particularly
revealing example is Qin Yaqing's glib use of the notion of the "tribute system," identified as one of the three principal sources for building the "Chi-

nese school." But the "tribute system" is a Western rather than a Chinese concept. Furthermore, by drawing almost entirely on the well-known work of John Fairbank, Qin seems unaware of the fact that the Fairbankian paradigm has come under severe attack from Fairbank's own students and other scholars at least since the 1980s.[34] In ignoring a wealth of new and solid research in the past three decades, Qin has reified the "tribute system" for privileged treatment without adequate scholarly justification.

A more general problem is that uncritical reliance on conventional wisdom or longstanding stereotypes has unfortunately led to essentialization of China's past—seeing its essence as peace and harmony while blithely dismissing inconvenient anomalies. Indeed, to many scholars, traditional Chinese thought appears to consist of nothing more than Confucianism.[35] One wonders where Legalism, Daoism, Mohism, and other schools of thought have gone. Such sleight of hand does serious injustice to China's rich and multiple traditions.[36] A supreme irony is that while many claim to be faithful explorers and followers of China's past, they are in fact only thinly or even deceptively historical and cultural. If the "Chinese theory" project is to succeed, its members must be more deeply and critically historical.[37]

Fourth, with respect to the "Chinese School" project, one puzzle is why we would need a school named as such from a scholarly point of view. In other words, why can't we just let the academic and theoretical enterprise run its own course according to its own internal dynamics? Why can't we build new theories just by discovering existing anomalies and proposing remedies with help from whatever sources—be they traditional Chinese thought or the latest Western scholarship—necessary? The explicit call for a "Chinese School" when it does not yet exist requires an explanation. Such an explanation is hard to come by from a strictly scholarly perspective.[38]

Fifth, there are some problems internal to Qin's conception of the "Chinese School." That his argument is based on a selective and somewhat problematic literature of the philosophy of science has already been noted.[39] Another problem concerns the nature and importance of a "theoretical problematic." Qin claims that U.S. and British IR have developed out of their respective problematics: hegemonic maintenance for the former and international society for the latter. He then contends that Chinese scholars' difficulty in producing a Chinese school is due to their lack of awareness of the importance of a distinct theoretical problematic and proposes that China's peaceful integration into the world can be one such problematic.

Finally, perhaps the most serious flaw in the "Chinese theory" project is that it is too self-limiting for the healthy development of the Chinese IR discipline.[40] It is a sort of "theoretical exceptionalism," implying that new theories will have to be primarily grounded in Chinese sources and above all for Chinese problems, rather than in a broad base including both Chinese and non-Chinese sources and for both Chinese and non-Chinese problems.

Overall, then, the "Chinese theory" project, despite its scholarly ambition and courage, faces some inherent problems and limitations. This is not to suggest that Chinese theories of IR are impossible. Rather, it is to emphasize that the conception of "Chinese theory" as currently envisioned by many scholars is too narrow and self-limiting. A broad and open-minded approach, recognizing both the importance of using traditional Chinese resources and the need to draw on existing IR theories, while containing the exceptionalist urge as manifested in the "Chinese characteristics" and "Chinese School" projects, might better serve the Chinese IR discipline as a whole.

This essay has reviewed the history of China's IR discipline, focusing on one of its essential and most consequential developments: the rise, growth, and change in the "Chinese theory of IR" project. Two of the most notable intellectual movements in Chinese IR over the past two decades—"IR theory with Chinese characteristics" and the "Chinese School of IR"—are seen, together with their varied criticisms, as subprojects and intellectual currents within the larger "Chinese theory" project. I have attempted to explain both the overall disciplinary development of Chinese IR and the more specific "Chinese theory" project by developing a model based on four factors: state-society relations, China's international standing, the historical and intellectual tradition, and the intellectual structure of Chinese IR. It appears from this analysis that while the "Chinese theory" project has some inherent problems and limitations, the debates surrounding it have improved Chinese scholars' understanding of the weaknesses and promises of Chinese IR. In this sense it is heralding a new stage in China's IR discipline: a more self-conscious attempt to supply Chinese IR with a solid and independent disciplinary foundation, as well as to develop it into a distinctive brand in the global IR field.

NOTES

1. See, e.g., Qin Yaqing, "Why Is There No Chinese International Relations Theory?" *International Relations of the Asia-Pacific* 7, no. 3 (2007): 313–40; Wang Yizhou, "Xulun" [preface], in *Zhongguo Guoji Guanxi Yanjiu 1995–2005* [IR studies in China 1995–2005], ed. Wang Yizhou and Yuan Zhengqing (Beijing: Peking University Press, 2006), 1–60; Ni Shixiong, Su Changhe, and Jin Yingzhong, "Zhongguo Guoji Wenti Yanjiu 60 Nian" [China's international studies in sixty years], in *Duiwai Guanxi yu Guoji Wenti Yanjiu* [Foreign relations and international studies], ed. Yang Jiemian (Shanghai: Shanghai People's Press, 2009), 211–17.

2. See, e.g., Ole Wæver, "The Sociology of a Not So International Discipline: American and European Developments in International Relations," *International Organization* 52, no. 4 (1998): 687–727; Barry Buzan and Lene Hansen, *The Evolution of International Security Studies* (Cambridge: Cambridge University Press, 2009).

3. Wæver, "Sociology of a Not So International Discipline," 694–95.

4. The following account draws on works listed in note 1.

5. Shi Bin, "Guoji Guanxi Yanjiu 'Zhongguohua' de Lunzheng" [Debates on the 'Sinicization' of international relations study], in Wang and Yuan, *Zhongguo Guoji Guanxi Yanjiu 1995–2005,* 518–45, at 522; Ren Xiao, "Zou Zizhu Fazhan Zhilu: Zhenglun zhong de 'Zhongguo Xuepai'" [Taking the independent development route: The "Chinese School" in dispute), *Guoji Zhengzhi Yanjiu* [International politics quarterly] 2 (2009): 15–28, at 17.

6. Qin, "Why Is There No Chinese International Relations Theory?" 317.

7. Ibid., 45.

8. Qin Yaqing, "Zhongguo Guoji Guanxi Lilun" [Chinese theories of international law], in *Zhonguo Quiwai Guanxi Zhuangxing 30 nian* [The transformation of China's foreign relations in thirty years], ed. Hang Yizhou (Beijing: Social Sciences Academic Press, 2008), 306–43, at 338.

9. China's leading theorist Qin Yaqing's latest term for the phenomenon is "Chinese paradigm of IR theory." See Qin, "Zhongguo Guoji Guanxi Lilun."

10. Shi Bin, "Guoji Guanxi Yanjiu 'Zhongguohua' de Lunzheng," 521–22.

11. Ibid., 522–24.

12. Liang Shoude, "Zhongguo Guoji Zhengzhixue Lilun Jianshe de Tansuo" [Explorations into the construction of international political theory in China], *Shijie Jingji yu Zhengzhi* [World economics and politics] 2 (2005): 16–21.

13. Zhu Feng, "Zhongguo Tese de Guoji Guanxi yu Waijiao Lilun Chuangxin Yanjiu—Xin Yicheng, Xin Kuangjia, Xin Tiaozhan" [Innovative research on international relations and foreign policy theories with Chinese characteristics—new agenda, new framework, new challenges], *Guoji Zhengzhi Yanjiu* 2 (2009): 1–14.

14. See Song Xinning, "Building International Relations Theory with Chinese Characteristics," *Journal of Contemporary China* 10, no. 26 (2001): 61–74; Shi Bin, "Guoji Guanxi Yanjiu 'Zhongguohua' de Lunzheng," 522–24.

15. Wang Yong, "Shilun Jianli Guoji Guanxi Lilun de Shizheng Fangfa: Jianping Guoji Guanxi Lilun de 'Zhongguo Tese'" [Empirical methods in the creation of international relations theory: With commentary on "Chinese characteristics" in international relations theory], *Guoji Zhengzhi Yanjiu* 4 (1994): 34–41, at 39.

16. Li Bin, "Guoji Guanxi Lilun yu Bentuhua Wenti" [Theories of international relations and indigenization], *Shijie Jingji yu Zhengzhi* 4 (2003): 69–71.

17. Shi Bin, "Guoji Guanxi Yanjiu 'Zhongguohua' de Lunzheng," 527–29; see also Qin, "Zhongguo Guoji Guanxi Lilun," 320.

18. Ren, "Zou Zizhu Fazhan Zhilu," 16.

19. Ibid.

20. Qin Yaqing, "Theoretical Problematic of International Relationship Theory and the Construction of a Chinese School," *Social Sciences in China* (English edition) (Winter 2005): 62–72; Qin Yaqing, "Guoji Guanxi Lilun Zhongguo Xuepai Shengcheng de Keneng he Biran" [A Chinese School of international relations theory: Possibility and inevitability], *Shijie Jingji yu Zhengzhi* 3 (2006): 7–13. See also Qin, "Why Is There No Chinese International Relations Theory?"

21. Qin, "Zhongguo Guoji Guanxi Lilun," 338.

22. Wang Yizhou, "Xulun," 54.

23. Wang Jisi, *Guoji Zhengzhi de Lixing Sikao* [Rational reflections on international politics] (Beijing: Peking University Press, 2006), 32. See also Ni, Su, and Jin, "Zhongguo Guoji Wenti Yanjiu 60 Nian," 227.

24. Shi Bin, "Guoji Guanxi Yanjiu 'Zhongguohua' de Lunzheng," 537–43.

25. Ni, Su, and Jin, "Zhongguo Guoji Wenti Yanjiu 60 Nian," 221.

26. Yan Xuetong, "Why Is There No Chinese School of IR Theory" (in Chinese), in Yan Xuetong, Xu Jin, et al., *Wangba Tianxia Sixiang jiqi Qidi* [Thoughts on world leadership and its implications] (Beijing: World Knowledge Press, 2009), 294–301; Yan Xuetong, "Guoji Guanxi Lilun shi Pushixing de" [IR theory is universal], *Shijie Jingji yu Zhengzhi* 2 (2006): 1–22.

27. Qin, "Zhongguo Guoji Guanxi Lilun," 339.

28. Shi Yinhong, "Guoji Guanxi Lilun Yanjiu yu Pingpan de Ruogan Wenti" [Several problems in the research and evaluation of IR theory], *Zhongguo Shehui Kexue* [Social sciences in china] 1 (2004): 89–91.

29. Robert W. Cox, "Social Forces, States and World Orders: Beyond International Relations Theory," *Millennium: Journal of International Studies* 10, no. 2 (1981): 126–55.

30. Zhu, "Zhongguo Tese de Guoji Guanxi yu Waijiao Lilun Chuangxin Yanjiu," 1.

31. Zhao Kejin and Ni Shixiong, *Zhongguo Guoji Guanxi Lilun Yanjiu* [China's international relations theory research] (Shanghai: Fudan University Press, 2007).

32. These are principally those of the "Tsinghua School": Yan Xuetong and Xu Jin, *Zhongguo Xianqin Guojiajian Zhengzhi Sixiang Xuandu* [Pre-Qin Chinese thoughts on foreign relations] (Shanghai: Fudan University Press, 2008); Yan, Jin, et al., *Wangba Tianxia Sixiang ji Qita*.

33. Wang Yizhou, *Tanxun Quanqiu Zhuyi Guoji Guanxi,* 383–84; Ren, "Zou Zizhu Fazhan Zhilu," 26.

34. See Zhang Feng, "Rethinking the 'Tribute System': Broadening the Conceptual Horizon of Historical East Asian Politics," *Chinese Journal of International Politics* 2, no. 4 (2009): 545–74.

35. See, e.g., Qin, "Zhongguo Guoji Guanxi Lilun," 326.

36. In the foreign relations area, see Michael H. Hunt, "Chinese Foreign Relations in Historical Perspective," in *China's Foreign Relations in the 1980s,* ed. Harry Harding (New Haven: Yale University Press, 1984), 1–42.

37. Victoria Tin-bor Hui, "Goujian 'Zhongguo Xuepai' Bixu Zhengshi Lishi" [Constructing the "Chinese School" must confront history], *Shijie Jingji yu Zhengzhi* 5 (2010): 124–38.

38. See a similar point in Lu, "Chuangjian Zhongguo Guoji Guanxi Lilun Sizhong Tujing de Fenxi yu Pingjia," 59.

39. Lu, "Chuangjian Zhongguo Guoji Guanxi Lilun Sizhong Tujing de Fenxi yu Pingjia," 60.

40. I am indebted to William Callahan for this observation and the preceding one on the British school. For Callahan's earlier view of the "Chinese theory," see William A. Callahan, "China and the Globalisation of IR Theory: Discussion of 'Building International Relations Theory with Chinese Characteristics,'" *Journal of Contemporary China* 10, no. 26 (2001): 75–88.

2

Confucianism and Chinese Politics

5

Contemporary New Confucianism

Background, Varieties, and Significance

Liu Shuxian

BACKGROUND

During the Song (960–1279) and the Ming (1368–1644) dynasties, China developed one of the most advanced civilizations in the world. In the seventeenth century, Jesuits who visited China, such as Matteo Ricci, who died in Beijing in 1610, maintained good relationships as well as fruitful scholarly exchanges with Chinese intellectuals. They tried to find common ground between Chinese and Christian traditions. During the Qing Dynasty (1644–1912), Emperor Kang Xi continued the Ming Dynasty policy and held a tolerant attitude toward Christian missionaries. However, he insisted that the Chinese rites of ancestor worship and public homage to Confucius were civil rather than religious ceremonies and could continue to be practiced by Christian converts. Yet during the controversy over these rituals, the Vatican ruled against the Jesuits and forbade Catholic missionaries to follow Kang Xi's orders. The emperor responded with an order of expulsion against all those who refused to sign a certificate accepting Kang's position. This mutual hard line wrecked the power base of the missions and effectively prevented the spread of Western teaching and science in China. Unfortunately, it was during the next couple of hundred years that scientific progress in the West produced the Industrial Revolution. Imperialism is not possible unless there is a vast difference in national powers, and China paid a heavy price for adopting a closed-door policy. In the nineteenth century, Western powers used their gunboats to open up ports in the Far East, and China was forced to change her traditional ways. The crisis was nothing short of the twin crises of order and meaning. Institutional Confucianism, along with its super-stable structure, came to an end with the fall of Qing, the last dynasty, in 1912, replaced by the Republic of China.

The challenge the Chinese culture has had to face over the last two hundred years has been far more stringent than anything it experienced in the past. As the mother culture in the Far East, it had never encountered another culture that was superior or even equal to itself. Now suddenly it was under the onslaught of a superior Western civilization. A paradigm shift was forced on China, and she was left with no choice but to make drastic changes, if only for the sake of survival; otherwise her fate would be worse than that of a subcolony, as Sun Zhongshan (Sun Yat-sen, 1866–1925), the founder of the Republic of China, observed.

China's responses to the West were much slower and less efficient than those of Japan, which was used to borrowing from outside sources. China tried very hard to maintain her pride and keep her traditional ways, but to no avail. Zhang Zhidong (1837–1909), a great advocate for railroads and heavy industry, made the famous statement that we should take "Chinese learning for *Ti* [substance], and Western learning for *Yong* [function]." However, as later scholars know, Western learning has its own substance and function, which cannot be separated from each other. Kang Youwei (1859–1927) made a valiant attempt to push for radical reform within the Confucian framework. He belonged to the modern-text school that interpreted the *Spring and Autumn Annals,* believed in the secret message of the classics, and took Confucius to be someone who tried to carry out the reform of systems or institutions in his own time in the name of returning to the ancient ways. Yet the so-called Hundred-Day Reform promoted by Kang under the reign of the young Emperor Guang Xu was crushed by the Empress Dowager and failed miserably. With it the reformers' last rays of hope were gone, and finally revolutionaries succeeded in overthrowing the Qing Dynasty in 1912. A new page was turned in China's history.

In 1919 the central government was under the control of warlords. Idealistic university students protested against secret agreements between the government and Japan; they initiated the so-called May Fourth Movement, which turned into the vigorous New Culture Movement, potent for a few years. It became the vogue to put all the blame for China's problems on the Confucian tradition; popular slogans included "Down with the Confucian shop!" and "Throw the stitched volumes into the toilet!" It seemed that China was on the road of no return.

The undisputed leader in the trend to Westernize or modernize was Hu Shi (1891–1962), who upheld the ideals of freedom, democracy, and science. He had studied under John Dewey at Columbia University, promoted pragmatism in China, and used new methods to investigate Chinese philosophy in the ancient period. However, his proposal for gradual reform could not meet the demands of the time. China had to face both serious internal problems and domination by foreign powers, culminating in the Japanese invasion that led to World War II. China tended to adopt more and more radical means for her survival. Eventually, all these led to the establishment of the People's Republic of China in 1949 under the leadership of Chairman Mao Zedong (1893–1976) and drove the Nationalist regime to the island of Taiwan. The official ideology of the Communist regime on Mainland China is Marxism-Leninism-Maoism, another foreign import adapted to the Chinese environment. Under the direction of Mao and the Gang of Four, the anti-Confucius campaign reached its climax during the disastrous Cultural Revolution (1967–1977). It was only after the death of Mao that China returned to a more moderate policy, and the fortunes of Confucius as well as of Confucianism have gradually changed in recent years. Despite the prediction of Joseph Levenson in the late 1960s that Confucianism would become something dead that could only be found in museums, it appears to be thriving; in the new century and millennium, it is like a phoenix reborn from the ashes.

VARIETIES OF CONFUCIANISM

Confucianism may mean different things to different people. Unless we make clear what we understand by the term, there cannot be meaningful discussions of the topic. I adopted a threefold division to distinguish among three distinct but related meanings of the term:

1. *Spiritual Confucianism:* the tradition of great thinkers such as Confucius, Mencius, Cheng and Zhu, and Lu and Wang that has been revived by Contemporary New Confucians as their ultimate commitment.[1]

2. *Politicized Confucianism:* the tradition of Dong Zhongshu, Ban Gu, and others that served as the official ideology of the dynasties and absorbed ingredients from schools of thought such as Daoism, Legalism, and the Yinyang school.
3. *Popular Confucianism:* Belief at the grassroots level that emphasizes concepts such as family values, diligence, and education and can hardly be separated from beliefs in popular Buddhism and Daoism, as well as various kinds of superstitions.

It goes without saying that on the conceptual level the three must be kept distinct, even though in reality they are intricately related to one another. However, since the demise of institutional Confucianism with the fall of Qing in 1912, Confucianism no longer occupies the center but has moved to the periphery. Under such circumstances, Confucianism certainly does not belong to the mainstream of Chinese thought. Yet that does not mean that it can be uprooted altogether either. Not only have some of its ideas and practices become such long-entrenched habits of the Chinese that they have inadvertently produced beneficial as well as harmful consequences, but some leading intellectuals have refused to abandon the Confucian cause. In fact, the most creative talents in contemporary Chinese philosophy can be found in the camp of Contemporary New Confucianism. Thus, it is necessary to keep an eye on the Confucian tradition. The time now seems ripe for an in-depth reexamination of the tradition.

In 1986 Mainland China designated Contemporary New Confucianism (*Xiandai Xin Ruxue*) a national research program; it is understood to be one of the three powerful trends of thought in China, its significance on a par with Western liberalism and communism. As a matter of fact, not only has spiritual Confucianism been recognized as a vigorous movement of thought, but politicized Confucianism has also attracted a large number of admirers. *Time Magazine* (June 14, 1993) used Confucius's portrait on its cover and reported that Francis Fukuyama, author of *The End of History,* was of the opinion that the kind of soft authoritarianism practiced in Singapore posed a greater challenge to Western liberalism than did Islam. Some sociologists such as Peter Berger believe that vulgar (popular) Confucianism has contributed a great deal to the economic miracles accomplished since the 1970s by Japan and the so-called Four Mini-Dragons: Taiwan, Hong Kong, Singapore, and Korea. All these deserve to be explored further. Naturally, my own effort will concentrate only on an inquiry into spiritual Confucianism.

The scope of the so-called New Confucianism is not clearly defined. It may include scholars with various backgrounds, such as scholar-thinker Liang Shuming (1893–1988), scholar-statesman Zhang Junmai (Carsun Chang, 1887–1969), historian Qian Mu (1895–1990), and leading intellectual historian and political commentator Xu Fuguan (1903–1982). After broad consultations and extensive discussions under the guidance of Fang Keli and Li Jingquan, directors of the program to research Contemporary New Confucianism, ten case studies were completed in a span of ten years. In addition to the four listed above, the program also examined the work of Xiong Shili (1885–1968), Feng Yu-lan (1895–1990), He Lin (1902–1992), Fang Dongmei (Thomé H. Fang, 1899–1977), Tang Junyi (1909–1978), and Mou Zongsan (1909–1995). When the research program's directors made arrangements with the China Broadcasting and Television Publishing Company in Beijing to publish the selected writings of fifteen New Confucian scholars, the names of four younger scholars were also included: Yü Ying-shih (1930–), Liu Shuxian) (1934–), Cheng Chung-ying (1935–), and Du Weiming (1940–). Among the older generation Ma Yifu (1883–1967), a noted scholar in classics studies, was also added. Eventually, fourteen volumes were in print, as the Qian Mu volume has not been published because of copyright issues. This may not be the best list of Contemporary New Confucians, but it is difficult to come up with something better. Thus, while I accept this list, I go further to assign the fifteen scholars to four groups in three generations:

The First Generation
    Group 1: Liang, Xiong, Ma, and Zhang
    Group 2: Feng, He, Qian, and Fang
The Second Generation
    Group 3: Tang, Mou, and Xu
The Third Generation
    Group 4: Yu, Liu, Cheng, and Du

Liang, Xiong, and Ma have been recognized as the three elders in the first generation. Liang is seen as the person who first blew the horn that initiated the whole movement. It was Xiong, however, known only in a small scholarly circle, who became the spiritual leader of *Dangdai Xin*

Rujia (Contemporary New Confucianism in the narrower sense). As the three most important representatives of *gang tai Xin Rujia* (Hong Kong and Taiwan New Confucianism), Tang, Mou, and Xu, were all his disciples. The three elders chose to remain in Mainland China in 1949, but Zhang, as the leader of a third-force political party, fled overseas, promoted New Confucian ideas in the United States, and became a representative of *Hai-wai Xin Rujia* (Overseas New Confucianism).

The scholars of the first generation in Group 2 were somewhat younger. Feng took a course with Liang while still a student at Beijing University, although he was only a couple of years younger than Liang. He went abroad to study at Columbia University in 1919 and developed his own philosophy during World War II. He based his ideas on a reinterpretation of Zhu Xi's (1130–1200) *Lixue* (learning of principle). His colleague He Lin believed that the future of Chinese philosophy should lie in a reinterpretation of Wang Yangming's (1472–1529) *Xinxue* (learning of the heart-mind). Both chose to remain in Mainland China after 1949, which meant the end of the development of their philosophy. Qian, on the other hand, decided to flee to Hong Kong. He and Tang became the two most important founders of the New Asia College in 1949, which has since then been recognized as a center for Contemporary New Confucianism. Yu was one of the first graduates of the institute. Later, in 1963, the college became one of the foundation colleges of the Chinese University of Hong Kong. Fang fled to Taiwan, where, as a young professor, he taught Western philosophy (Tang had once been his student in Nanjing). He published his most important works on Chinese philosophy in Taiwan and taught a younger generation of scholars, including Liu and Cheng, at Taiwan University.

Without question, the mainstay of Contemporary New Confucianism is represented by the second generation of scholars: Tang, Mou, and Xu. While Tang started the New Asia College in Hong Kong, Mou and Xu fled to Taiwan. When a liberal Christian institute, Donghai University, was established in 1955 in Taizhong, first Xu and then Mou joined the faculty, making it the second center of Contemporary New Confucianism for a decade, from the mid-1950s to the mid-1960s. Liu was recruited to teach in 1958. Du was a graduate from Donghai in 1961. Finally, Tang, Xu, and Mou all ended their careers at the New Asia Research Institute, a private institute that was separated from the Chinese University of Hong Kong in 1975. On New Year's Day of 1958, the famous "Manifesto for a Reappraisal of Sinology and Reconstruction of Chinese Culture" was published. It has been regarded as a landmark for the emergence of the Contemporary New Confucian movement in the narrower sense. The manifesto was drafted by Tang, urged by Zhang, revised by Mou and Xu, and put into final form only after extensive discussions among them. Eventually, only these four scholars signed the manifesto. Qian did not sign the document for various reasons I cannot specify here. As a result, he is not included in the camp of Contemporary New Confucianism in a narrower sense. It may be said that their goals were similar, but their approaches were different.

Finally, the third generation of scholars, in Group 4, were all disciples of Hong Kong or Taiwan New Confucians. They went abroad to earn their advanced degrees and have (or once had) teaching careers in the United States. As they have lived a long time in both Chinese and Western cultures and have moved freely between the two worlds, naturally they have a more international perspective; they have become representatives of overseas New Confucianism. They are now in their sixties or early seventies, so there is still room for further development in their thoughts and scholarship. Even though their directions are clear, nothing definitive can be said about scholars in this group. Moreover, the story of New Confucianism certainly does not end here, as the fourth generation of scholars is still in the making; for the time being they have not yet earned the stature of their predecessors and so are not studied by current research projects on the movement.[2]

As my interest here is primarily philosophical, it is understandable that my emphasis in the following will be on Contemporary New Confucianism in the narrower sense. In the three generations of scholars, my attention will be on Liang and Xiong in Group 1, Feng and Fang in Group 2, and Tang and Mou in Group 3.

Liang initiated the movement in 1920. The debate between scientists and metaphysicians broke out in 1923, with Zhang representing the New Confucian position, which echoed Liang's thought. However, that was only a prelude for the movement. It was not until the Japanese invasion threatened to turn China into a colony that Feng developed the first Contemporary New Confucian philosophical system. He learned from *Yijing* (The book of changes) that a bright moment would follow the darkest moment, just as early spring would follow severe winter. In 1939 he published *Xin Lixue* (New learning of principle), intended to be a reinterpretation of Zhu Xi's Neo-Confucian philosophy; this work was followed by five more books, with the last volume published in 1946. He Lin was the first to use the term *Xin Rujia* (New Confucianism) in the contemporary sense, in an article published in 1941. He saw the future of Chinese philosophy in a *Xin Xinxue* (new learning of the mind). However, he himself was not able to develop a philosophical system of his own. His expectation was fulfilled by the publication of the vernacular version of Xiong's *Xin Weishi Lun* (New doctrine of consciousness-only) in 1944.

Xiong was older than Feng by ten years, but he was known only within a very small circle of scholars. When Liang prepared to leave Beijing University in 1922, he recommended Xiong to teach *Weishi* (consciousness-only) Buddhism in his place. In the process of preparing his lecture notes, however, Xiong came to question more and more the teachings of *Weishi,* which he had learned from his teacher Ouyang Jingwu (1871–1943) at the China Institute of Buddhism in Nanjing from 1920 to 1922. Eventually, he turned to the philosophy of creativity in *Yijing* and published the first draft of *Xin Weishi Lun,* written in classical Chinese, in 1932, which caused many debates in the Buddhist circle. Yet he insisted on his own course, holding onto his lone lantern; he published his magnum opus in 1944, attracted a number of bright students, and inadvertently became the spiritual leader of the New Confucian movement. As Chen Rongjie noted: "Liang, in giving the Confucian concept of *jen* [*Ren*] a new interpretation of dynamic intuition, exerted tremendous influence on the New Culture Movement in the 1920's, but he did not evolve a philosophical system of his own. Hsiung [Xiong] has done this. Besides, he has influenced more young Chinese philosophers than any other contemporary Chinese philosopher."[3] Among those influenced were, of course, Tang and Mou. Fang was another solitary figure. In his early career, he concentrated on the study of Western philosophy and showed his preference for classical Greek philosophy over modern European philosophy, as he detected a nihilistic turn in the latter. His research was also disrupted by the war. He gave public lectures in the manner of Fichte to reawaken the spirit of the Chinese people, and he studied Buddhist scriptures when he could have access to them in the temples. He wrote his major works on Chinese philosophy in Taiwan and developed a grand scheme of a philosophy of culture, which covers classical Greek, modern European, Indian, and Chinese cultures. Unfortunately, he did not get to finish this project, although he did influence younger generations of scholars such as Liu, Cheng, and Fu Weixun (Charles Wei-hsun Fu).

Ironically, the movement did not become vigorously intellectual until some of the scholars were driven out of their homeland and became refugees in Hong Kong, Taiwan, and overseas. None of Xiong's disciples, such as Tang, Mou, and Xu, followed their teacher's approach: starting with a critique of consciousness-only Buddhism and then returning to the classics of Confucianism. In fact, they all disagreed with Xiong's interpretation of the classics during his later years. Rather, they were inspired by his spirit, which went far beyond his publications. Although Tang and Mou never went abroad to study, they were well versed in Western philosophy, and each had a comprehensive and comparative perspective. In temperament, Tang appeared to be more Hegelian, while Mou was more Kantian. In 1953 Tang published *The Spiritual Values of the Chinese Culture* (in Chinese), presenting a comprehensive overview of traditional Chinese culture, as he understood it. He acknowledged that he had been influenced by Xiong and Mou in his understanding of Chinese philosophy and also by Fang in his appreciation of the sentiment of life and the sense of beauty found in Chinese culture. When he died in 1978, Mou praised his friend as a giant in the cosmos of cultural consciousness. Mou probably was the most original thinker of his generation; he had great powers of conceptualization and personal charisma. Moreover, as he lived longer, naturally he exerted even greater influence on the next generations of scholars.

Liang Shuming as Pioneer

In the following, I shall devote myself to finding clues to answers to the two most puzzling questions that have deeply bothered me in connection with the movement. First, how is it possible that the emergence of Contemporary New Confucianism came right after the iconoclastic May Fourth Movement in 1919? Second, how is it possible that only a few refugee scholars could initiate the Contemporary New Confucian Movement under the most difficult circumstances? It was initially ignored; then gained some recognition overseas; and finally earned respect even in Mainland China after the fierce anti-Confucian campaign that lasted a whole decade during the disastrous Cultural Revolution, which ended in 1977. In order to answer the first question, we must reexamine the circumstances in which Liang's thoughts emerged and review the situation that led to the breakout of the debates on science and metaphysics. In order to answer the second question, we must study the significance of the declaration issued on New Year's Day of 1958. In this section, I shall focus on the first question, and in the next section I shall turn to the second.

The first thinker who reflected in depth from a New Confucian perspective on the problems of culture was undoubtedly Liang. At first, he did not seem to fit the stereotype of a conservative. He had been exposed to Western learning at a tender age. As a young scholar, he was greatly attracted by Buddhist philosophy and believed that only Buddhism could provide the ultimate answers about life. He very much wanted to become a monk. It was not until 1921 that he changed his mind in a decisive manner and got married to start his own family, in order to fulfill his worldly duties as a Confucian before he could renounce his family and retreat into the quiet life of a monastery. In 1917, when he was invited to give lectures on Indian philosophy at Beijing University, he was already under pressure to respond to the problems of culture. After the May Fourth Movement broke out in 1919 and turned into the vigorous, iconoclastic New Culture Movement, he engaged in developing his ideas of comparative culture and started to write on the subject. He gave his first lectures on East-West cultures and their philosophies in 1920 on the campus of Beijing University.[4] Then he was invited to give a series of lectures at Jinan First Middle School in Shandong Province in 1921. A book based on his lecture notes was published the same year. In 1922, a new edition was printed in large characters. It became a bestseller and has exerted broad influence ever since.

His ideas may appear to be overly simplified from our perspective today, but they did touch upon certain fundamental problems for the development of culture and were thought-provoking in those days. He took a comparative approach and found that Western, Chinese, and Indian cultures have opted for three different directions in life. According to him, the guiding spirit of Western culture is a belief that the Will always strives forward, its characteristics the conquest of nature, the scientific method, and democracy. The guiding spirit for Chinese culture, on the other hand, is that the Will aims at achieving harmony and equilibrium, its characteristics contentment, adjustment to the environment, and acceptance of authority; such a culture would not invent steamships and trains or democracy. Finally, the guiding spirit of Indian culture is that the Will looks backward; the only thing it cares about is religious aspiration and liberation from worldly cares. Thus, Western culture values material gratification, Chinese culture values social life, and Indian culture values transcendence.

After examining these three directions of life, Liang felt he was ready to answer the question of what attitudes should be adopted today. Apparently, Liang changed his mind and deviated from his earlier views, as he found that the Indian and Chinese cultures were premature and had failed to fully develop their potentialities. His conclusions at the time were as follows: (1) that as the Indian attitude looks backward, it must be totally excluded; (2) that Western achievements must be adopted without reservation, but that the Western emphasis on striving forward only would cause serious problems and hence must be changed so that its undesirable consequences could be avoided; and (3) that the middle way of Chinese culture, which looks both forward and backward, should be revived from a critical point of view. Confucius's strength was that he found resources in life itself; both traditional shortcomings and modern diseases could be overcome in the future. Liang, of course, never showed how such a synthesis could actually be achieved, but instead of following the vogue of putting all the blame on the Confucian tradition, he was the first to suggest the revival of Confucianism as a way to face the contemporary situation.

Clearly, Liang could never be accused of being a reactionary thinker, as he opened his arms to embrace Mr. Democracy and Mr. Science from the West; however, he also saw the limitations of Western culture, which is well equipped to conquer nature but fails to find harmony among individuals. Even though he committed himself to reviving the Confucian spirit, he never took Confucianism as his ultimate concern. Thus, when Guy Alitto had the chance to pay a personal visit to Liang in Beijing, he was shocked to find that Liang rejected the label "the last Confucian" for himself—not only was he not the last Confucian, but he also looked beyond Confucianism to find messages for liberation from Buddhism, the last stage of development of life and culture as he saw it.[5]

With this background in place, we are now ready to answer some of the questions raised before. Clearly, Liang made a sharp distinction between spiritual Confucianism and institutional Confucianism. The rigid system of rites and ritual had died with the fall of the last dynasty; the remnants of the system were denounced by the New Culture Movement. The spirit of Confucianism, however, symbolized by Confucius himself and transmitted by Neo-Confucians, especially Wang Yangming (1472–1529) in the Ming Dynasty, never dies. It teaches a perennial philosophy and has significance not only for the Chinese but also for the rest of the world. Such is the fundamental message transmitted by Contemporary New Confucianism, even though expressions of this insight differ significantly from one individual to another. It is in this sense that Liang is honored as the initiator of the movement.

Throughout his life, Liang never changed his basic convictions. In 1924 he began to envision a book on the human mind and human life. In 1926 he even wrote a preface for the planned volume. He gave several lectures on the theme after that, and his lecture notes were preserved. In 1960 he started to write the book, with seven chapters completed by 1966. Then the Cultural Revolution broke out, and the project was disrupted. In 1970 he resumed writing, and the book was finally completed in 1975 but was not published until 1984. Without doubt, it reflects Liang's thoughts in his later years. He still maintained that Eastern cultures turn inward while Western culture turns outward. He paid tribute to the accomplishments of the People's Republic of China under the leadership of Chairman Mao. However, these achievements still put emphasis on the conquest of nature and, by extension, on class struggles. There was still a further need to return to the Confucian tradition, which could bring about harmony in the world of human relations; he also believed in a common human nature, over and above different class distinctions. Besides, as the spheres of religion and morality are different, he still found the need to find liberation from the bondage of the mind to the body by returning to the Buddhist tradition.

There is no doubt that Liang had a fiercely independent mind, and he is famous for his integrity, refusing to bend under external pressures. Yet some misconceptions need to be corrected. In 1953 he was severely criticized by Chairman Mao and Premier Zhou Enlai, as he had dared to speak out against some of the farm policies practiced at the time. In 1955 there was even a nationwide movement against Liang's "reactionary" thoughts. However, he stood his ground and cited Confucius's saying as his defense: "The commander of three armies may be taken away, but the will of a common man may not be taken away from him." His courage earned him great admiration overseas. Still, it is wrong to project him as the opposite of Mao. Actually, throughout his life he showed great admiration for the so-called great helmsman. As he saw it, if Mao had not made a correct social analysis, he could not have succeeded in bringing about the revolution and becoming the founder of People's Republic of China in 1949. In general, he agreed with Mao on egalitarian socialist ideals; he was only unhappy about certain practices. He also blamed himself for not speaking to Mao in the proper manner and thus arousing Mao's anger. Although he criticized Mao's failures and confusion in his later years in a letter sent to *Baixing*, a Hong Kong magazine, in January 1982, he nevertheless considered Mao's direction to be correct. This was his understanding during the disastrous

Cultural Revolution. An unpublished manuscript included in *Collected Works of Liang Shuming* has confirmed that such is the case.[6]

In sum, Liang always maintained that some sort of evolution through the process of Westernization is necessary; otherwise China cannot survive. However, there is no need to take the capitalist road and repeat the mistakes made by the West, which have produced dire consequences. A far better alternative is to adopt the socialist approach. As he saw it, China under the leadership of Mao had taken such an approach and, in so doing, had shown the world its great creativity. Furthermore, this approach, which emphasizes unselfish drives to form a civilization that takes care of the welfare of the people, will prepare China for a smooth transition to the next stage of the development of culture, one dominated by the Confucian ideal of harmony.

Because China was isolated from the rest of the world for a long time, Liang felt the desire to see China as the leader in the process of creating a higher civilization for humankind. Then the Cultural Revolution ended in 1977, and the Gang of Four fell after Mao died in 1976. Under the leadership of Deng Xiaoping, a more realistic open-door policy was adopted, which continues at the present time. Capitalism is now seen as a necessary stage before socialist ideals can be put in practice. In his later years, Liang seemed to be out of sync with current developments. Eventually, he died in 1988. The major problem faced by Liang and other intellectuals who chose to remain in Mainland China after 1949 was that due to political intervention, they were no longer allowed to develop their own ideas freely but were forced to twist their thoughts to respond to the demands of self-criticism and reform authority imposed on them in a closed society. They were deprived of intellectual resources, lacked information on outside developments, and were somewhat inadvertently forced to rationalize their thoughts within the limits set by authority. Some of them still tried very hard to maintain their integrity, even at the price of their lives; those lucky enough to survive could not help but be influenced by their environment, as reflected in their publications after 1949.

Liang was a case in point. He failed to understand the power of market forces, which caused the breakup of the Soviet Union and the fall of the Berlin Wall. Even more important, he failed to appreciate the checks-and-balances system of Western democracy. It is exactly because of the lack of such a system that the disastrous Cultural Revolution could take place in China. Here lies one of the main differences between the New Confucians who chose to remain in Mainland China and those who chose to flee to Hong Kong, Taiwan, and overseas: the latter realized that pure moral ideals alone will not suffice and that the checks-and-balances system of Western democracy, which has never been developed in a traditional culture, is the only thing that can prevent tyranny from trampling on the basic human rights of people. Democracy may not be a good system, but we have not found anything better. Consequently, the only alternative is to have an elected government with limited powers; the promotion of moral ideals must depend on other nongovernmental forces. From the above, we can see that Liang was indeed the first to start the contemporary New Confucian Movement, but he was not a factor in the rise of the Hong Kong, Taiwan, or overseas New Confucian movements.

THE SIGNIFICANCE OF NEW CONFUCIANISM

In 1941 the Japanese bombed Pearl Harbor, which was the turning point of World War II. Eventually, the Japanese surrendered in 1945. However, the civil war between the Nationalists and the Communists raged on, until the former were driven to Taiwan, and the People's Republic of China was established in 1949 under the leadership of Mao Zedong. This marked the parting of the ways for the New Confucians. Liang Shuming, Xiong Shili, Ma Yifu, Feng Youlan, and He Lin chose to remain in Mainland China, and consequently the development of their thought was interrupted by political interventions. Zhang Junmai, Qian Mu, Fang Dongmei, Tang Junyi, Mou Zongsan, and Xu Fuguan, on the other hand, refused to live under Communist rule, chose to be refugee scholars, and fled overseas to Hong Kong and Taiwan. Under severe hardship they upheld their ideals; luckily, however, circumstances allowed them to develop their scholarly careers and become mainstays of Hong Kong, Taiwan, and overseas New Confucianism.

On New Year's Day of 1958, "A Manifesto for a Reappraisal of Sinology and Reconstruction of Chinese Culture," signed by Zhang, Tang, Mou, and Xu, appeared in *Minzhu Pinglun* (Democracy review) and *Zaisheng* (Rebirth) magazines. It is without a doubt the most important document issued by this group of scholars and has been regarded as a landmark for the Contemporary New Confucian Movement. As the title suggests, the manifesto was addressed to Sinologists in the West who had failed to take the proper approach in studying Chinese culture. They were urged not to view Chinese culture through the eyes of missionaries, archeologists, or political strategists, but with a sense of reverence and sympathetic understanding. According to Tang and his colleagues, the wisdom of Chinese thought is crystallized in its philosophy of mind and nature, an unmistakable reference to New Confucianism. According to them:

> Chinese culture arose out of the extension of primordial religious passion to ethical moral principles and to daily living. For this reason, although its religious aspects have not been developed it is yet pervaded by such sentiments, and hence is quite different from occidental atheism. To comprehend this, it is necessary to discuss the doctrine of *"xin-icing bit"* [concentration of the mind on an exhaustive study of the nature of the universe], which is a study of the basis of ethics and forms the nucleus of Chinese thought and is the source of all theories of the "conformity of heaven and man in virtue." Yet, this is precisely what is most neglected and misunderstood by Sinologues.[7]

Once the spirit of Chinese culture is grasped, its limitations can clearly be seen. It excels in the development of the moral subject but is not sufficient in the development of the political subject, the knowing subject, and the technological subject, which is the strength of Western culture. Western culture has pluralistic origins, such as Greek reason, Hebrew faith, and Roman law. Chinese culture, on the other hand, puts emphasis on *Yiben* (one foundation). It follows a different course of development with less emphasis on competition and diversity. There is no need to impose Western ways on it, as that would not work anyway. Nevertheless, it certainly needs to expand its scope for its own good. It should wholeheartedly learn from the West its systems of logic, natural sciences, technological inventions, and institutions of democracy. Moreover, the two cultures are not that far apart from each other.

The traditional Chinese political ideal has always taken people as the basis for dynasties to hold on to their political power. The adoption of the democratic system would avoid the tyranny of despots and in practice could move closer to the Confucian ideal of a government of humanity: a government not only for the people but also of the people and by the people. Then the Confucian tradition would never be misunderstood as teaching only secular ethics. In fact, the ideal of *Tian Ren Heyi* (heaven

and humanity in union) certainly has a transcendent aspect and hence
a religious import, which has been improperly ignored by missionaries
on one hand and by atheists on the other. It was wrong for the West to
impose its ways on other cultures, as if they were the only true and universal ways. Although there is no dispute that the West has become the
leader of the world during modern times, that does not mean that Western culture does not have serious limitations or even defects—as can be
seen by the two world wars. Thus, the West is urged to reflect deeply on
both cultures, of East and West, and to learn these five things from Chinese thought:

> In the first place, the West needs the spirit and capacity of sensing
> the presence of what is at every particular moment (*Dangxia Jishi*),
> and of giving up everything that can be had (*Yiqie Fangxia*).
>   The second element the West can learn from the East is all-
> around and all-embracing understanding or wisdom. . . .
>   The third point that the West can learn from the East is a feel-
> ing of mildness and compassion. . . .
>   Fourthly, the West can obtain from the East the wisdom of
> how to perpetuate its culture. . . .
>   The fifth point the West can learn from the East is the attitude
> that the whole world is like one family. . . .
>   Our list is, of course, by no means exhaustive. What we have
> pointed out is that the West must also learn from the East if it is
> to carry out its task as the world's cultural leader. These things are
> certainly not entirely alien to Western culture. However, we would
> like to see their seeds bloom into full blossom.[8]

Surely, there are a number of assumptions behind this statement, and
its tone seems apologetic. The document was totally ignored at the time of
its publication: who would want to listen to the advice of a few refugee Chinese scholars? However, the situation changed a great deal in the latter half
of the twentieth century. Since multiculturalism became a popular movement, the document appears to be prophetic, and many leading Western
intellectuals now are willing to listen to voices from other cultures.[9] The
time is ripe to introduce Contemporary New Confucian philosophy to
Western audiences. I have ventured to give a very general picture of where
Contemporary New Confucian scholars stand, as follows:

Metaphysically, there is a creative ontological principle that works incessantly in the universe; without it there would be nothing in the world.

Epistemologically, this metaphysical principle can be known through a realization of "the depth of reason" inherent in every human being, but it cannot be reached through either logical inference or empirical generalization.

Axiologically, there are intrinsic meaning and value in the existent beings in the world. If there were not a common source of all values, then it would inevitably follow that our values are arbitrary and relative.

Cosmologically, the function of the creative ontological principle finds its manifestation in the formative process of the natural world, and man is a unique product of the evolutionary process of nature.

Scientifically, since there are regular patterns in changes of nature, they may be studied by the intellect; general laws of patterns may be established by way of empirical generalization. In the process concrete details and individual differences are ignored from a methodological point of view in favor of abstract formulas and quantitative differentiation. Even though past Chinese achievements in science and technology should be preserved, Western approaches to science and technology must be thoroughly learned by the Chinese and the rest of the world.

Psychologically, human beings are endowed with the depth of reason and the ability to realize the truth about the creative ontological principle and the intrinsic value of their own life. Therefore, the approaches of behavioral psychology and depth psychology have not exhausted the field of the psychological study of humanity. There should be room for a branch of psychology that studies the transformative process of sages and worthies from a spiritual point of view.

Ethically, humans are endowed with the depth of reason, and so they are by nature moral beings, thereby answering the question: "Why should human beings be moral?" We must try our best to mold ourselves into moral and creative beings.

Socially, as we cannot isolate ourselves from fellow human beings, the commitment to the basic family and social structures must be preserved, indeed vigorously guarded. Every human being is not only an intimate part of nature but also an intimate part of society.

Politically, the traditional ideal that takes politics as an extension of ethics must be revised. Even though the government exists to ensure the welfare of the people, and acknowledging that a government under the leadership of a sage-emperor may achieve a good deal more than a democratic government, the fact remains that there are not many sage-emperors and that a concentration of power may lead to terrible consequences. Hence, contemporary New Confucian scholars are convinced that the Western practice of democracy through election is preferable to traditional practices. A government for the people is not enough; it must also be a government of the people and by the people. Procedural and substantive matters must be equally emphasized.

Culturally, contemporary New Confucian scholars still believe that popular tastes should not dominate people's lives. More refined cultural aspirations should be vigorously promoted and encouraged.

Educationally, knowledge of science and technology must be emphasized in the school curriculum, but these subjects do not exhaust the whole range of education. Humanistic and moral education should also be emphasized. How to achieve a balance between the two is one of the most important concerns of modern educators.

Finally, economically, people should be allowed to earn a good living, but infinite accumulation of wealth should not be the goal of life. There is certainly a sort of socialist tendency among Confucian scholars. However, in the meantime they have also realized the importance of the right to own property, as it has proved to be a necessary measure for the protection of the freedom of people.[10]

NOTES

1. Please note I prefer to use the term "Neo-Confucianism" to refer to this group of scholars, as they professed to succeed the lines of Song-Ming Neo-Confucianism, with *xin zing phi xue* (learning of mind and nature) as its core teaching.

2. Recently I have observed that there were four waves in the movement, each lasting about twenty years. In the 1920s Liang initiated the movement; in the 1940s Feng and others formulated their philosophies; in the 1960s Contemporary New Confucians in the narrower sense developed their theories; in the 1980s there was an international dimension in the third generation.

3. See Wing-tsit Chan [Chen Rongjie], *A Source Book in Chinese Philosophy* (Princeton: Princeton University Press, 1963), 765.

4. These lecture notes were published in the daily reports of Beijing University from Oct. 1920 to Feb. 1921 and were only recently found. The content is somewhat different from the book he later published. In the very beginning he argues that what is important is not to discuss East-West cultures on an equal basis, but

rather to see whether Eastern cultures could survive under the present circumstances at all.

5. See Guy S. Alitto, *The Last Confucian: Liang Shuming and the Chinese Dilemma of Modernity* (Berkeley: University of California Press, 1979).

6. *China: The Country of Reason* (in Chinese) was written between 1967 and 1970. It is to the credit of his descendants that several manuscripts, not known to the public, were included in the collected works of Liang. Especially important is the one mentioned above. It was written during the most difficult years of the Cultural Revolution. Liang gave up some of his former views and endorsed certain official positions held by the government, then controlled by Mao and the Gang of Four, that were judged to be erroneous after the Cultural Revolution was over. He was asked by his close relatives and associates to revise the manuscript but lacked the energy to do the work. His conversion at that time was genuine. These documents were preserved for research purposes only.

7. See Carsun Chang and others, "A Manifesto," in Carsun Chang, *The Development of Neo-Confucian Thought*, 2 vols. (New York: Bookman Associates, 1957), 2: 461.

8. Wing-tsit Chan [Chen Rongjie], *Source Book in Chinese Philosophy*, 476–81.

9. In the 1970s, e.g., credits earned for courses on Chinese philosophy were not recognized by the Philosophy Department at the University of California, Los Angeles. However, the mode at the present time is totally different. The second edition of *The Cambridge Dictionary of Philosophy*, published in 1999, includes many items on Chinese philosophy; I alone contributed forty items, some of which are on contemporary Neo-Confucian philosophy. One key feature of the volume is that it has more entries on non-Western and non-European philosophy than any other comparable volume, including African, Arabic, Islamic, Japanese, Jewish, Korean, and Latin-American philosophy.

10. Liu Shu-hsien [Liu Shuxian], "Confucian Ideals and the Real World," in *Confucian Traditions in East Asian Modernity*, ed. Du Weiming (Cambridge, MA: Harvard University Press, 1996), 92–111, 358–60. I borrow the term "depth of reason" from Paul Tillich but use it in a totally different sense. Since Tillich's "depth of reason" points to faith in a transcendent God, only the Chinese have been able to find the true "depth of reason" in humans.

6

Modernity and Confucian Political Philosophy in a Globalized World

Chen Ming

The pressure of modernity and globalization on Chinese society in the last century has been unprecedented in all dimensions. The preservation and contemporary legitimacy of Confucianism depend on whether it can provide effective responses to the problems that have been generated by modernization and globalization. These responses should not be confined to pure academic study but should also aim at realizing its ideals in practice.

I believe that Confucianism faces the onerous task of providing solutions to three major problems of contemporary Chinese society: namely political reconstruction, cultural identity, and religious faith. These are actually the major issues that the field of Chinese contemporary political philosophy has to address. So-called Confucian political philosophy is scholarship that embraces a set of political ideals that are indigenous to China, as distinguished from liberalism and New Leftism, when confronting these three important problems. Before I start discussing this field, it is necessary to briefly compare Confucianism and Western political philosophy.

COMPARATIVE PERSPECTIVE: THE *POLIS* AND THE "KINDREDOM"

The term *political philosophy* is a Western concept, deriving from the Greek word *polis,* which is very different from the historical and sociological environment where Confucianism originated. *Zheng Zhi,* the Chinese phrase equivalent to *politics,* consists of two different characters, *Zheng* and *Zhi.* According to the Chinese classic *The Book of History,* the word *Zheng* refers to various activities like the preservation of material well-being, ancestral worship, foreign affairs, and military expedition. The word *Zhi* means governing, which is close to the contemporary Western meaning of the word *politics.* It is important to compare and distinguish the Chinese terms for politics with the Western political philosophy that is derived from the affairs of the *polis.*

The main reason for the difference between the two perspectives is that Western political philosophy is derived from the *polis,* yet Confucian political philosophy is derived from "kindredom." The *polis* is based on a contractual agreement that is a human-made reconstruction, but the kindredom is based on blood lineage, which is an extension of nature. Therefore, in his *Politics,* Aristotle begins with the statement that "the construction of all social entities is to accomplish some common good."[1] To construct a social entity depends on the construction of institutions. An institution is in fact a system of rules and laws specifying rights and obligations. It is pertinent to ask the following questions: Under what conditions will the need to construct rights and obligations become necessary? Under what conditions will these rights and obligations become normative? Under what conditions will different bearers of rights and obligations seek to cooperate in order to fulfill their own goals? The *polis* that Aristotle described seeks to address these questions. The *polis* is an independent unit consisting of many citizens who perform different rights and obligations. The so-called citizens are defined in terms of birth and property; slaves, masons, foreigners, and even merchants are excluded. In contrast to the units of family, those people who perform different functions come together for a common purpose to comprise the political entity known as the *polis.* The military force and blood lineage are not part of the building blocks. Therefore, the establishment of a contract or constitution is necessary. In other words, so-called political science refers to the art of accomplishing the common good of the *polis.* This may have something to do with Aristotle basing his political philosophy on the teleological view that politics originates from family, which is then transformed into the village and the *polis.*

While Aristotle acknowledged that political power originates from patriarchy, and the *polis* originates from family structure, his conception of the *polis* totally excludes blood lineage. He believed Plato made a grave mistake by not differentiating patriarchal power from political power. He not only linked the origin of politics with the *polis* but also believed that men are by nature political animals. This laid the legal and moral foundation for Western political philosophy.

From the perspective of cultural anthropology, this Greek political background is quite unique, rather than universal. But the concepts of patriarchal power and political power are helpful for us to understand the characteristics of Confucian political philosophy. On the basis of archeologists Su Binqi[2] and Elman R. Service,[3] we can modify Aristotle's evolution of "family-village-*polis*" to the historical evolution of "chiefdom-kindredom-empire." This model can help us understand where Confucianism originated in the historical evolution from chiefdom to kindredom and empire.

Man as the basic unit in the *polis* is referred to as a citizen; man as the basic unit in the kindredom is referred to as a member of the family. According to Chinese historical records, the system of kindredom was designed and created by Zhou Gong. It established the King of Zhou as the universal king under heaven, also called the son of heaven. The family of the king is the primary clan. The vassal lords who shared the family name of the king owing to their blood lineage are called secondary clans. This clan system, which was based on blood lineage, was extended to the governing structure of the whole country when the King of Zhou conquered the whole country. Likewise, every noble family is constructed on the same clan principles. Such a system is designed to combine the king, lords, high officials, intellectuals, and commoners into a moral entity. In some sense, the discourse of Confucian political philosophy revolved around the question of how to interpret, justify, and adjust such a system.

In *The Ancient Society,* Morgan proposed two modes of government. As he stated, sequentially, the first type of government is based purely on individuals and can be called society; the second type is based on geography and property and can be called the state. While Morgan's characterization of the state as the benchmark of civilization reveals some degree of ethnocentrism, his distinction between society and the state parallels the distinction between the *polis* in Western political philosophy and the kindredom in Confucianism. For the sake of easy understanding, we can call naturally formed society the primary institution and the state that defines the political relationship among men the secondary institution. This may help us better understand Chinese thought.

With different focuses—the *polis* focusing on individuals and Confucianism focusing on family—the two different schools of thought are concerned with different questions. *Polis*-centered political philosophy focuses on how to organize the relationship among individuals in order to realize individual goals and achieve social justice. Confucianism is more interested in the question of political legitimacy and how the government or the king as the representative of the collective interest should perform its role and obligations effectively. While both schools of thought are concerned with how to pursue the common good, Western political philosophy tends to focus on law—passionless wisdom—to pursue human happiness, and Confucianism tends to emphasize government by virtuous kings and ministers to maintain social order and world peace. In terms of normative value, one type stresses individual rights and freedoms, and the other stresses obligations and collective interests over individual rights. In terms of reasoning, one emphasizes the importance of the public will as the basis of political legitimacy, and the other often refers to the will of heaven as the basis of political legitimacy. For example, phrases like "Heaven sees through the eyes of the people, heaven hears through the ears of the people," and "Heaven gives birth to the people, and gives them the king and the teacher," can help us have a better grasp of the difference between Western political philosophy and Confucian philosophy, which came about due to different historical evolutions.

One last point to add is that Confucius, the first sage-cum-scholar who transmitted a body of classical thoughts from antiquity that came to be known as Confucianism, was born in the disorder era. He merely transmitted and reinterpreted the Chinese tradition in the hope that virtuous kings would come about to keep peace for all-under-heaven, rather than pursuing self-interest. But the political systems adopted by the Qin and Han dynasties were centered around kingship and based on material power as preached by the Legalist School of thought, which stressed the use of naked force to rule the country. Confucian political philosophy mainly relied not on the government but on society, where Confucian scholars played an important role in balancing the influence of the Legalist government. As a philosophy that existed to check the government, Confucianism evolved into a kind of "antistatist" political philosophy. As the contemporary Confucian scholar Mou Zongsan points out, China is not a country but a civilization; it has the concept of all-under-heaven, but it does not have the concept of the nation-state. The Chinese people can be said to be a moral entity in the ethical sense, but not a political entity.[4]

JIANG QING AND HIS POLITICAL CONFUCIANISM

The onslaught of modernization and globalization has put great stress on cultural diversity and national integrity. As part of modernization and globalization, the spread of Western individualism, the market economy, democracy, and rationalism has posed a great challenge to Chinese traditions. It is against this background that a number of so-called contemporary New Confucians, represented by Jiang Qing, Kang Xiaoguang, and Chen Ming, have emerged in Mainland China to respond to the challenge of modernization and globalization in recent years.

Jiang Qing is mainly concerned with the loss of Chineseness and the reconstruction of Chinese identity. He states that Confucianism has historically been the cultural foundation defining the Chinese identity, which is characterized by *Ren* (benevolence), *Yi* (justice), *Li* (rites), and *Zhi* (wisdom) in the moral dimension and by the kingly government (*Wang Dao*) in the political dimension. Confucianism is derived from the teachings and revelations of the Confucian sages. Their teachings and revelations come directly from heaven or the law of heaven (*Tian Li*). This is why Jiang Qing firmly believes in the sanctity and validity of Confucianism. His view of Confucianism in an ontological sense has made it impossible for him to appreciate the Western concepts of liberty, democracy, and rationalism. It rather leads him to appraise the question of modernity and globalization from the vantage point of East-West cultural differences and the destiny of human society. Therefore, his political philosophy can be summarized in several aspects, including his critique of Western culture and his belief in the importance of the preservation of Confucian tradition and the reconstruction of Confucian politics.

As he believes, "the Westernization of politics is the core of Westernization."[5] His critique of the Western political system concentrates on the concept of human nature as developed by Western liberals, the concept of liberal democracy, and the effect of Social Darwinism. The following are some excerpts of his writings:

> If liberty is the defining basis for a man to really become a man, then it is to suggest the complete abolition of morality and ethics for human beings. . . . From the perspective of Confucianism, to be a man is not to realize his liberty, but to manifest his conscience, to restore his original or natural propriety. Such conscience and

propriety exist in the human nature a priori. They define a man as a man and distinguish a man from an animal.[6]

In the guise of modernity, men become animals full of desire. . . . My understanding of tradition as opposed to modernity is that human desire must be somehow restricted by heavenly law (*Tian Li*). The Western scholarship of politics, economics, law, ethics, religion, arts, history and philosophy that emerged in the modern era has been developed to serve the gratification of human desire. Western intellectuals are unaware of this fact and think they are pursuing truth through rationalism. But in fact they confuse gratifying human desire with the meaning of life.

I believe the major problem of liberal democracy is that it treats the pursuit of selfish human desire as the first priority of politics. But the traditional Chinese view of politics is that the reason politics is legitimate is because it embodies a certain transcendental value or ethics. From the Confucian perspective, the sum of selfish individual desire is still selfish individual desire. A selfish aim is a selfish aim regardless of whether it is based on an individual, or a group, or a nation, or the world. "Selfish interest will not become a just interest just because many more people are involved and served."

The major problem of liberal democracy is that it totally separates politics from ethics. Liberal democracy deals only with procedural legitimacy and has nothing to do with ethical value.

Social Darwinism will destroy the human race ultimately. Confucianism put its ultimate wager of human salvation on the reemergence of a sage king. . . . Only the reemergence of a sage king can rekindle human conscience and bring the human race out of the Social Darwinist dilemma.

That Confucianism survives the onslaught of modernity is not only fortunate for the Chinese people, but also for the people of the world. . . . Only Confucianism can rescue the world from the savagery of Social Darwinism.[7]

Jiang Qing believes that Confucianism consists of two parts: political Confucianism, developed on the basis of the Gongyang scholarship of the Han dynasty; and ethical Confucianism, developed by the Neo-Confucians of the Song dynasty. Political Confucianism is the crux of Confucianism. But people have gradually forgotten political Confucianism and mistaken the ethical Confucianism of the Song era as political Confucianism, attempting the impossible task of developing a political system out of ethical Confucianism. Thus, modern attempts to build a Confucian political system have been based on the acceptance of Western science and democracy, which is tantamount to the de facto Westernization of China. Jiang Qing thinks the Gongyang scholarship of the Han era represents the orthodoxy of Confucianism because the Gongyang scholarship relies on the interpretation of major classics of Confucianism such as *Chun Qiu* and *Analects* to build political institutions. The following summarizes Jiang Qing's views of Confucian political philosophy based on Gongyang scholarship:

The kingly government (*Wang Dao*) refers to the conduct of political affairs by the rule and laws set forth by sage kings in the ancient time. To be more precise, it refers to the rule and laws governing the country and pacifying the world as practiced by the sage kings of the three ancient dynasties (Xia, Shang, and Zhou), which were transmitted by Confucius to the people of the later age.[8]

The crux of the kingly government is that its political legitimacy derives from its compliance with rules and laws in three dimensions: the will of heaven, the will of the earth, and the will of the people.[9] Or to put differently, a kingly government must know how to please the wills of these three elements. Only by complying with the wills of these three dimensions can a government be called a kingly government, and only such a government can be called a legitimate government. The will of heaven refers to the transcendental and sacred will of heaven or god. The will of the earth refers to the rules and laws of historical and cultural legitimacy because historical and cultural rules and laws are created in particular times and spaces and must be respected. The will of the people refers to the will of ordinary people, which is similar to the notion of popular will in the context of Western political philosophy.

Jiang Qing thinks this political system of three-pronged legitimacy was put in practice in the Han era and has since evolved into a unified political ideology for Chinese politics. Thus, he has proposed a three-chamber legislature, in correspondence with the three-pronged political legitimacy of the ancient system. The three proposed chambers include the *Su Ming Yuan* (the House of Commoners), which represents the popular will; the *Guo Ti Yuan* (the House of National Polity), which represents the will of the Chinese aristocracy; and the *Tong Ru Yuan* (the House of Confucian Scholars), which represents the transcendental and sacred will of heaven or god. By creating the *Tong Ru Yuan*, Jiang Qing thus elevates Confucianism to the status of state religion. Obviously, the sacred heaven is the essence, the foundation, and the prerequisite of all these chambers.

As Jiang Qing writes, "The restoration of Confucian religion can restore China's historical and cultural destiny, or Chineseness. . . . Confucian religion had performed three functions historically: First, it provides political legitimacy for Chinese government by laying a transcendental and sacred foundation for politics. Second, it provides ethical norms to regulate the social conduct of Chinese people on the basis of rites; third, it provides religious faith for the people on the basis of transcendental and sacred values as interpreted by the Confucian sages. These three functions are not obsolete in the contemporary world."[10] He makes it clear that it is important to integrate Confucian religious faith with Confucian politics and to use the political system as a carrier to promote the Confucian faith.

Jiang Qing's work is very significant, but it has some problems also. Its significance lies in Jiang Qing's astute understanding and appreciation of ancient Confucian scholarship and in its direct relevance to understanding contemporary practical problems in China and the world. Jiang Qing reminds people that the ancient sages' deep understanding of heaven, human nature, and politics continues to have strong relevance in the contemporary world and that the issues and questions that concerned the ancient sages are the same as those that continue to concern people in the contemporary world. The problems of Chinese cultural identity, political reconstruction, and religious faith that have confronted contemporary Chinese people have been cleverly addressed by Jiang Qing. Without a doubt, he opens up a completely new perspective for modern Chinese people to look at and understand the world and politics. For this reason, Jiang Qing has established himself as the leading Confucian scholar in contemporary China at the turn of the twenty-first century.

But Jiang Qing's writing is not without its problems. They can be approached from the perspectives of problem sensing, epistemology, cultural value, and practicability.

For Jiang Qing, both the Marx-Leninization of political life and the modernization of social life belong to the process of "Westernization," so they are the opposite of the construction of "Chineseness" and should be cleaned away. Many aspects of Jiang's "Westernization" actually are some forms of modernity. They are connected to industrialization and urbanization and have to do with modern production, living, and thinking styles, rather than certain values and ideologies. In this sense, they are universal. Therefore, Jiang's problem sensing is more a response to the vehement polemic of cultural encounters in recent history rather than an accurate mastery of contemporary realities. If it is still meaningful, its meaning would only reside in cultural theories. It may come from a certain revelation or enlightenment, but its foundation is mainly sentimental or emotional, even though it has gained some sympathizers and followers.

From the epistemological aspect, it is a historical fact that the Chinese political system after the early Han era directly inherited the Legalist system of the Qin empire; therefore the system included a mixture of Confucianism and Legalism. The Confucian influence existed superficially on the administrative level in order to reduce the operational cost of government. This system is otherwise known as the "Legalist system with a Confucian cloth." If the Han system was designed according to Confucian principles, as suggested by Jiang Qing, how do we explain the power usurpation by the maternal relatives of the emperors and the eunuchs with the suppression of Confucian scholars in the late Han dynasty, which lasted for a long period? One wonders what Confucius would think of this. Will this part of history help to inject more confidence in Confucianism or make the people lose confidence in Confucianism? Jiang Qing also relegated the famous Confucian ethical principles of cultivating virtues, managing family affairs, governing the country, and pacifying the world, as recorded in the classical *Great Learning,* to the status of political administrative strategy. This challenges the mainstream consensus view that has formed since the Song dynasty. Thus emphasizing the paramount importance of Gongyang scholarship while downgrading the long-recognized mainstream classics only creates confusion in the study of Confucianism and cannot lead to the healthy development of new scholarship.

Confucian political philosophy promises to find a heavenly destiny for ordinary people. This necessitates meeting ordinary people's material desire for survival. The principle of the people's material needs as heavenly needs is the oldest political wisdom. Likewise, Confucius put the material nourishment of people before education. Huang Zongxi, the famous Confucian scholar of the early Qing period, also wrote that people are concerned about their own self-interest and self-benefits. Thus, Jiang Qing's suggestion that democracy is problematic because it makes people's own interest the top priority of politics is ambiguous. Democracy seeks the citizens' maximal participation in politics and the maximal realization of the citizens' self-interest. It has no direct relationship with human nature. From the perspectives of sociology and political science, the crux of the kingly government is to respect social forces, institutions, and the expression of ethical values in political institutions. The richness of democracy and the pursuit of justice cannot be covered by or subsumed under the concerns of moral teaching.

The neglect of basic historical facts and important modern values has made people very critical of this kind of political Confucianism and made it very difficult for it to become practical and operational. The project of making Confucianism a state religion should be based on the existence of a corresponding Confucian culture in civil society. Yet when such a precondition is absent, it is very difficult to talk about a Confucian state religion. In my opinion, that Jiang Qing is trying to elevate a Confucian culture that historically existed in civil society to an integral component of the state structure may lead to the danger of creating an antisocietal superstate; in the end, society may be hollowed out, and the Confucian culture that provides the basis of the cultural identity and religious functions for such a society may also collapse. Modern society is characterized by civil society; the reforming motto of "small government and big society" should be in correspondence with the mode of modern production and the modern mode of thinking. The opportunity to revive Confucianism and Confucian politics should be found in this direction.

CHEN MING: CULTURAL POLITICS

Chen Ming approaches Confucianism from its historical role in ensuring Chinese national survival and creativity in particular historical contexts. The relationship between Confucianism and the Chinese nation is the relationship between cultural molding and expression. As a cultural expression, Confucianism represents the will and desire of the Chinese nation, as well as its perception of the world. As the cultural molder, it represents mastery and adaptation and the creation of national self-consciousness.

Thus, Confucianism is not a priori self-sufficient or fundamental. On the one hand, it is the expression of national will and desire; on the other hand, it is the construction of historical and social contexts. From the angle of cultural construction, Confucianism is the molder of Chinese national ethos. From the angle of cultural expression, Confucianism is the Chinese national pathway to realizing the meaning of life.

If Jiang Qing is trying to return Confucianism to its cultural core in the context of recent history, post–Cultural Revolution, and if Kang Xiaoguang is focused on how to utilize the soft power of Confucianism to reconstruct Confucian religious China, Chen Ming aims to reconstruct Confucianism and make it adaptable to modern political reality on the basis of the historical role of Confucianism. Chen Ming thus takes the effective response of Confucianism to contemporary realistic problems as the starting point and the goal of his thought. He borrows the words *foundation* and *use* from ancient philosophy and proposes the idea of "practical use as foundation" (*Ji Yong Jian Ti*) as the criterion for reconstructing Confucianism. Chen Ming cites many examples from cultural anthropology, cultural phenomenology, and existentialism to support his views.

Chen Ming has long paid significant attention to the political aspect of Confucianism and is against classifying the Neo-Confucianism of the Song-Ming era as the main foundation of Confucianism, as proposed by the New Confucian scholars of Hong Kong and Taiwan. He believes that the problem of collective action is the first problem that Confucianism set out to deal with. This suggests that the issue of creating kingly government (*Wai Wang*) to deal with collective action is the foremost question of Confucianism. The cultivation of inner sanctity (*Nei Sheng*) is the instrument or pathway to the realization of kingly government. The creation of kingly government is the ultimate goal of Confucianism. The cultivation of inner sanctity can only be realized through the creation of kingly government.

According to Chen Ming, traditional society is based on agrarian economy, and the common interest of the agrarian economy is larger than the sum of individual interests. Thus, there is less competition but more cooperation in traditional society, and social relationships are stable. But modern society is characterized by commercial and industrial economy, whereby individual rights and interests form the basis of the modern society. Moreover, there is much more competition and less cooperation, and social relationships are less stable but more fluid. These new conditions in modern society require new methods of political governance. The political philosophy of Confucianism, which is based on personal relationships, should adapt itself to the impersonal relationships in modern society. While Chen Ming is vigilant about modern culture, he is guardedly open to the modernization of politics. Concretely speaking, he thinks that the Western ideas of human rights and individual liberty should be incorporated into the discourse of Confucian political philosophy.

He believes that this does not contradict the Confucian tradition. While the saying that "the sage has no fixed mind but is based on the minds of all people under heaven" comes from the Taoist tradition, he believes that this is consistent with the Confucian saying that "whoever wins the hearts of all people under heaven gets to rule over the people," or the sayings from the *Analects* that "a ruler should do what the people like but avoid doing what the people hate" and "do not do to others what you do not like others to do to you." All these ideas suggest that people have some fundamental rights and interests that rulers need to respect. This traditional Chinese emphasis on the practical needs (*Shi Shi*) and human relationships (*Ren Jing*) of ordinary people is consistent with the Western ideas of individual liberty and human rights and the modern liberal institutions that seek to protect these rights.

Put differently: if the political philosophy of Confucianism wants to connect with the modern mainstream political life, then it is necessary to develop a new set of political concepts from Confucianism that suits modern society. The main characteristic of Confucian political philosophy is its emphasis on restricting the role of the state to ensure the welfare (food and material supply) of the common people. In other words, the legitimacy and justice of political governance is judged on the sole criterion of political effectiveness, rather than on the basis of institutional design and principles, as in modern Western political philosophy. Modern society faces a multitude of complex issues and needs, which traditional society never experienced. Such difficult issues cannot be dealt with by Confucian political philosophy, which was derived from blood lineage and the clan system. While the Confucian concepts of "love one's parents" and "respect seniors" are compatible with the modern concepts of harmony and order and provide a counterbalance to modern people's overemphasis on rationality and efficiency, it is important to focus on the institutional aspects of ethics, on the improvement of the legal system, and on the building of a fair and just political system for political competition if Confucianism is to be made adaptable to modern society. In building institutional ethics, Chen Ming focuses on the concept of *Yi* (justice) in the *Book of Great Learning* and interprets it to mean fairness in the institutional dimension, rather than traditional virtue.[11] He sees the Western political theoretical approach as the pathway to realizing the reinterpretation of Confucian political philosophy.[12]

Nonetheless, Chen Ming believes Confucianism can perform some kind of active function in modern society. As he writes, "Constitutional institution needs to be built on a concrete historical tradition. This tradition can only be Confucianism."[13] First, as a local body of cognitive knowledge and the embodiment of the national ethos, it provides a link allowing foreign ideas to settle in China; second, as the indigenous Chinese cultural foundation, it can supplementally function to support the practice of Western liberalism in China. Last and most important, it provides a cultural and national foundation for the construction of liberal institutions in China, rather than treating individuals as the foundation of public institutions, as originally proposed by liberals. Therefore, the principles and wisdom of Confucianism can provide a counterbalance to the extreme individualism that has become a problem in Western liberal democracies. Thus, the Confucian principle of the Mean as the pathway to the realization of eternal peace becomes embedded in the liberal institutions to be constructed.[14]

Institutions are constructed on the basis of competition. The greater number always prevails in competition over the smaller number. Therefore, in contrast to Jiang Qing's top-down approach, Chen Ming stresses the importance of the bottom-up approach, that is, the need to rely on the societal influence of the state in reconstructing and promoting Confucianism. In his article "Promoting Confucianism as Civic Religion," he writes that civil religion plays an important and sacred role in facilitating the effective operation of a political system: "While the religious sacredness as embodied in the *Doctrine of the Mean* and the *Great Learning* is well-known, their relevance for modern political life is also self-evident." "Modern society," he notes, "emphasizes small government and big society. The autonomy of society plays a significant role in modern political life because society has a tremendous amount of social capital. Confucianism is just such important social capital because Confucianism develops out of the primordial clan-based society."[15] Thus, Chen Ming is different from Jiang Qing in his emphasis on the bottom-up approach to reconstructing Confucian politics and religion.

The dichotomy of state versus society is central to the liberal discourse on politics. While Chen Ming uses the state-society dichotomy as his ana-lytical framework in his first book, *The Historical and Cultural Function of Confucianism*, he goes further, using the state-society dichotomy as the basis for the reconstruction of Confucianism.[16] By stressing Confucianism as originating from clan-based society, he attempts to graft liberalism onto Confucianism while preserving the historical and cultural continuity of Confucianism.

This brings up the issue of cultural identity. As Chen Ming argues, cul-tural identity is a collectively shared set of values and beliefs in a given nation that are used to make sense of the world and to guide national behaviors. Historically, the tradition of Confucianism was ingrained in the minds of the Chinese people, and the issue of cultural identity was not an issue. But in the recent past, several factors have caused Chinese cul-tural identity to become an acute issue. First, the Chinese encounter with the West and the subsequent military defeat in the nineteenth century led many Chinese elites to blame Confucianism as a backward culture, hold-ing it responsible for the defeat. Second, through political movements such as the Cultural Revolution, the ruling party targeted Confucianism as the main ideological rival to be removed. Third, liberal-oriented Chinese intel-lectuals have also sought to destroy Confucianism from the perspective of universalism and modernization and ignored the importance of cul-tural identity. Fourth, the ideology of Chinese nationality during the Qing Dynasty did not catch politicians' and thinkers' attention, because of the anti-Manchu movement and the Cold War. As a result, we Chinese, who have had a rich and proud culture, finally got lost in the onslaught of glo-balization and modernization. We do not know who we are, where we are from, or where we are going.

As Chen Ming believes, the political aspect of cultural identity is an objective reality. This is determined by culture, people, and blood lineage. The function of cultural identity is to forge national unity while excluding those who do not share the same cultural traits and blood lineage. This is why there was a popular saying in ancient times: those who are not from our own clan must have a different heart. Nonetheless, Confucianism does not emphasize the exclusiveness of cultural identity but stresses unity among all-under-heaven. This Confucian view of harmony and universalism may be a better choice for China, which is in a weak position in contemporary world politics. The Confucian view of universalism and inclusiveness is also a better choice to promote national unity for a multinational country such as China. But in the world, where the clash of civilizations prevails, Chen Ming thinks it is necessary to emphasize the clan- and blood-lineage-based origins of Confucianism, stressing that Confucianism represents the ethos of the Chinese nation. He admits that by doing so he has revised the idealistic worldview of Confucianism. But he insists that the emphasis on blood-based human relations is consistent with the Confucian view of graded love. He believes that culture is the ideology of a nation. Therefore, every country should consider national self-interest as of primary importance and the common interest of the world as of secondary importance. Again, this is consistent with the Confucian view of graded love.

As Chen Ming believes, the successful recovery of Confucianism as the main foundation of Chinese cultural identity depends on the success of reconstructing Confucianism politically and recovering its function as the foundation anchoring Chinese religious faith. Historically, Confucianism was not the most important religion in China, compared with Taoism and Buddhism. This has to do with Confucian rationalism. But Confucian religious ideas are closely connected with the popular religions that existed in society. The traditional worship of heaven and earth, of ancestors and sages, shared by both Confucianism and popular religions, has been preserved in Chinese society to this day. While it can be said that the religiousness of Confucianism is weak, it can be deemed strong if one takes into consideration its impact on the secular lives of ordinary Chinese. Therefore, Chen Ming thinks it is more precise to regard Confucianism as a civil religion.

This is how Chen Ming approaches the restoration of Confucianism on the basis of the historical development of Confucianism as a religion. He believes that by looking at Confucianism as a civil religion, Confucianism can be brought back to the politics of society, where it originated, allowing people to examine the societal function of Confucianism as a religion and transforming the Confucian religion into something like Zen Buddhism or Protestantism, existing in society independent of the state. Civil religion is both the symbol of the restoration of Confucianism and the pathway to its restoration.

Chen Ming tries to distinguish himself from fundamentalist Confucianism in his emphasis on national life as having a higher priority than Confucianism. He also differs from the liberals who advocate the total Westernization of China in his stress on the relevance of Confucianism to contemporary society. Therefore, his ideas of "practical use as foundation" and Confucianism as civil religion have been criticized by both conservative Confucian scholars and liberals.

Conservative Confucian scholars criticize Chen Ming's idea of "practical use as foundation" as having no basis, thus hollowing out the most fundamental values of Confucianism and leaving it to become just a body of truncated symbols. Some even label him as a pseudo-Confucian scholar. Liberals criticize Chen Ming as being too pragmatic by transforming Confucianism into the main basis of Chinese nationalism, which contradicts liberal concerns about individual rights and liberty. Others think his pragmatic treatment of Confucianism to suit nationalist goals represents not just a logical contradiction but, more important, the intense conflict between nationalist passion and scientific reason that has been a tragic problem for many modern Chinese intellectuals. For Christians, the question is why Confucianism should be the civic religion rather than Christianity or another religion.

Clearly, these criticisms have touched some deep problems in contemporary thought and culture. But Chen Ming is concerned with how to revive Confucianism within the Han nationality and maintain its role as the civic religion in public life. However, here lies a dilemma: on one hand, the activation of Confucianism within the Han nationality needs the "arithmetic of addition" to consolidate its core tenets and facilitate its revival in theory, organization, and activities; on the other hand, in order to become the "overlapping consensus," Confucianism needs the "arithmetic of deduction" to weaken its core and guarantee its role as the civic religion. For Chen Ming, these problems are all inevitable challenges, not only theoretically but also practically.

KANG XIAOGUANG: BENEVOLENT GOVERNMENT AND CULTURAL CHINA

The main concern of Kang Xiaoguang is how to maintain social and political stability as China undergoes rapid transition and how to improve China's economic efficiency, social justice, and international competitiveness. He discovers the relevance of Confucianism in the midst of China's modernization and globalization.

Kang Xiaoguang is an empiricist who believes the Western experience cannot be used to chart China's future development. As a nationalist, he takes national restoration as his ultimate yardstick in accepting or rejecting certain theories. Basically he believes China should reject Western liberalism but create a benevolent government on the basis of Confucianism in order to maintain long-term social stability. To achieve a benevolent government, it is necessary to Confucianize China. The hallmark of Confucianizing China is to turn Confucianism into a state religion, which becomes Kang Xiaoguang's basis for sketching the picture of a cultural China.

As a sociologist, Kang Xiaoguang believes that contemporary China is characterized by the separation of state from society, with society controlling a huge part of the national wealth and resources, in contrast to the political system of the recent past. Thus, the legitimacy of government and the question of social stability become acute issues. Kang is against the liberal formula to establish constitutional democracy in China. He thinks the Western model is not useful for China because of its decadent values and because China's performance in the areas of economic growth, social justice, and incorrupt governance is not inferior to that of Western governments. Liberal democracy also tends to promote national division. Even if liberal values are good, they have not been realized in Western countries because of the hypocrisy of Western governments.

As Kang Xiaoguang believes, the ruling party in China has been trying very hard to gain political legitimacy in order to meet the new circumstances that have accompanied rapid economic transformation. In the early years of the reform, the ruling party's legitimacy came mainly from what Samuel Huntington calls "performance legitimacy." The most immediate problem that the ruling party faces right now is how to establish a new theory of political legitimacy to justify its continued political rule. To be more precise, Kang is concerned with the question of what kind of authoritarianism is most legitimate, or so-called substantive legitimacy rather than procedural legitimacy. That is to say, it is more important to know how political power is used, rather than to know how political power is acquired in the first place.

Kang Xiaoguang thinks Confucian political philosophy treats collective interests, rather than individual interests, as its top priority. Confucianism, in his view, is also against the equality of humans and popular sovereignty and is consistent with modern authoritarianism. Therefore, Kang concludes that Confucianism can become a new source of political legitimacy for China's authoritarianism. He believes that benevolent government is a mixed polity, with elements of monarchy, oligarchy, and democracy. Every social class has an institutional channel allowing it to express its needs to the government. This is a structure of social strati-fication, but not a class-based dictatorship. The system Kang Xiaoguang proposes includes benevolent authoritarianism, a market economy, corpo-ratism, a welfare state, and the Confucian state religion, a system of coor-dination, cooperation, and checks and balances among different social classes. He cites the executive-directed political system in Hong Kong as his ideal type of government and believes such a system can promote effi-ciency and social justice as well as political legitimacy.

Kang's theory of benevolent government includes the following. First, benevolent government is based on Mencius's principle of people as fun-damentally important. Kang purports Confucians value elitist politics but treat people's interests as top priority, with a corresponding form of pater-nalistic politics. To put it differently, Confucian politics is about the nour-ishment and education of the people. Second, benevolent government takes good care of the people by providing material abundance. Third, it practices the ancient principle of rotation for the succession of political power by selecting talented and virtuous officials on the basis of the will of heaven and the will of the people. Fourth, it forwards the ideal of the world being united. The Confucian notion of benevolent government is the present goal; the unity of the world is the idealistic goal of the future.[17] The benevolent government is founded on the dictatorship of Confucian scholars (*Shi*) because only Confucian scholars know the will of heaven.

While Kang does not believe that benevolent government was ever fully practiced in Chinese history, he thinks it can provide a point of reference or a yardstick to evaluate contemporary politics. The Confucianization of China is the pathway to realizing his ideal of benevolent government. The process of Confucianization consists of two parts: "To confucianize the Chinese Communist Party and to confucianize Chinese society. When Confucianism replaces Marxism-Leninism as state ideology and Con-fucian scholars replace the communist cadres, the process of creating a benevolent government is complete."[18] He also advocates the elevation of Confucianism as an essential part of national education. He believes that key to the creation of benevolent government is making Confucianism the state religion and the embodiment of the new values and ideals of the Chi-nese people in the new era. He accepts that the ancient Chinese political system integrated state and religion and believes that now a new polity needs to be created that integrates state and religion.

Kang Xiaoguang believes that cultural nationalism not only performs a traditional role but also helps a given nation enhance national unity and gain competitiveness in a globalized world. He highly admires both Kang Youwei, the famous Confucian reformer of the late Qing dynasty, and the Harvard professor Samuel Huntington. He believes that the clash of civilizations may become the major source of international conflict in the aftermath of the Cold War and calls for the restoration of Confucianism to build a cultural China transcending the physical boundary of the political China.

The supporters of Kang Xiaoguang praise him for the insightfulness and persuasiveness of his argument. They think Kang proposes an entirely new solution to China's problem that is different from the Western solution but rooted in cultural conservatism and authoritarianism.

Nonetheless, Chinese liberals are very critical of Kang's proposals. This is not an appropriate place to examine the intense debates between liberals and Kang, but liberals seem to think that institutional reform alone can determine the national destiny of China, which is really a myth. But conservatives who totally deny the values of human rights and democracy are also wrong. Rather than being a hindrance, the ideas of liberty and democracy, if they take root in China, may actually be a precondition for China's national restoration.

Moreover, while Kang is concerned about the changing social conditions of China and expansion of the market economy and wants to propose new political institutions to suit such changes, the Confucian ideas that he cites as solutions are exactly the same as those of classical Confucianism. How can he ensure that unchanged classical Confucian ideas can adapt to the rapid changes in China's socioeconomic conditions?

Finally, there are two civilizations within the Chinese cultural history, namely the nomadic and the agrarian. These two not only constituted the most fundamental and vehement contradictions in Chinese history but also pose a severe problem in contemporary reality. Responding to the "clash of civilizations" thesis with our traditional "China versus barbarians" framework is obviously a double-edged sword: externally, it could enhance unity and pool strengths, but internally, it could cause disputes and strife. But if the internal world cannot be integrated and consolidated, what is the use or the meaning of a cross-boundary Confucian China? Civilization as the boundary of international politics is proposed by Huntington, but take the examples of the Arab world and of North-East Asian

politics: what is the significance of cultural symbols in the face of conflicting interests?

Without a doubt, Confucian scholarship in China is in the process of restoration. Its historical missions are twofold: it should become the preserver
of the Chinese national character; it should also become the promoter of
China's modernization. More or less, these objectives are in conflict with
each other. To realize the former objective, it is necessary to stress historical continuity and consistency, which requires us to reexamine and justify
the preservation of classical Confucian ideas and values in order to provide
spiritual support for Chinese cultural identity and social cohesion. As for
the latter objective, it is necessary to reinterpret some part of classical ideas
and values and link them with modern values such as liberty and justice
and democracy. In some sense, Jiang Qing is concerned with the former
objective in his efforts to justify the continued relevance of classical Confucian values in modern society. Chen Ming is more concerned with the
latter objective in his emphasis on linking classical Confucian values with
modern and Western values. Kang Xiaoguang is somewhere between the
two. Kang's understanding of Confucianism is closer to that of Jiang Qing,
but Kang's methodology of studying Confucianism (such as his instrumental use of Confucianism) is closer to that of Chen Ming.

Just like the predicament that Judaism faced when confronted with
the European enlightenment, we can see the strands of Confucian orthodoxy, conservatism, and reformism in the writings of Jiang Qing, Chen
Ming, and Kang Xiaoguang as they confront the challenges of modernization and globalization. While their writings are still rudimentary, they
can be expected to mature, rooted as they are in a rich old culture with
five thousand years of historical continuity and anchored in a huge population of five billion people who are eager to embrace modernity and
globalization.

NOTES

1. Aristotle writes that "the *polis* consists of citizens. . . . When some citizens
assembled into a political unit, it becomes a *polis*." See Aristotle, *Politics,* 109, 118.

2. Su Bingqi, *The New Discovery in Chinese Civilization* (in Chinese) (Beijing:
Jointly Press, 1999).

3. Elman R. Service, *Primitive Social Organization: An Evolutionary Perspective* (New York: Random House, 1962).

4. Mou Zongsan, *The History of Philosophy* (in Chinese) (Guiling: Guangxi Normal University Press, 2007), 170–72.

5. Jiang Qing, *Political Confucianism* (in Chinese) (Beijing: Jointly Press, 2003), 3.

6. Ibid., 352.

7. Jiang Qing and Sheng Hong, *To Nurture Virtue with Virtue* (in Chinese) (Shanghai: Jointly Press, 2003), 184, 187, 189, 56, 59, 58, 161.

8. Jiang Qing, *Political Confucianism,* 202.

9. Jiang Qing, "The Kingly Government Is the Future Direction of the Chinese Political Development" (in Chinese), *Yuan Dao* (Beijing), no. 10 (2003).

10. Jiang Qing, "On the Reconstruction of Confucian Religion in China" (in Chinese) Beijing: Communication in the Study of Confucianism, no. 1.

11. Chen Ming, *Ru Zhe Zhi Wei* [The dimension of Confucianism] (Beijing: Beijing University Press, 2004).

12. Chen Ming, "Yuan Dao and the Reconstruction of New Confucianism in the Mainland," *Yuan Dao,* no. 12 (2005).

13. Chen Ming, "The Reconstruction of Confucianism to Incorporate Constitutionalism" (in Chinese), *Nan Du Zhou Kan* [Southern city metropolitan weekly], May 25, 2007.

14. Chen Ming, "Reconstruction of Confucianism to Incorporate Constitutionalism."

15. *Yuan Dao,* no. 14 (2007).

16. Chen Ming's treatment of state-society relations is built on John Locke's view that society is more important than the state.

17. Kang Xiaoguang, *Benevolent Government: The Third Road to China's Political Development* (in Chinese) (Singapore: 2005).

18. Kang Xiaoguang, *Benevolent Government,* vii–xlix.

7

Four Models of the Relationship between Confucianism and Democracy

He Baogang

Confucianism is not a conceptual monolith but rather has a variety of traditions, versions, and forms including imperial, reform, elite, merchant-house, and popular Confucianism. Just as Confucianism is multidimensional, democracy is also multifaceted, including liberal, developmental, social, deliberative, and republican conceptions. The relationships between democracy and Confucianism therefore must be multiple and complex. Much of the controversy stems from the fact that scholars use different conceptions of democracy and different interpretations of Confucianism to support their positions.[1] Any single conceptualization about correlations between democracy and Confucianism will therefore, of necessity, be narrow, one-sided, and incomplete. It seems inappropriate to start with a monocular definition of Confucianism or democracy because such an approach will exclude others. It is better to remain open to other definitions and interpretations, because different understandings and conceptions of Confucianism and democracy, together with historical contexts, cultural backgrounds, power relationships, and geopolitics all play their part. In building democracy, changing interpretations and reconstructions of Confucianism often come into play.

In the past the debate has focused on the question of whether Confucianism is conflictive or compatible with democracy. In this regard, Huntington and Fukuyama offer different evaluations of Confucianism.

According to Huntington, the core values of Confucianism are not compatible with liberal democracy.[2] By contrast, Fukuyama argues that the
Confucian examination system, education, fairly egalitarian income distribution, relative tolerance, tradition of dissent and protest, and tendency
toward egalitarianism are not only compatible with but actually promote
liberal democracy.[3]

The two models of understanding above are largely framed by a tra-
dition-versus-modernity mentality and a West-versus-East outlook. This
essay argues that we need to *go beyond these two conventional models*
and explore alternative ways of thinking about the relationship between
democracy and Confucianism.

The search for alternatives comes from the real world. In the last
decade the processes of Chinese local democratization, the development of village elections, and the struggle for human rights, deliberative
forums, and intraparty democracy reveal that in practice there is a mix-
ing of Chinese traditions and new democratic institutions. This gives rise
to a mixed model for rethinking the relationship between democracy and
Confucianism. Unfortunately the mainstream thinking on Confucianism
and democracy is still confined to either the conflict or the compatibility
model. Importantly, the last two decades have witnessed the development
of a post, critical, or New Confucianism.[4] With the revival of Confucianism in the 1990s,[5] and in particular in the context of the rise of China, some
Chinese have become more confident in their tradition of Confucianism
than before. They have reflected upon and criticized electoral democracy
and developed a new critical model of rethinking the relationship between
democracy and Confucianism.

Some creative Chinese scholars have departed from conventional
models and developed a number of approaches. First, the convention-
ally close association between Confucianism and authoritarianism has
been deconstructed.[6] Jiang Qing distinguishes *politicized Ruxue,* which
was often used to maintain autocracy, from *political Ruxue,* which seeks to
uphold social justice by criticizing the government, its institutions, and its
policies.[7] Often an idealized version of *Ruxue* has been developed so that
its moral and political principles offer new criteria for rethinking democracy. Second, there are plural truths and multiple ways of reconsidering the
relationship between democracy and Confucianism. Traditional Western
liberal democracy is not the final truth or criterion by which to judge all
political systems. There are different models of democracy, ranging from

direct and representative democracy to communitarian and deliberative democracy. Democracy itself needs to be opened up and subjected to criticism from different cultures. In this context, Confucianism is presented as a counterbalance to excessive individualism and narrowly defined electoral democracy. Third, there is a continuing attempt to transcend the boundary between tradition and modernity, as well as West and East, which can therefore recover the traditional value of Confucianism and blend it with modern democratic values.

This chapter examines *the ways and models of thinking in which questions regarding Confucianism and democracy are raised and answered.* The various answers depend, first, on the attitudes of political actors and scholars toward Confucianism; second, on the selection of which key elements of Confucianism are emphasized; and third, on different conceptualizations of Confucianism and democracy.

Four ideal-type models of the relationship between Confucianism and democracy—*conflict, compatible, hybrid,* and *critical*—constrain or condition our questions and answers concerning the relationship. Huntington and many others work from a conflict model, holding that Confucianism is an obstacle to Chinese democratization. This view stresses the negative and inhibiting factors of Confucianism, such as orientations favoring authoritarian statecraft, collectivist hierarchical behavioral traits, and unequal distribution of power.

By contrast, scholars such as de Bary, Nathan, and Friedman have adopted a *compatibility* approach, which points out elements in Confucian culture that are positive in relation to democracy.[8] Chinese scholars such as Liang Shuming, Yu Yingshi, Cheng Zhongying, and Lin Yusheng have also emphasized some aspects of compatibility between Confucianism and liberalism.[9]

The conflict and compatibility models largely look at how democratic and Confucian ideas, beliefs, and values can be conflictive or reconciled. The *hybrid* model, in contrast, goes against both the conflict and the compatibility models and occupies a middle position. It examines complex institutional and behavioral practices and holds that the practice of democratization in East Asia is always a mix of Western and Confucian cultures. This model is used to describe the mixture of democracy and Confucianism in a variety of ways at different levels. It asks the empirical question of what is the best proportion of the different ingredients from each culture for different times and places. It reveals the complex relation between democracy and Confucianism in practice. Under the seemingly smooth combination of democratic and Confucian elements, however, subtle tensions remain. This differs from the compatibility model, which assumes a simple view of convergence.

The critical model reverses the conventional thinking and turns the logic upside-down. In both the conflict and the compatibility models, democracy is the judge and final truth, while Confucianism is deemed passive: either it should be abandoned for the sake of democracy, or it should be modified to make it compatible with democracy. In the critical model, however, the primary orientation is from the Confucian point of view, rather than from the Western perspective. Confucianism is now regarded as the active arbiter of the political norm rather than the passive listener or beneficiary. From a Confucian perspective, electoral democracy is full of deficiencies and flaws, while deliberative democracy is a more acceptable form of government and decision making. It should be noted that the critical model is not a simplistic form of the conflict model, because it recognizes and respects the core values of liberal democracy. It does not reject liberal democracy, but it operates from an awareness of its problems and suggests that Confucianism can be used to address them.

There are variations on each of these models. Thus, rather than one critical model, there are many versions, which have a complex relationship with the conflict model. Below I examine the strengths and weaknesses of each model in turn.

THE CONFLICT MODEL

The conflict model is used to maintain that all of the ideological structures of Confucianism and democracy are in conflict. In this model Confucianism is seen as a product of an agricultural society that constructs a political order to meet its specific social and economic conditions, while liberal democracy is seen as the political construct of an industrial society seeking to meet such modern conditions as the rise of commerce and individual interests. Theorists who work from the conflict model hold that the original ideas of Confucius do not harmonize with liberal ideas.

Three key concepts from Confucius's original doctrine, *Ren* (benevolence, humaneness, or simply goodness), ritual, and the gentleman, indicate a political order in which the rule of the gentleman prevails, duty is central, political inequality is taken for granted, moral concerns override the political bargaining process, and harmony prevails over conflict. This, it is argued, conflicts with a democratic order in which the rule of law prevails, rights are central, political equality is taken for granted, the political bargaining process overrides moral consensus, and conflict is seen as a necessarily normal condition of political life. The Confucian notion of the sage undermines the idea of equality. Confucian unity undermines plurality, and Confucian harmony undermines the necessity of conflicts. The Confucian ideal of *Ren* is incompatible with utilitarian calculation.[10] In Confucian culture the government must proceed on the basis of harmony rather than conflict (which leads to suppression of dissidents and renders compromise morally repugnant); the interests of the collective must not be challenged by lesser groups and individuals (which is less favorable to the actions of individual citizens); and finally, rights have to be treated as something granted by the state, not inherent in the person (which is less favorable to the institutional protection of individual rights).

According to Confucianism, a political party should embody moral correctness. *Junzhidang* (gentleman party) is concerned with moral principle and public interests, while *Xiaorendang* (villain party) cares for material interest. (Similarly, Edmund Burke draws the line between factions and honorable connections.) This moralized notion of party precludes competitive intraparty politics and effectively bans factions.

Today, the Chinese Communist Party bans "factional" activities and denies the existence of any form of factionalism or of any factional strife in elite politics. The philosophical objections to factions, according to Confucianism, are that politicians should represent the interests of the whole community and that factions seek to articulate only their own narrow interests at the expense of the broader general interest. In addition, the Confucian-inspired aversion to competition makes the Chinese hierarchy even more distrustful of factionalism. This leads to a concern with removing the causes of factionalism, which leads to the inexorable destruction of liberty. Western liberalism, too, is concerned with controlling the more destructive effects of factionalism but holds that neither moral nor religious motives can be relied on as an adequate control because they are as ineffective in the face of malevolent intent on the part of an individual as they are in the face of a passionate majority. As long ago as 1787, James Madison concluded that a polity that valued both liberty and representation would be hard put to totally control the existence of factions or the problems arising from their existence.[11] Related to the above discussion is the issue of political opposition. The idea of unity is the key concern of both Confucianism and Legalism. Both hold that plurality creates disunity. Nevertheless the motto "harmony with differences" encompasses the idea that people can be allowed to dissent within a broad underlying framework of agreement. This idea has a background in the tradition of political opposition by moral scholars to corrupt rulers and in the position of the imperial censor, or *Jianguan,* an official whose duty was to advise and even criticize the emperor.

The conflict model is confirmed by the East Asia Barometer Survey, conducted in South Korea during February 2003. Findings revealed that attachment to Confucian values makes it harder to reject authoritarian rule than to embrace democracy.[12] The conflict model is also confirmed by the histories of East Asia. Japan's moral culture was preeminently Confucian in 1890, when Tani and Torio thought that the constitution and the Imperial Diet would give rise to an unhealthy sense of individualism among the Japanese, making each of them think only of himself or herself. As a result, the development of Japanese parliamentary institutions was to some extent limited by these ultraconservative attitudes.[13] In modern China, Yuan Shikai used Confucianism to suppress democratic movements in the 1910s. Chiang Jiang Jieshi (Chiang Kai-Shek) also employed Confucianism in the 1930s and 1940s to contain the trend toward democratization in Mainland China and in the 1970s in Taiwan. In South Korea, two negative elements of Confucianism—orientations of authoritarian statecraft and collectivist hierarchical behavioral traits—have been used by the political elite in their effort to maintain authoritarian rule and arrest the process of democratization.[14]

The conflict model was further contested in Singapore in the 1980s, when Confucianism was used to argue for Asian values and against Western democracy. Confucian respect for authority is seen not to favor an opposition movement, which is interpreted as an attempt to undermine authority in Singapore. It is believed that Confucianism operates in politics as an overriding ideology and a set of moral codes to regulate political behavior and to ensure discipline and loyalty. Today, the Confucian idea of *Ren* is openly used by Kang Xiaoguang to justify what he calls the Chinese "benevolent authoritarian polity."[15] Chen Ming endorses a new authoritarianism in order to secure some sort of funding and political patronage for *Ruxue.*[16] Whether Confucianism will play out the same "Beijing opera" of inhibiting democratic movement in contemporary China remains to be seen.

THE COMPATIBILITY MODEL

Those who adopt this model hold the view that some elements of Confucianism are democratic or are compatible with democratic ideas and institutions.[17] The Confucian idea of *Minben* and the idea of heaven in relation to the idea of the people are seen as supporting democratic institutions. The principle of the people in particular can be used to support democratic ideas such as votes, parliament, and parties. The tradition of a local gentry (*Shenshi*) class can be interpreted as a self-governing local community, a sort of local autonomy and even a primitive form of local democracy. The very idea of leaders coming from and representing the local community facilitated the development of local democracy in China.[18] The Confucian institution of *Xuedang* is a public forum where the intellectual elite discuss and debate moral, social, and political issues, and this can be transformed into a modern civil society.

In addition, other Confucian political institutions can be transformed into something to support democratic development. The Confucian tradition of scholarly criticism could be transformed into a formal opposition force if the practice of criticism could be afforded a genuine political significance. Confucian rituals can be quite easily modernized into political procedures. Confucian tolerance of plural religions can promote liberal toleration. As Daniel Bell argues so well, it would be possible to take the Confucian idea of gentry and institutionalize it as a Confucian chamber in a democratic assembly.[19] The Confucian balance-check system can be transformed into a modern system of checking powers. All these may be compatible with liberal democracy.

Both Confucianism and liberalism recognize and respect the self and the idea of dignity. *Ren* as a form of love and a psychological principle is inherently rooted in each individual. If *Ren* plays its role, it will go against tyranny and support democracy. *Ren* is concerned with individuality and the equality of individual moral values. *Ren* could provide a theoretical basis for the idea of human rights.[20] Japanese scholars such as Itagaki argue for liberty according to these Neo-Confucian forms.[21]

De Bary notes that individualist and liberal elements exist in the Confucian tradition,[22] and Nathan argues that traditionally based Chinese values, such as the morally autonomous individual, the absolutely just ruler, the responsibility of the government for the people's welfare, and the ordinary person's responsibility for the fate of the nation, served as the main justification for the growth of a pressure movement demanding democratization in a Schumpeterian direction.[23] With its emphases on selecting the government administration through civil service exams, the duty to protest unjust policies, the disapproval of benighted government, and decentralization and openness to all religions, China is extraordinarily replete with traditional tendencies favorable to democratization.[24] Seeking justice from a Confucian moral principle has been a principal basis for demanding democracy. Democracy is seen as an enterprise for justice for the people, and the acquisition of power is required to deliver social justice.

The Confucian examination system can be developed into a system of equal access to public office and as a way of ensuring a meritocracy. Confucianism allows for equal opportunity for political positions, open to all scholars through an open examination system.

There are two different approaches to the compatibility question. One is soft, something like color matching. This is subject to normative and individual variations. The above arguments about compatibility fall into this category. It is easy to identify Confucian terms that seemingly look like the notion of liberty or the social contract in order to argue that there is a Confucian source for democracy. This method, however, according to the conflict model, is misleading in the sense that it ignores the whole structure in which different ideas operate and develop their basis. The Confucian tradition of *Minben* indeed contains some democratic elements. *Minben*, however, lacks democratic institutions and methods such as elections or a party system allowing the voice and views of the people to be articulated. *Minben* is only "for people" in its concern for their well-being, security, and prosperity. It is not "by people." As Liang Qichao has said, "Our ancestors knew that the will of the people ought to be respected; they did not make a serious study of the method by which the ideal might be realized."[25] Therein lies the weakness of Confucian thinking on political institutions.

The other approach is objective and focuses on institutions. It asks the question of whether there is a fit between a particular key and a particular locker. It can be argued that Confucian institutions are much less compatible with democracy than Confucian ideas are. The fact that the positive (not negative) liberty of Confucianism has been mentioned and stressed indicates the lack of institutionalized liberty in the Confucian tradition. In other words, there are many more conflicts and tensions between liberal democracy and Confucianism in the area of institutions than in the area of abstract ideas. This institutional structural approach tends to support the conclusion that there is inherent tension between Confucianism and democracy.

Continuing with the key-and-locker metaphor, there are two ways of approaching this dilemma: to make democracy and Confucianism institutionally compatible, it is necessary either to change the "locker" or to cut a new "key." This consideration leads to the transformation approach discussed below.

At least three factors explain the apparent compatibility. First, Confucian society has undertaken a transformation. Nowadays, more than 40 percent of the South Korean population are Christians who might or might not practice Confucian traditions. Liberal intellectuals who have pushed democratization in both South Korea and Taiwan received their education in the West.

Second, one significant but less emphasized transformation is the retreat of Confucianism as a state ideology from political life. One of the reasons why contemporary Confucianism can coexist with democracy in Japan, South Korea, and Taiwan is that Confucianism has retreated from public life and politics and become a doctrine of private life, as demonstrated by the Confucian heart-mind doctrine developed in Hong Kong and Taiwan in the 1980s. When the core value of Confucianism has receded, Confucian personal ethics and customs indeed help to build democratic institutions. In this way, Confucianism does not conflict with liberal democracy directly, and the transformation of Confucianism has converged toward democracy. This is similar to the way in which Buddhism has withdrawn from a dominant role in the political life of Thailand. Contemporary Confucianism and Buddhism constitute a lesser obstacle to democracy than Islam because the former retreated from politics, while the latter is still very much part of the political machinery.

Third, center-peripheral relations come into play. The South Korean and Japanese versions of peripheral Confucianism have found it much easier to adapt to and then adopt cultural and political changes than does Chinese indigenous Confucianism. This is because in South Korea and Japan Confucianism could be more easily given up and discarded because such abandonment did not carry with it issues of national pride, Confucianism having been "borrowed" from China in the first place. Thus, Korea was the first to abandon the examination system in East Asia, and Korea is now taking the lead in synthesizing liberalism and Confucianism in East Asia. It was likewise easy for Japan to borrow democratic institutions from the

West because some elements of Confucianism could be abandoned quickly without a sense of intellectual guilt. It has been much harder and slower for indigenous and orthodox Confucianism in China to accommodate democratic institutions than it was for the peripheral Confucianism of Korea and Japan.

THE HYBRID MODEL

It seems that neither Confucianism nor democracy alone can offer a desirable solution to the complex problems China faces. A better solution may be found by combining the best of each in a mixed regime, striking a balance between authority and liberty and effectively coping with the complexities of modernity while maintaining stability. China has been making historical and contemporary efforts to combine Confucianism with democratic values and systems.[26] Based on the Western idea of three divisions of power and drawing on Confucian traditions, Sun Zhongshan (Sun Yat-Sen) developed the idea of five divisions of power, adding the examination *Yuan,* which is responsible for the nation's civil service system, and the control *Yuan,* which is the highest watchdog organization of the state, exercising powers of impeachment, censure, and audit. Liang Shuming, in the 1920s–1940s, attempted to integrate democracy into the program of village reconstruction and advocated the New Confucian model of democracy, characterized by the combination of Western notions of rights and liberty with Chinese emphasis on responsibility and ethical education and of Western majority rule with Chinese ethical rationality, while criticizing Western individualism and substituting an advocacy of communitarianism.[27] Similarly, in Japan, Itagaki devised the terms *patriot* and *public* to revise the Confucian ideal of disinterested public service so as to combat individualist attempts to advance personal ambition or sectional interests.[28]

In the Chinese practice of village election, the institutional materialization of the idea of democracy in China was undertaken by converting the ancient principle of *Xuanju* into election. The vote is seen as a method for selecting a good leader or electing a moral and able person. By contrast, the liberal interpretation of voting stresses a method of controlling officials by subjecting their tenure to periodic electoral tests, and a populist interpretation emphasizes a method for citizens to participate directly in making law.[29]

The development of Chinese deliberative democracy in the last five years has heavily drawn on the Confucian tradition of public consultation blended with Western theories of deliberative democracy and social science methodology for deliberative polling.[30] Take the example of Wenling city, in which, from 1996 to 2000, more than 1,190 deliberative and consultative meetings were held at the village level; 190 at the township level; and 150 in governmental organizations, schools, and business sectors. In particular, from 2005 to 2009 Zeguo township in Wenling city, Zhejiang Province, has held a series of public consultations utilizing deliberative polling techniques whose results have direct impact on the township's budgeting process.[31] Such meetings are called *Kentan,* meaning "sincere heart-to-heart discussion," imbued with a special local flavor drawn from the Confucian tradition. In this mixed practice, Western deliberative democracy and Chinese Confucian elements are present and make their own distinct and unique contributions. It is difficult to claim that this practice of local deliberative democracy is purely a Chinese local phenomenon or that it is merely the result of Western influence.

THE CRITICAL MODEL

The critical model has emerged against the background in which the marketization of politics has caused the degeneration of the moral dimension of politics, in particular concern for the public good. Contrary to the conflict model, where Lucian Pye sees Confucian morality as an obstacle to bargaining politics and democratic institutions, new and critical Confucianism attempts to return to classic Confucian moral principles and find a new type of moral politics to enhance the quality of democratic life. The Confucian ideal of politics denies the market of politics, attempts to remedy the extreme excesses of individualism, and seeks the perfectionism of moral life.[32]

Kang Xiaoguang and Jiang Qing have developed a critique of liberal democracy; they are examples of the new school of Confucianism in contemporary China. Kang questions the effectiveness and legitimacy of electoral democracy and advocates benevolent government and Confucian mechanisms for the expression of public opinion.[33] Jiang rejects the will of the people as the source of political legitimacy and seeks a legitimacy "established on transcendent sacred origins" and "extolling unification" (*Dayitong*).[34] Their critique is sharp and centered on Confucianism, but it is flawed in that it fails to address the need for an institutional form of modern legitimacy and goes too far in rejecting elections completely. These critics have not addressed whether it is feasible to return to a Confucian utopia in the contemporary world. In order to develop a more appropriate mixed model, it is necessary to examine the Confucian critique of the philosophical foundations of liberal democracy.

THE CONFUCIAN CRITICISM OF AN INDIVIDUALISTIC THEORY OF RIGHTS

First of all, Confucianism does necessarily entail the idea of rights. The idea of reciprocity carries with it implicit rights. Mencius's idea of the right to rebel is similar to Locke's notion of the right to revolution. Legitimate interest groups have the right to be heard and to contribute to consensus formation. Such a right is not based on "natural law," but rather on Confucian communitarianism, in that "a broadly defined consensus can only emerge when all interested parties are consulted and their differences accommodated or rationalized."[35]

There also has been a great liberal tradition of Confucianism as stressed by de Bary. Some key concepts that express "Confucian liberalism" are "learning for the sake of one's self," "getting it oneself" or "finding [the Way in] oneself," and "taking responsibility [the Way] oneself."[36] A Confucian notion of liberty is perfect liberty or positive liberty, which is not decided by material conditions. The sage is an ideal self who has the highest liberty, or an inner freedom, which combines moral autonomy with happiness and peace. The rich Chinese traditions of positive liberty are similar to the French and German traditions of positive liberty, but they lack the English tradition of negative liberty.[37] One can draw on the Confucian notion of positive liberty to launch a critique of an individualistic theory of rights.

The first criticism centers on the individualistic basis of rights. According to Confucianism, individuals are social beings and have duties to their communities and societies. An individualistic starting point for rights faces serious problems in achieving a balance between rights and duties. Non-relational individual rights—for example, the right to private property, the right to drink, and the right to watch pornography at home—overlook duty to others. In addition, the rights of others—say, the right to self-determination in East Timor—are a *weak* basis upon which to ground a duty, the duty to defend the right of others. Instead, it is the Kantian duty per se that constitutes a moral basis to support the rights of others. Indeed,

Amnesty International promotes the development of our duty to protect human rights.

The second criticism targets the priority of rights over goods. Confucianism emphasizes the priority of *Ren* (compassion) over rights.[38] Rights, according to Joseph Chan, are seen as supplementary or auxiliary: when virtues do not obtain, or human relationships clearly break down, rights are a fall-back auxiliary apparatus.[39] Rights ought to promote *Ren*. As Hsieh argues, "Whatever freedom you want, you should not violate this ethical principle of freedom to choose the good."[40] The integration of Confucian goodness with rights discourse has the capacity to promote human rights enterprises.

Third, an individualist rights theory contains the idea of the right to do wrong. Jeremy Waldron articulates this well: P has a moral right to do wrong, P's doing A is morally wrong, and it is morally wrong for anyone to interfere with P's doing A.[41] Of course Waldron notes that it is morally permissible for someone to interfere with P's doing A. Confucian criticism of a right to do wrong is based on the concept of the priority of goodness over rights. The Confucian *communitarian* idea of a political community necessitates order and authority and justifies paternalistic intervention. The existence and development of community have priority over an individualistic emphasis on the right to do wrong. The problem with the idea of the right to do wrong is its emphasis on rights as entitlement; as a result the very ancient distinction between right and wrong has lost importance.

MORAL POLITICS AND THE CONFUCIAN CRITIQUE OF LIBERAL NEUTRALITY

In contemporary liberal society, where individuality is taken seriously, morality has become rule-following. Government has no authority to impose on individuals any particular moral vision. When a moral world is based on individualism, there is inevitably a lack of moral unity. An individualistic regime of rights leads to a diverse, fragmented, and instrumental world of moral life. The liberal idea of the neutrality of the state justifies the inaction of the state in promoting a moral life. In modern liberal societies the government has no power to enforce moral action. Jiang Qing criticizes democracy, as it is devoid of a moral dimension. The democratic notion of "people" is based on an abstract idea of the social contract that ignores individual responsibility.[42]

By contrast, in both the ancient Greek and the Chinese worlds, moral action and responsibility were united, and individual and political moralities were linked. In Greek society, those who supported war had a duty to join the army. In modern life, moral speech or action can be separated from moral responsibility. For example, those who supported the independence of East Timor on moral grounds did not have a moral duty to engage in military activities, although they may carry with them an obligation to some sort of action. It can be argued that moral statement without moral action is no statement at all, but empty rhetoric.

There is no morality at all if we simply talk about individual rights and self-love. Rights-based moralities cannot allow granting intrinsic moral value to virtue and the pursuit of excellence. Rights are only a *means* (not a purpose) by which individuals achieve their life goals. Morality makes sense when we help others and makes more sense when we make sacrifices. Morality is always directed outward toward others, like the family, the local community, the state, and the global village (surely, many individualist thinkers would call this morality). Self-love or egoism directed toward oneself is not morality at all. The exercise of an individual right itself has nothing to do with morality, although the institutional protection of individual rights has a moral implication in terms of the endorsement of the idea of equality.

The Confucian notion of justice as a substantial moral principle and rationality provides a strong critique of the market-dominated society, the capitalist principle, and excessive individualism. It goes against an instrumental rationality. According to Confucianism, a political society or community is just if moral principles are to be satisfied. The ideal of a just Confucian society is a knowledge-dominated society where morality with knowledge constitutes the first social rank, power the second, and money the third. Knowledge is required to provide service to community and society. Confucian society is much more just than a money-dominated society, for individuals cannot inherit knowledge; thus, a knowledge-dominated society can reduce the inequality between generations spawned and exacerbated by the unequal distribution of wealth. Both power-dominated and money-dominated societies are unjust. Confucianism can limit the power of capital, redistribute resources in favor of the poor and disadvantaged, and regulate profit-making activities.

Confucian theory and practice provide a strong, and in many ways unique, communitarian response to liberalism, without fundamentally invalidating humanistic principles.[43] Confucianism concurs with Western communitarianism or republicanism in stressing the value of a cultural community, the republican spirit, and the diversity of democratic models. In the opinion of Confucianism, the state is not an instrument for class or group interests. The state reflects the interests of the whole community. Statesmen have a moral origin: they are born for the commonwealth. This contrasts with the divine rights doctrine, which asserts that heaven selects rulers for people; with the Legalist explanation that the absolute power of a ruler is required to avoid the state of nature where people kill each other; and the Marxist explanation that the state is an instrument for class struggle.

According to Confucianism, politics is one way to achieve morality or to satisfy a moral principle. Politics is about how to select upright and able persons in government, and moral persons should manage politics. In the Confucian tradition, the state is based on family or an extension of family; management of the state begins with management of family. The moral principle that manages the family is filial piety, and the moral principle that manages the state is loyalty. Today, the principle of equality applies to family and state.

Confucianism holds that politics is an instrument for moral improvement, rather than a function for the articulation of individual interests: "If one is guided by profit in one's action, one will incur much ill will." "The gentleman understands what is moral. The small man understands what is profitable." "He (the gentleman) has not lived in vain who dies the day when his is told about the Way." Politics is seen as a place where one can transcend oneself. *Zhengzhi* means that ill politics should be guided and corrected by moral principle, which leads to an orderly society. Democracy is seen as an instrument of realizing and improving moral life and of facilitating communication between rulers and citizens.

Confucianism rejects the idea of the neutrality of the state. In liberal theory, states have a neutral position to set up rules and procedures and to punish those who break those rules. Liberal states, however, have no right to impose a particular moral life on individuals. Asian countries challenge the idea of the neutrality of the state in that substantial concern about the good life is a moral issue, and substantial justice is a principle for how to organize a society. This argument allows and justifies the right to interfere in and dictate the moral life of individuals. It is justifiable in East Asia to impose moral education. Political institutions are able to force people to have a better moral life. Confucianism emphasizes the state's educative role in promoting a moral life. The state, with the aid of intellectuals, has a role to play in providing a moral example. The Department of Education in Singapore organized and produced a textbook for the Confucian moral code. Zhejiang Province in China made a law to punish those who do not save the lives of others who are in danger. In China, the politics of example tends to set up a good example in the mass media, talking more about the success of those who have found a new job through self-effort, rather than about the unemployment rate. The moralist approach to politics may improve the quality of politics, but in so doing it may well constrict the bargaining power of politics and thus repress negative liberty.

Confucianism challenges the liberal neutrality principle on the grounds that it does not allow for the moral significance of supererogation. Acts are said to be supererogatory if their performance is praiseworthy and yet it is not morally wrong to omit them. There is no obligation to act in a supererogatory way in the framework of rights-based morality. As Joseph Chan asserts, rights constitute neither human virtues nor virtuous relations. In a healthy, close relation, parties should best ignore rights and focus on the norms of mutual caring and loving. Even if there are problems in a relationship, it would be best to repair the relationship by refreshing the partner's commitment to the ideal of mutual caring, rather than by introducing or invoking rights.[44]

There is a link between the egalitarian ideal and the forms of the state. If the function of the state is to reduce unequal distribution among provinces and regions and to help poor regions (*Fupin*), the state has the right to redistribute resources to help poor regions. In the age of globalization, Confucian humanism should entail the invocation of a care ethic that looks after alienated neighbors on the one hand and promotes an ecofriendly worldview on the other.[45]

THE BLUEPRINT FOR CONFUCIAN DEMOCRACY

Mou Zongsan, a New Confucian scholar in Hong Kong, developed the doctrine of the "self-generation of democracy," which attempts to overcome the weakness of Confucian representation. According to Mou, *Ren* does not directly require sages or statesmen but first institutionalizes itself through a constitution. This is an indirect way for New Confucianism to use its own internal logic to generate democracy.[46] Sor-hoon Tan blends

Confucius and Dewey, two great philosophers separated by more than twenty-five hundred years, and injects Dewey's ideas of government by the people, participation, and collective inquiry into Confucianism. Tan's ideal Confucian democracy is a "harmonious community in which every member contributes, participates, and benefits according to his or her abilities and needs."[47] Daniel Bell also proposes a modern Confucian democracy characterized by a parliament of scholar-officials, a house of scholars selected on the basis of competitive examinations.[48] Cheng Zhongying outlines a Confucian way of democratization, that is, democratization via government for the people, who are "ruled with their ends and needs satisfied by a ruler"; a Confucian philosophy of virtue is seen as "a dynamic agency of democratization that is also bidirectional: virtues to become powers and powers to become virtues."[49] In 2009 the Hangzhou government developed a new project of improving people's welfare through democracy.

Today, Chinese local democratization needs critical Confucian ethics to contain excessive individualism. Nowadays, to solve difficult local problems, local officials attempt to use democratic means such as public hearings and consultations. But often a few individuals demand high compensation by using the language of rights, while refusing to pay their contribution. This leads to the postponement of some public projects at the expense of the others and even makes it difficult to make embryonic democratic institutions viable. In this context, a Confucian ethics is used to combat individualistic egoism, enhance the quality of democratic life, and strike a balance between the individual and the collective and between rights and duties. It is necessary to search for an appropriate and stable balance between the need for liberty and the need for community. Confucianism has much to offer in this regard.

Each model reveals one particular relationship between Confucianism and democracy. Stressing one model while ignoring others produces a one-sided view and tends to raise one-sided questions. Empirically, the conflict model was much more accurate than the compatibility model in the early stages of democratization in East Asia. Nevertheless, the conflict model overstates the negative role of Confucianism and overlooks the option of compatibility, consequently downplaying the likelihood of a Confucian contribution to democratization and blinding one's eyes to the prospect of a hybrid model.

The compatibility model has its strengths: it leads us to look at the rich resources of Confucianism that favor democratic enterprise and helps us to create a constructive transformation of Confucianism. However, it may "distort" both Western and Chinese democratic ideas in the process. While the compatibility model celebrates the seeming congruence between the two worldviews, it takes for granted the assumptions that democracy is the ultimate goal and that Confucian culture eventually will converge with Western democracy.

The hybrid model goes beyond the conflict and compatibility models in examining the mixed practices occurring in the real world, catching and reflecting the complex reality. However, it lacks clarity regarding what dominates in the mixed model and how different elements operate in reality. Further empirical study of these complexities is necessary.

The critical model goes beyond the conflict and the compatibility models, offering a fresh perspective, reversing the conventional wisdom regarding the negative or secondary role of Confucianism and reconstructing Confucian democracy. Nevertheless, the practical construction and application of this idealized version of Confucian democracy in the real world are much more complex than theoretical constructs might imply. One dangerous possibility is that a simplistic understanding of the critical model may well be co-opted to suit the predilections of the authoritarian state. If this happens, the validity of the conflict model will be enhanced. How the critical model will unfold remains to be seen. Whether it will develop into innovative institutions is dependent upon the hard work of practical Chinese intellectuals. They should not talk about Confucian democracy alone, but rather engage in a series of social experiments like combining deliberative polling techniques with Confucian traditions. The ultimate test will be whether the critical model can be institutionalized in a way that supports the development of true democratization in China.

The four models can be seen to play their different roles in the democratization process. Use of the conflict model emphasizes tension, causing the rejection of Confucianism and the defense of Western standards of democracy. The drive is to implement Western democratic ideas and institutions without compromise and distortion. In the compatibility model the contribution of Confucianism is stressed, and an attempt is made to find proto-democratic ideas within Confucian traditions. The critical model can play dual and conflicting roles: on the one hand, it can develop and promote a desirable Confucian democracy, while on the other, it may be used to inhibit democracy if it is co-opted as a narrow definitive feature of

Chinese nationalism. The hybrid model aims to mix different elements of Confucianism and democracy to produce something suitable to local conditions. In this model, actors often interpret how best to devise and choose institutional embodiments for democracy according to local conditions. This is the most creative approach.

NOTES

1. Joseph Chan, "Democracy and Meritocracy: Toward a Confucian Perspective," *Journal of Chinese Philosophy* 34, no. 2 (2007): 179–93.

2. Samuel P. Huntington, "Will More Countries Become Democratic?" *Political Science Quarterly* 9, no. 2 (1984): 193–218.

3. Francis Fukuyama, "Confucianism and Democracy," *Journal of Democracy* 6, no. 2 (1995): 20–33.

4. For a critical model, see Liu Shuxian, "Democratic Idea and Practice: A Critical Reflection," *Journal of Chinese Philosophy* 34, no. 2 (2007): 257–75.

5. See John Makeham, *Lost Soul: "Confucianism" in Contemporary Chinese Academic Discourse* (Cambridge, MA: Harvard University Asia Center, 2008).

6. Russell Fox criticizes the view of Confucianism as necessarily authoritarian. See his article "Confucian and Communitarian Responses to Liberal Democracy," *Review of Politics* 5 (1997): 561–92.

7. Makeham, *Lost Soul*, 265.

8. William Theodore de Bary, *The Liberal Tradition in China* (Hong Kong: Chinese University Press, 1983); Andrew Nathan, "The Place of Values in Cross-Cultural Studies: The Example of Democracy and China," in *Ideas across Cultures: Essays on Chinese Thought in Honor of Benjamin I. Schwartz,* ed. Paul Cohen and Merle Goldman (Cambridge, MA: Harvard University Press, 1990), 293–314; Edward Friedman, "Democratization: Generalizing the East Asian Experience," in *Politics of Democratization: Generalizing the East Asian Experience,* ed. Edward Friedman (Boulder: Westview Press, 1994), 27–28; He Baogang, "Dual Roles of Semi-Civil Society in Chinese Democracy," *Australian Journal of Political Science* 29, no. 1 (1994): 154–71.

9. Chung-Ying Cheng, "Transforming Confucian Virtues into Human Rights," in *Confucianism and Human Rights,* ed. William Theodore de Bary and Du Weiming (New York: Columbia University Press, 1998), 142–153; Lin Yu-sheng, *Zhongguo Chuantong de Chuangzaoxing Zhuanhua* [The crisis of Chinese consciousness: Radical antitraditionalism in the May Fourth Era] (Beijing: Sanlian Shudian, 1988).

10. Guy S. Alitto, *The Last Confucian: Liang Shuming and the Chinese Dilemma of Modernity* (Berkeley: University of California Press, 1979).

11. Clinton Rossiter, "Madison's No. 10," in *The Federalist Papers,* by Alexander Hamilton, James Madison and John Jay (New York: New American Library, 1961).

12. Chong-Min Park Shin and Doh Chull, "So Asian Values Deter Popular Support for Democracy in South Korea," *Asian Survey* 46, no. 3 (2006): 341–61.

13. R. H. Mason, *Japan's First General Election* (Cambridge: Cambridge University Press, 1969), 122–23.

14. Kim Kyong-dong, "Social and Cultural Developments in the Republic of Korea," in *Democracy and Development in East Asia,* ed. Thomas W. Robinson (Washington, DC: AEI Press, 1991), 137–54.

15. Kang Xiaoguang, "Confucianization: A Future in the Tradition," *Social Research* 73, no. 1 (2006): 77–120.

16. Makeham, *Lost Soul,* 197.

17. See Albert H. Y. Chen, "Is Confucianism Compatible with Liberal Constitutional Democracy," *Journal of Chinese Philosophy* 34, no. 2 (2007): 195–216.

18. J. Fincher, *Chinese Democracy: Statist Reform, the Self-Government Movement and Republican Revolution* (Tokyo: Institute for the Study of Languages and Cultures of Asia and Africa, 1989), 231.

19. Daniel A. Bell, *Beyond Liberal Democracy: Political Thinking for an East Asian Context* (Princeton: Princeton University Press, 2006).

20. Cheng, "Transforming Confucian Virtues"; Lin, *Zhongguo Chuantong.*

21. R. H. Mason, *Japan's First General Election* (Cambridge: Cambridge University Press, 1969).

22. de Bary, *Liberal Tradition in China.*

23. Andrew J. Nathan, *China's Crisis: Dilemmas of Reform and Prospects for Democracy* (Columbia: Studies of the East Asian Institute, Columbia University, 1990), 308–11, 384.

24. Friedman, "Democratization," 11–12.

25. Liang Qichao, "The Confucian School," in *History of Chinese Political Thought during the Early Tsin [Qin] Period* (London: Kegan Paul Ltd., 1930), 150–52.

26. He Baogang, *Rural Democracy in China* (New York: Palgrave, 2007), 222–27.

27. Hung-yok Ip, "Liang Shuming and the Idea of Democracy in Modern China," *Modern China* 4 (1991): 481–87.

28. Mason, *Japan's First General Election,* 76.

29. He, *Rural Democracy in China.*

30. Chen Shengyong, "The Native Resources of Deliberative Politics in China," in *The Search for Deliberative Democracy in China,* ed. Ethan Leib and He Baogang (New York: Palgrave, 2006).

31. He Baogang, *Deliberative Democracy: Theory, Method and Practice* (Beijing: China's Social Science Publishers, 2008).

32. Joseph Chan, "Legitimacy, Unanimity and Perfectionism," *Philosophy and Public Affairs* 29, no. 1 (2000): 5–42.

33. Kang Xiaoguang, "Confucianization," 86–94.

34. Jiang Qing, *Zhengzhi Ruxue: Dangdai Ruxue de Zhuanxiang, Tezhi yu*

Fazhan [Political Confucianism: The development, characteristics, and reorientation of contemporary Confucianism] (Beijing: Sanlian Shudian, 2003).

35. Chua Beng-Huat, *Communitarian Ideology and Democracy in Singapore* (London: Routledge, 1995), 197.

36. William Theodore de Bary, *Ch'ien Mu Lectures: The Liberal Tradition in China* (Hong Kong: Chinese University Press, 1983), 9.

37. If one accepts Isaiah Berlin's praise for negative liberty, it may be argued that the Confucian account of positive liberty is a great weakness.

38. Lin Yusheng, "The Evolution of the Pre-Confucian Meaning of Jen and the Confucian Concept of Moral Autonomy," *Monumenta Sinica* 31 (1974–75): 172–204.

39. Joseph Chan, "Asian Values and Human Rights: An Alternative View," in *Democracy in East Asia,* ed. Larry Diamond and Marc Plattner (Baltimore: Johns Hopkins University Press, 1998).

40. Yu-wei Hsieh, "The Status of the Individual in Chinese Ethics," in *The Chinese Mind,* ed. Charles A. Moore (Honolulu: University of Hawaii Press, 1967), 313.

41. Jeremy Waldron, "A Right to Do Wrong," *Ethics* 92 (1981): 21–39.

42. Jiang Qing, *Zhengzhi Ruxue,* 385–87.

43. Fox, "Confucian and Communitarian Responses."

44. Joseph Chan, "An Alternative View," *Journal of Democracy* 8 (1997): 35–48.

45. Young-Bae Song, "Crisis of Cultural Identity in East Asia: On the Meaning of Confucian Ethics in the Age of Globalisation," *Asian Philosophy* 12, no. 2 (2002): 103–25.

46. Mou Zongsan, *Zhengdao yu zhidao (Zhidao)* (Taipei: Taiwan Xuesheng Shuju, 1974). Lin Anwei criticized Mou for failing to demonstrate how democracy could be developed out of Confucianism. See Makeham, *Lost Soul,* 179.

47. Sor-Hoon Tan, *Confucian Democracy: A Deweyan Reconstruction* (Albany: State University of New York Press, 2003), 201.

48. Bell, *Beyond Liberal Democracy.*

49. Chung-Ying Cheng [Cheng Zhongying], "Preface: The Inner and the Outer for Democracy and Confucian Tradition," *Journal of Chinese Philosophy* 34, no. 2 (2007): 152, 154.

8

Confucianism and Democracy

Water and Fire? Water and Oil?
or Water and Fish?

Ni Peimin

The dominant view today still holds that Confucianism and democracy are like water and fire, totally incompatible and antagonistic to each other. According to this view, Confucianism is authoritarian, repressive, and typically associated with totalitarian policies, uniformity of ideology, social hierarchy, and discrimination against women. Democracy is the very opposite: It is government of the people, by the people, and for the people. It tolerates and embraces multiplicity, upholds equality and liberty. The conclusion from the contrast seems obvious—Confucianism should be rejected. In the past one hundred years or so, Chinese people have struggled hard to overcome the dominance of authoritarian governments and obtain basic human rights and democracy. As William Theodore de Bary says:

> In the paroxysms of revolution, and especially in the May Fourth Movement of 1919, which, as the great breaking point between old and new, is celebrated as the highest expression of the liberationist spirit, Confucianism was made to stand for all that was backward and benighted in China. It bore all the burden of the past, charged with innumerable sins of the old order: political corruption and repression, the suppression of women, concubinage, female infanticide, illiteracy, etcetera, etcetera.

Even today, de Bary says, Confucianism is still used to justify rulership by a political elite, by a party dictatorship allegedly for the people. The dramatic appearance of the "Goddess of Democracy" at Tiananmen Square would never be identified with any Chinese or Confucian tradition.[1] Even the Marxists condemn Confucianism as a feudalist ideology, worse than bourgeois democracy, and consider the rejection of Confucian social and political philosophy a prerequisite for the development of capitalism, on the basis of which the proletarian revolution will take place, leading eventually to the emancipation of all individuals.

This view, however, has been seriously challenged. Many scholars have questioned it and proposed alternative theories of the compatibility of Confucianism and democracy and a new evaluation of the two. Some have argued that Confucianism and democracy are both valuable in their own right. Like water and oil, they are incompatible with each other, and neither one can be inserted into the other without sacrificing the values of one or the other, but they are capable of peaceful coexistence. Others have gone far beyond and argued that Confucianism and democracy are actually compatible. They cite well-known passages from the *Shujing*—"Heaven sees through what the people see, Heaven hears through what the people hear" (11: 10); "The common people are the root or foundation of a society" (6: 3) —and mention the Confucian teaching "In instruction, there is no such thing as social classes" (*Analects*, 15.39) and Mencius's tenet holding that "the common people are of supreme importance, the altars to the gods of earth and grain come next; last comes the ruler" (*Mencius*, B:14),[2] and so on, to show that there are resources in classical Confucianism for developing a communitarian form of democratic society. While some who try to identify resources for democracy in Confucianism presuppose the legitimacy of a liberalist notion of democracy, and tailor Confucian resources accordingly, others are critical of rights-based democracy. They even suggest that the lack of rights-based democracy in China is an advantage instead of a liability. Peter Woo, for instance, argues that, because of their Confucian belief in an underlying harmony, Chinese people did not feel any urge to fight for rights and freedoms against each other or against the state.[3] Roger Ames and others have argued that rights-based democracy is detrimental to society. The emphasis on rights and the neglect of duties in the West account for many of its social ills.[4]

Among the critics of Western liberal notions of democracy, Henry Rosemont is certainly one of the most vocal and thorough. He argues that Western liberal notions of democracy and human rights are based on the

Enlightenment notion of the rights-bearing, autonomous, rational individual. This notion, as a descriptive term, is deeply flawed. "For most of the world's peoples," he says, "there are no disembodied minds, nor autonomous individuals; human relationships govern and structure most of our lives, to the point that unless there are at least two human beings, there can be no human beings. . . . The contemporary philosophical and social scientific stereotype of a disembodied, purely logical and calculating autonomous individual is simply too far removed from what we feel and think human beings to be."[5] Rosemont further argues that when the flawed Enlightenment notion of the individual is applied to our social practice as the basis of prescriptive principles, it generates deep social problems. Since individual rights and social justice are very likely incompatible, there is no way we can resolve the "prisoner's dilemma" and maldistribution of the world's wealth on the basis of the Enlightenment's notion of a human being. The collective good will never be obtained, and everyone will be worse off.

Rosemont argues that the Confucian notion of an embodied, relational, duty-bearing person is much more in accord with our moral intuitions. We are human beings with concrete bodies in specific spatiotemporal locations, which generate impulses, emotions, and attitudes; these inclinations are deeply affected by our social relations and cultural traditions. We are so essentially related that we don't just *play* the roles of being a father, a teacher, a friend, and so on. We *are* these roles.[6] The role-based concept of the person allows each member of a society to have a clear sense of mutual dependence on other people and to develop a sense of caring for the interest of others. He suggests, therefore, that Confucianism can be a valuable resource and a great alternative.

Rosemont's view has been criticized in a number of ways. In the following sections of this essay I will try to articulate and discuss his view by addressing two criticisms that I find most significant and challenging. To be clear: Rosemont does not make a sweeping rejection of democracy. What he rejects are the liberalist notions of democracy and human rights. These concepts are based on a false and harmful notion of human being— the Enlightenment notion of an autonomous rational individual. He does think that the notion of democracy based on the Enlightenment notion of the individual is incompatible with Confucianism and should be rejected. However, Rosemont does not denounce democracy (or human rights) entirely. In *The Chinese Mirror,* Rosemont says clearly that he is suggesting "a somewhat different philosophical view of democracy," not a view against democracy in general. His criticism of the Enlightenment notion of persons and his recommendation of the Confucian notion of persons as an alternative are intended to build a solid basis for actualizing the ideal of genuine democracy.

To the question of whether we can find resources for democracy and human rights in classic Confucianism, Rosemont says his answer is both yes and no. If we define human rights and democracy as the public and political rights of autonomous rational individuals to claim their interests regardless of any conflict with the genuine interests of the community, then his answer is negative. If we define democracy and human rights as the right and duty of every member of the community to participate in public affairs and take the public welfare of all the other members as one's own, his answer is positive.[7] This Confucian notion of democracy is fully in accord with the spirit of democracy—a way of social and political life in which democracy not only means a formal procedure that protects individuals from being forced upon but promotes the life of each member of the community to be a vital part of the society of, by, and for the people. The key Confucian constituent in this theory is that there can be a good life over and above individual preferences. In this alternative democratic community, "the desired would not be equated with the desirable, and democratic political participation—being a citizen—would involve engaging in collective dialogue about the appropriate means for achieving agreed-upon ends." Within Confucian democracy, the participation of each individual in politics is not merely an expression of personal preferences. It is a dynamic interaction and dialogue with other members of the community, which does not and will never occur in "the economic and political marketplaces of capitalism."[8]

COMPARISON AND ASYMMETRY

One criticism of Rosemont's view is that he compares the ideal Confucian system of righteous rulers, which has seldom, if ever, existed in practice, with the worst consequences in actual practice of liberal ideas.[9] To compare the best of an idealized and distant Confucian theory with the worst aspects of a liberal Western reality, of course, inevitably works to the former's favor.[10] It is asymmetrical and therefore unfair. One might even suggest that Rosemont's approach succumbs to a romantic longing for a lost traditional ideal and an old tendency to romanticize a foreign society when facing problems in one's own.

There is indeed an asymmetry in Rosemont's comparison. He tells us that the Confucianism he advocates is not the kind that was practiced by "authoritarian rulers, self-serving officials, exploitative parents, [and] dull pedants"; it is rather classic Confucianism, the ideal of which was never realized in imperial China.[11] Therefore, he is not defending a dogmatic insistence on social hierarchy, authoritarianism, and a repressive form of government. Instead, he is advocating loving and caring relationships, a nurturing reciprocity between people in different social positions.

Now if we take the ideal of democracy, we might also be able to paint a beautiful picture of the real core of democracy as government of, by, and for the people, claiming that this ideal, though implemented in some countries with certain levels of success, has never been realized completely anywhere in the world. If, on the other hand, we look at the actual social consequences of Confucianism and liberal democracy, we find disheartening problems with both.

But the asymmetry is intentional. As we put Rosemont's point into broader perspective, we can see that the asymmetry is itself a counterbalance for correcting an opposite asymmetry. Responding to the charge that he is partisan in his writings about China, Rosemont writes: "Partisanship does not entail an unbalanced account; on the contrary, one of my major purposes in presenting it was to offer a balance to what I regard as ideologically skewed standard accounts, accounts that are all too common in sinological scholarship on contemporary China, and in the commercial television and print coverage of the country."[12] Another reason for choosing the asymmetry is explained in his essay "Whose Rights? Which Democracy?" Using Alasdair MacIntyre's words, Rosemont explains his approach: "The only way to approach a point at which our own standpoint could be vindicated against some rival is to understand our own standpoint in a way that renders it from our own point of view as problematic as possible and therefore as maximally vulnerable as possible to defeat by that rival."[13]

It should be obvious, then, that the asymmetry does not entail that there are no values in liberalism that Rosemont could accept. He says that his criticisms of liberalism actually are mostly derived from the very values endorsed by liberals themselves. But since these basic values are deeply in conflict with some other values central to liberalism, they cannot be realized within the modern liberal tradition. As Rosemont tells us in his

recent book *Rationality and Religious Experience:* "Whether we are ultimately autonomous individuals or co-members of the human community
is of course not an empirical question, and I know of no conclusive rational
argument for one or the other, a priori or otherwise. Worse, these differ-
ing views are in many ways self-prophetic; the more we believe ourselves
to be essentially autonomous individuals, the more easily we become such."
Exactly because "this view is very deeply rooted in contemporary Western
culture, especially in the U.S.," and is "largely responsible for much of the
malaise increasingly definitive of it," Rosemont calls our attention to it.[14]
Similarly, because the Confucian vision entails resources for us to overcome this malaise, he tirelessly advocates it as an alternative.

The asymmetry also does not entail that he thinks Confucianism has
no need of critical examination and modern transformation. For example,
Rosemont admits that classic Confucianism must be modified to accommodate the development of contemporary moral consensus on such issues
as gender equality and the acceptance of different sexual orientations.[15] But
he points out that these modifications only make the respective parts of
Confucianism more fully consistent with the core values of Confucianism.

The asymmetry does entail, moreover, that Chinese people need to
understand their own tradition in a way that renders it as problematic as
possible and therefore as maximally vulnerable as possible to defeat by
rivals. In this regard, some of my Chinese predecessors have done quite
well. Contemporary New Confucians Xu Fuguan (1903–1982) and Liu
Shuxian, for instance, have both made critical and stimulating reflections
on Confucianism. Both Xu and Liu were confronted with the charge that
Confucianism provided an outdated basis for the Chinese political system
and, even worse, that its fundamental flaws made it responsible for two
hundred years of social and political crises and evils. They both believe,
however, as Rosemont does, that the real spirit of Confucianism is quite
compatible with the ideal of democracy. But they point out that Confucianism lacks something for it to work effectively at some stages of social
and human development. According to classical Confucianism, says Xu,
"the people were not merely 'the ruled' who were below the rulers; they
were the representatives of Heaven and the gods, above the rulers."[16] Why
then are there evils contrary to the Confucian ideal? Xu says that Confucianism lacks two things: (1) external standards of conduct and (2) a
democratic political system. First, since Confucianism grounded morality
internally in human nature rather than in an external source, a person can

make a moral stand without relying on anything external; yet because of its internal basis Confucian morality cannot be as indisputable as the size and weight of an object and so can easily be manipulated. For example, when Confucius's disciple Zai Yu argued with Confucius over whether a three-year period of mourning was necessary, Confucius asked him whether he felt that his own heart-mind was at ease or not. When Zai Yu replied that he felt his heart-mind was at ease, Confucius could do nothing but say, "if that is the case, so be it." While it is disputable whether the form of three years of mourning is really necessary, the passage shows, as Xu puts it, that "even though those who are 'gifted' and well-cultivated are able to take their stand by their innate strength, the less gifted and not well-cultivated still have to rely largely on external forces to stand up."[17]

Recently there have been discussions about the resources within the Confucian tradition with regard to external moral constraints on rulers. Du Weiming points out that while Confucianism allows more political power in the hands of the rulers, it also puts more moral requirements on them. Quoting the saying that "rituals do not apply to ordinary people" Du says that the higher up he or she is in the social political power, the less free a person is: "I would say that the emperor was the least free of all, because the operation of rituals makes him constrained."[18] David Wong further points out that the way rituals work in political life has a unique advantage. He says that since a set of universally recognized moral values or an overlapping consensus is hard to obtain, it is a mistake to take the search for overlapping consensus as the main strategy for ensuring a democratic system. Rituals, however, allow us to have the balance between the two extremes, that is, simply letting disintegration happen on the one hand and using harmony as an excuse to eliminate healthy disagreements on the other. Rituals require the participants in an encounter to have the proper attitude demanded by the particular ritual setting, and rituals themselves can stimulate, enhance, and enforce this attitude. Direct appeals will lack the force that can generate the attitude of mutual respect necessary for people to listen to others, think about what others are saying, and reach consensus. There is no language of discourse involved in ritual activities. Rationality is ambiguous in rituals, and yet the resonance of feelings is rich in content and meaning. The openness and ambiguity allow people with different life orientations to unite and provide an emotional basis for harmony, beyond rationality.[19]

Xu Fuguan points out that there is another external constraint—

historical records. Confucians made great efforts to establish historical records and embed moral judgments into them so that all rulers, while they may enjoy unlimited political power, are reminded that they may also face moral condemnation by ten thousand future generations. Historically this served as a powerful constraint on rulers.

These points are illuminating and worthy of serious investigation. But rituals function on the basis of a firmly established tradition, and in Chinese history the tradition of rituals has been greatly modified to favor the rulers. It would take generations of collective effort to restore or establish a set of rituals able to implement the Confucian ideal. Moreover, for the moral condemnation of history to be effective, it must go through a person's internal moral conscience and have its relevance recognized. Xu's point that Confucianism lacked an effective external constraint in a not-so-perfect society remains a valid concern.

This leads to the second point Xu makes. According to Xu's analysis, Confucianism lacked a democratic dimension. By this he means that the Confucian tradition was concerned with how the ruler should offer benevolent government to the ruled but failed to consider how the ruled might secure good government for themselves.[20] There was no room in the tradition for the political subjectivity necessary for political participation by the ruled. Consequently, Confucian political thought could do no more in Chinese history than reduce the harms of bad government, with no effective means for preventing them. Even when the emperors and ministers were morally conscientious, there was no group in society capable of supporting them. Furthermore, the lack of room for political subjectivity entailed that political change (at least peaceful changes) had to be initiated by the imperial court rather than the society. When intellectuals wanted to influence society, their only means of doing so was by influencing the imperial court. Because Chinese intellectuals lacked a tradition of pursuing knowledge for its own sake, the only social and economic ground for their existence was in the political circle as consultants or advisers. The Chinese phrases *You Shi* (wandering gentry) and *Yang Shi* (fostered gentry) clearly show this feature of Chinese intellectuals. "Wandering" indicates that they had no root in society; "fostered" reveals that they had no means of economic support other than being fostered by someone else. Yet both the realm of their wandering and the realm in which they were being fostered were political. So Chinese intellectuals were from the very beginning parasites of politics, beggars of the ruling class.[21]

Xu's analysis leads to the conclusion that the problem is not that Confucianism is inconsistent with a political system of the people, by the people, and for the people. It is rather that Confucianism lacks a structure that can effectively implement its ideals. Liberals such as Qi Liang are right when they point out that the idea that the people are the most important component of the society (*Minben*) does not in itself entail democracy. It does not extend beyond enjoining the rulers to take the people's interests seriously. This idea still emphasizes personal government by the ruler, which is contrary to democracy and the rule of law. It advises rulers about what they should do rather than telling them what is required of them, and it assumes that the people should be treated in a certain way, instead of placing them in a position to determine their own fate.[22]

Another contemporary New Confucian scholar, Liu Shuxian, makes a similar point. Based on the observation that Confucianism relies heavily on the moral cultivation of persons, especially rulers, with hardly any established procedure for eliminating or even regulating corrupt rulers, Liu claims that "we have to reject the tradition in order to reaffirm the ideal of the tradition." By rejecting the tradition, he means, of course, not rejecting the core values of Confucianism, but rejecting mere reliance on the moral character of rulers, rather than on objective democratic procedures as well.[23]

We should notice that Liu's suggestion is a contextualized one, namely, that it is offered for those countries (primarily China) that have not yet established democratic procedures. Whether an idea is good or not should be determined within a social and historical context. Confucianism was generated at a time when the people were burdened by heavy physical labor. They were in no position to actively participate in politics, as they lacked education, training, and time, and it was impossible for them to be well informed about governmental affairs. It was therefore natural for Confucians to expect rulers to be paternalistic and provide the best guidance for the people. After two thousand years the social conditions remain largely the same. Chinese sociologist Cao Jinqing, having spent a long time doing field studies at villages along the Yellow River, concludes that

> [Chinese] family-based farmers seldom reflect their own interests beyond the boundary of their village. The center of their concern is what is inside the walls of their fence. Generally speaking they are incapable of representing their own interests in political and public

realms and can only be represented by "someone else." This "someone else," according to Marx, has to be the emperor high above. Small farmers rely on the imperial power above them for their highest political ideals and hope that the rain and the sunshine can fall from above. . . . If this situation remains the same with no substantial improvement, regional political changes in China can only be taken as changes in political structure, not polity itself, and changes in political structure are in fact merely changes of political terminology.

Looking at the current rural political situation [in China], we have imported a lot of "modern" formalities: We have a "Villagers' Self-Governing Committee" that theoretically offers extensive self-governing powers to all villagers. We have a multilevel "People's Congress" system that gives people the rights to discuss politics, to play roles in the political decision-making processes, and to participate in governing public affairs in their community. However, for all the underdeveloped countries that are pressured by the developed ones to select the path of "modernization," importing a modern political system is merely a beginning. It is a far more difficult process to cultivate the "social-psychological culture" that is necessary for the effective operation of the modern system. From my observation, the imported terminologies currently introduced to our rural areas are still merely drops of oil floating on the surface of thick layers of traditional culture and modes of behavior.[24]

A democratic system will have less reliance on the moral quality of the rulers; the leader of a nation does not have to be a sage king. This is an advantage. But as J. S. Mill pointed out, democracy requires a certain level of maturity of its participants. To say the very least, a modest level of intellectual development is necessary for a workable democracy, since, as Joel Kupperman puts it with his typical humor, it "scarcely can flourish if most voters have very short attention spans and are easily captured by slogans."[25] The ideal of democracy has to rely on the moral quality of the participants as well. A democratic government may pass a law that allows child pornography as a freedom of expression. Socrates was condemned through a democratic procedure. It is obvious that if the ideal of democracy is to be fully realized, it has to be more than a procedure. It requires moral cultivation and a sense of connectedness, caring, and ultimately, as Rosemont points out, a role- and duty-based notion of persons. Xu Fuguan characterizes it well when he says that while the ideal of Confucianism has to be achieved by establishing democracy, a "democratic political system can be firmly established and fully utilized only when it takes a step forward to accept Confucian thought." In the ideal Confucian society the ruler and the ruled are in a morally reciprocal relation, not in a right-enforcement relation. Morality is the common ground that makes us all human. When we are all able to manifest our moral virtue to our best ability, we can live with others (and meanwhile forget the otherness) on the common ground of being human. That is the purpose and highest ideal of politics.[26]

The relationships maintained by legal rights are at their best external relations. External relations are not reliable and do not allow human nature to develop freely, unless they are grounded on internal relations. To govern by virtue is to establish internal relations between individuals through the moral virtues that everyone possesses. From the Confucian point of view this is the only natural and rational relation. In the ideal society, democracy and human rights may still be present, but few feel the need to use the language of rights. To use Zhuangzi's analogy: When the shoes fit, one forgets their existence. Or to make a Confucian analogy: A country is like a family. When the children are small, we expect good parents to guide the children, which sometimes requires the exercise of authority and paternalism. When the children grow up, good parents are able to exercise more democracy—respecting the children's privacy and right to make their own decisions. Finally in the ideal state every member of the family is able to live in the family with a feeling of full participation and mutual trust; no one feels the need to invoke the language of rights or to appeal to strict democratic procedure. Children normally do not have as much authority as adults, and the voices of those who have higher moral quality and wisdom are taken more seriously than others. But children are listened to and not disregarded simply because they are not yet eighteen years old.

LIBERALISM AND HUMAN RIGHTS

Another significant criticism of Rosemont's theory concerns his interpretations of liberalism and Confucianism. Li Xiaorong says, "Liberals do not need to be committed to the metaphysical 'person' as rendered in the Enlightenment model": "In fact, the liberal view is a moral imperative that individuals be free to question their participation in existing social practices and choose not to participate, if these practices should seem not worth pursuing upon critical reflection. Individuals may be born into and raised up to believe in particular religious, social, economic, sexual, or political relationships; but they do not have to see these relationships as the fixtures, essence, and core of the 'self.'"[27] A similar point is made by Joseph Chan, more specifically with regard to human rights:

> Human rights are rights that people have solely by virtue of being human, irrespective of sex, race, culture, religion, nationality, or social position. But this concept of human rights does not presuppose or imply that human beings can be thought of as having none of these attributes. What it asserts is rather a normative claim: one's sex, race, or culture is morally irrelevant insofar as one's entitlement to basic human rights is concerned. Similarly, the concept of human rights does not imply that humans are asocial beings with interests independent of and prior to society, quite the contrary. The international charters of human rights include rights that protect those interests of an individual that are social in nature.[28]

I am sure Rosemont would be relieved if liberalism were indeed not committed to the descriptive metaphysical view of autonomous individuals, since what worries him is exactly the fact that liberals characteristically rely on this metaphysical view as a basis for their normative principles, either explicitly or implicitly. A central tenet of liberalism is the right of individuals to be left alone to pursue their own ideas of the good, and liberal democracy is supposed to protect this right. But this tenet makes sense only if liberals maintain the idea of "the separateness of persons," as Robert Nozick puts it, or "the distinctness of persons," in John Rawls's words.[29] Marx also has characterized the liberal notion of a right as the right of "the separation of man from man."[30] Now if a liberal is willing to admit (consistently) that human beings are essentially related to other beings, he would have to give up the claim that "I don't need to care about the welfare of the others" (i.e., "I have the right not to take up my duty"), or "I desire this, and I don't care whether this is desirable or not" (i.e., "I have the right not to consider justice"). Though it is questionable whether one can remain a liberal without endorsing these claims, Rosemont would surely be happy if it were so.

Chan also complains that Rosemont failed to interpret Confucianism properly. With reference to Rosemont's role-based interpretation of Confucian ethics, Chan says, "Although the sites for the realization of *ren (Ren)* are commonly found in personal relationships such as those of father-son and husband-wife, there are *nonrelational* occasions when moral actions are also required by *ren (Ren)*. That is to say, not all moral duties in Confucianism arise from social institutions or relationships."[31] He cites Mencius's famous example of a child on the verge of falling into a well to show that "a man with *ren (Ren)* would be moved by compassion to save the child, not because he had personal acquaintance with the child's parents, nor because he wanted to win the praise of his fellow villagers, but simply because of his concern for the suffering of a human person." He also cites Confucius's saying that one should "love the multitude at large" (*Analects*, 1.6) to show that Confucian morality applies to everyone, not merely specified ones.

With regard to whether Confucian ethics extends to nonrelational occasions, we have to be careful about what we mean by "role" and "relational." If we interpret roles and relations narrowly, as strictly personal, then it is true that classical Confucianism goes far beyond that. Humans have very personal relations, as in father-son, husband-wife; they also have less personal roles and relations. A person is related, for example, to a family, a village, a larger community, and even human beings as a whole species. These less personal relations are nevertheless relations, and Confucians must specify their relations to each of these groups in order to act morally toward them. The well-known distinction between Confucian ethics and Mohist ethics is exactly that Confucian love and duty are specified according to different relationships, and Mohist love is not. It is also well known that the Confucian point is not that *we should not* love and care for those who are less closely related to us; it is rather that we should extend our love as broadly as possible, even though we start with, and give priority to, those who are more closely related to us. In the broadest sense, not only are "All within the four Seas" "brothers" (*Analects*, 12.5), but we are intrinsically related to the entire universe. This is exactly the metaphysical ground of Confucian environmental ethics, although obviously, when we compare, say, the value of a horse and the value of a fellow human being, the Confucian would definitely give priority to the latter (*Analects*, 10.17). For this reason I think Confucian environmental ethics is a different kind of anthropocentrism, or, as Du Weiming calls it, an "anthropocosmic vision." In Confucianism, humans are valued more highly than other species, but they are also responsible for caring for other species.

Li Xiaorong's criticism actually entails more than an interpretation of liberalism. Li says, "People are certainly embedded in specific ends or purposes shaped by communal values. But ends and purposes are not forever attached to particular, fixed communal values." She also points out that within Confucianism there is a recognition that, "though deeply entrenched in relationships, obligations and their conventional interpretations, human beings remain able, and should aspire, to question, re-examine, or reject socially given roles and ends upon reasonable, reflective judgment."[32] In his version of Confucian democracy, Rosemont seems to have overstressed the sharing of community values and engagement in "collective dialogue about the appropriate means for achieving agreed-upon ends" and to have neglected the critical reexamination and reformulation of the ends themselves.[33] This is particularly disconcerting because, says Svensson, "today's authoritarian regimes in Asia use the common good, defined by themselves, as a pretext to clamp down on individual dissent. In an authoritarian political system, to emphasize consensus and expect people to shoulder duties while ignoring their individual rights only serves to benefit the power holders."[34]

There is indeed a rich resource in classical Confucianism for an individual to dissent from popular or state-sanctioned values. Confucius was himself a dissident. Likewise, Qü Yuan, a famous dissident of the Chu state during the Spring and Autumn period, has been highly regarded by the Confucian tradition. "If we do not pay adequate attention to this side [of Confucianism], and only emphasize social responsibilities of individuals and the spirit of serving the society, then we would be neglecting many important resources in Confucianism since the pre-Qin period with regard to individual self-determination [*Zizhu*] and the spirit of resistance," says Du Weiming.[35]

Obviously, Li's criticism is based on a central idea of liberalism, namely that individuals should have the right to accept or reject communal values and have their voices heard in the political arena, regardless of their specific roles or beliefs. Her view is philosophically challenging because an adequate answer to her criticism has to address the issue of whether the recognition of free choice of values entails a denial of the relatedness that Rosemont repeatedly emphasizes. Does a person have to be constrained by socially and culturally constructed values, or can one make autonomous decisions? The answer requires a reconciliation of the Confucian notion of contextualized persons with self-determination, which is equally recognized by Confucianism.

I do not think Rosemont intends to reject the view that a Confucian must recognize both a person's ability and a person's right to critically examine and even reject existing social values and the moral imperative of exercising this ability and right. Indeed, Rosemont is himself an active critic of existing Western social values. What he means, I think, is that one cannot make choices out of nowhere. Choices must be situated within inclinations of the body, emotions of the heart, and social relationships of the community. I have argued elsewhere that the Confucian account of freedom is actually a very convincing alternative to the dominant Western notion of freedom. Here I will summarize the relevant parts of that essay to answer Li's challenge.

The Confucian account of freedom entails two major points. First, it denies the freedom of indifference, and second, it endorses the freedom of spontaneity. Not only is it impossible for anyone to be free from dispositions, but even if we assume that one could be totally indifferent to dispositions, such a person would be like Buridan's ass, which starved to death between two equally good piles of hay because it could not find a reason to go to one pile and not the other. Some may take Buridan's ass as an exceptional case, since people rarely confront alternatives that are exactly equal in goodness. But in every rational deliberation, if one does not have any inclination, how can one find reason to choose one alternative and not another? Furthermore, if freedom is indifference, the person should be indifferent to the choice she makes and be able to choose between making the choice and not making the choice. The person has to choose the choice, and for the same reason, she has to choose the choice to choose the choice. This regress will go backward infinitely. The result is obvious—the person will not be able to make any choice, unless at some point she lets it go and simply chooses! Once when Confucius was asked whether a person should think three times before taking an action, Confucius said, "twice is enough" (*Analects,* 5.20). Clearly Confucius was aware of the fact that too much deliberation is restrictive, and having to deliberate too much is a sign of lacking freedom.[36]

For Kant, our desires and aversions reflect the natural aspect of ourselves. They are governed by causation and cannot govern themselves. Only pure reason, in John Rawls's words, can be the "court of appeal concerning its own constitution and its principles and guidelines for directing its own activities."[37] The Confucian would say, however, that absolute spontaneity is still spontaneity—it is impossible for reason to appeal its own decisions endlessly. Second, if it makes sense to call absolute spontaneity a state of freedom, it makes more sense to speak of cultivated spontaneity as a state of freedom. In the Kantian absolute spontaneity, pure reason is not yet in harmony with inclinations and is therefore endangered by predeterminism from the natural forces of desires and aversions. In Confucian cultivated spontaneity, desires and aversions are attuned and are therefore no longer purely "natural" forces. They have been modified and purified by the subject and are therefore in harmony with moral reason. They become the embodiment or the materialization of moral reason. This harmony allows the individual's moral actions to be more fully her own than the Kantian absolute spontaneity, in which the moral actions are still partially against the agent herself.[38]

Second, Confucian freedom entails relatedness. Even though Confucius never dealt with the issue of freedom directly, we can speculate that he would endorse the view that relatedness is a necessary condition for one to be free! Just as a person swimming freely in water must have a harmonious relation with the water, and water is the necessary condition for the swimmer to have such freedom, a person can have freedom in a society only by recognizing the necessity of her relatedness to other human beings. This relatedness does not downgrade an individual human being; on the contrary, it affirms the uniqueness of the individual. Ames and Hall say it better than I can: "A particular person is invested in personalized relationships: this son, this daughter, this father, this brother. . . . In the absence of the performance of these roles, nothing constituting a coherent personality remains: no soul, no mind, no ego, not even an 'I know not what.'"[39] Shared ends are part of our relatedness. Without any shared ends with other members of the community, one has to either live apart from society or use external force to fight against it. Democracy works only when there is a minimum set of values shared by all its participants.

Now it is clear that Rosemont's emphasis on "agreed-upon ends" is again an intentionally chosen asymmetry—an emphasis on something that has not received adequate attention, in order to achieve the balance of the whole.

Yes and No

Having laid out the above analysis and arguments, it is now time to state my conclusion. Are Confucianism and democracy compatible? The answer from Rosemont is "yes" and "no."

It is "no" if we are speaking about the liberalist democracy of, by, and for autonomous rational individuals. Confucianism and this kind of democracy are more like fire and water than oil and water. They cannot coexist peacefully, as the insistence on autonomous individuals will inevitably damage the kind of human relationships that Confucians would like to build, and Confucian ideals would inevitably require that one live as a responsible member of the community.

The answer would be "yes," if we are speaking about the highest aims of democracy—human flourishing; a government of, by, and for the embodied and related people. Confucianism and this kind of democracy are like water and fish. Fish cannot survive without water, and water cannot become a meaningful habitat for fish without fish in it.

NOTES

1. William Theodore de Bary, *The Trouble With Confucianism* (Cambridge, MA: Harvard University Press, 1991), 103–8.

2. The translations of the *Analects* are mainly from Roger T. Ames and Henry Rosemont Jr., and the translations of the *Mencius* are from D. C. Lau.

3. Peter K. Y. Woo, "A Metaphysical Approach to Human Rights from a Chinese Point of View," in *The Philosophy of Human Rights: International Perspectives,* ed. Alan S. Rosenbaum (Westport, CT: Greenwood Press, 1980), 116.

4. See James C. Hsiung, ed., *Human Rights in East Asia: A Cultural Perspective* (New York: Paragon, 1986), 25; Yong Xia, *Renquan Gainian Qiyuan* [The origin of the concept of human rights] (Beijing: Zhongguo Zhengfa Daxue Chubanshe, 1992), 190–91; Roger T. Ames, "Continuing the Conversation on Chinese Human Rights," *Ethics and International Affairs* 11 (1997): 192; David Hall and Roger T. Ames, *The Democracy of the Dead* (LaSalle, IL: Open Court, 1999), 35–40.

5. Henry Rosemont Jr., *A Chinese Mirror: Moral Reflections on Political Economy and Society* (LaSalle, IL: Open Court, 1991), 63.

6. Ibid., 72.

7. Henry Rosemont Jr., "Whose Rights? Which Democracy?" (in Chinese), in *Rujia yu Ziyou Zhuyi* [Confucianism and liberalism] (Beijing: Sanlian Shudian, 2001), section 5.

8. Rosemont, *Chinese Mirror*, 93, 98.

9. Li Xiaorong, "Can a Confucian Person Have Rights? A Critique of Confucian Communitarianism," *China Rights Forum* (Fall 1998): 16–17.

10. Marina Svensson, *Debating Human Rights in China: A Conceptual and Political History* (Lanham, MD: Rowman and Littlefield, 2002), 57–58.

11. Rosemont, *A Chinese Mirror*, 74.

12. Ibid., 2.

13. Alasdair MacIntyre, "Incommensurability, Truth, and the Virtues," in *Culture and Modernity: East-West Philosophic Perspectives,* ed. Eliot Deutsch (Honolulu: University of Hawaii Press, 1991), 121.

14. Henry Rosemont Jr., *Rationality and Religious Experience: The Continuing Relevance of the World's Spiritual Traditions* (Chicago and LaSalle, IL: Open Court, 2001), 91.

15. Rosemont, *Chinese Mirror,* 75.

16. Xu Fuguan, *Xueshu yu Zhengzhi Zhijian* [Between politics and scholarship] (Taipei: Xueshen Shuju, 1980), 51.

17. Ibid., 179–80.

18. Du Weiming, "Confucianism and Liberalism: A Dialogue with Professor Du Weiming" (in Chinese), in *Rujia yu Zhiyou Zhuyi* [Confucianism and liberalism], 79.

19. David Wong, "Harmony, Disintegration, and the Ritual of Democracy," in *Civility,* ed. Leroy Rouner (Notre Dame: University of Notre Dame Press, 2000).

20. Xu Fuguan, *Xueshu yu Zhengzhi Zhijian,* 54–55.

21. Ibid., 182.

22. Qi Liang, *Xinruxue Pipan* [Critique of New Confucianism] (Shanghai: Sanlian Shudian, 1995), 438–40.

23. Liu Shuxian, "Cong Minben dao Minzhu" [From people-as-the-root to democracy], in *Rujia Sixiang yu Xiandaihua* [Confucian thought and modernity] (Taipei: Zhongguo Guangbo Dianshi, 1992), 34.

24. Cao Jinqing, *Hunghe Bian de Zhongguo* [China along the Yellow River] (Shanghai: Wenyi Chubanshe, 2000), 76–77.

25. Joel J. Kupperman, *Value . . . and What Follows* (New York and Oxford: Oxford University Press, 1999), 142.

26. Xu Fuguan, *Xueshu yu Zhengzhi Zhijian,* 49, 53, 60.

27. Li Xiaorong, "Can a Confucian Person Have Rights?" 17.

28. Joseph Chan, "A Confucian Perspective on Human Rights for Contemporary China," in *The East Asian Challenge for Human Rights,* ed. Joanne R. Bauer and Daniel A. Bell (Cambridge: Cambridge University Press, 1999), 216.

29. See Robert Nozick, *Anarchy, State, and Utopia* (New York: Basic Books, 1974), 34; John Rawls, *A Theory of Justice* (New York and London: Oxford University Press, 1971), 27, 29.

30. Karl Marx, "On the Jewish Question," in *Karl Marx: Early Writings,* trans. and ed., T. B. Bottomore (New York: McGraw-Hill, 1964), 24–25.

31. Chan, "Confucian Perspective," 218.

32. Li Xiaorong, "Can a Confucian Person Have Rights?" 18.

33. Rosemont, *Chinese Mirror,* 93.

34. Svensson, *Debating Human Rights in China,* 57–58.

35. Du Weiming, "Confucianism and Liberalism," 74.

36. Ni Peimin, "The Confucian Account of Freedom," in *The Examined Life:*

Chinese Perspectives, Essays on Chinese Ethical Traditions, ed. Jiang Xinyan (Binghamton, NY: Global Publications, 2002), 125.

37. John Rawls, *Lectures on the History of Moral Philosophy,* ed. Barbara Herman (Cambridge, MA: Harvard University Press, 2000), 280.

38. Ni Peimin, "Confucian Account of Freedom," 127.

39. Hall and Ames, *Democracy of the Dead,* 209.

3

Post-Maoism
and the New Left

9

The Dialectic of the Chinese Revolution Revisited

Desublimation and Resublimation in Post-Mao China

Ci Jiwei

Thirty years after China set off on the path of reform that has changed it beyond recognition in so many ways, what I have called the dialectic of the Chinese revolution has yet to run its full course.[1] The contradictions that make up this dialectic—between the idealism of a lingering socialism, however threadbare and calculated, and the sheer materialism of a brave new quasi-capitalist world—retain all their potency, and in this sense China is still very much in the transition from Mao's social order to a new one. We live amid the ever-renewed fallout of that transition, one of whose most telling features is a moral crisis to which no solution is yet remotely in sight. A phenomenon worth serious reflection in its own right, this moral crisis is also a point of entry into other problems, such as that of legitimacy, that have dogged the reforms from the start to the present day. It is for its significance in both respects that I shall examine, once again, the moral crisis in post-Mao China.[2]

What is particularly striking about this moral crisis is that it has endured and even worsened alongside determined official attempts to maintain leadership and indeed monopoly in the propagation of systems of belief and meaning. Despite the gradual relaxation of central control in the economic sphere and in many aspects of everyday life, the propagation of systems of belief and meaning, in morality no less than in politics, remains the prerogative of the state alone. It is one of the few crucial domains of life on which state political control is still strictly imposed.

This domain is distinctive, however, in that it has an internal dimension—the "internalization" of belief and meaning—as well as an external one—the propagation itself—and yet only its external dimension is amenable to effective monitoring and management. Not surprisingly, such management has succeeded in one way but failed, or succeeded less, in another. It has succeeded in preventing alternative systems of belief and meaning from emerging or at least from acquiring sufficient critical mass to compete with the official one. Yet it has fallen some way short of getting the official system of belief and meaning understood, accepted, and absorbed—in a word, internalized—by the populace. Up to a point, people still have to act, in public, as if they embraced this official system; but more and more of them have learned to cope by going through the motions without taking up the spirit. What is the spirit anyway? This creates a troubling situation: systems of belief and meaning that might have a chance to be internalized and help give significance and direction to everyday life are not allowed much room to develop, on the one hand, and the only system that is given free rein offers little that lends itself to internalization, on the other, and the result is an *inner* vacuum of belief and meaning.

UTOPIANISM AND SUBLIMATION

This situation has been much analyzed in terms of a "moral vacuum" (*Daode Zhenkong*), a "crisis of belief" (*Xinyang Weiji*), and so on, and various official solutions have been tried. I do not disagree with this line of analysis,[3] but I want to push it further by working with a more expansive sense of what a moral crisis involves and thus providing a new perspective on the composition of the crisis and on the logic of the official attempts to cope with it. To this end, I want to begin by reproducing here a set of claims I first made in 1994—claims that can usefully serve as a point of departure for this essay and that it is part of my purpose to refine and modify.

In *Dialectic of the Chinese Revolution,* I proposed an account of the Chinese communist experiment in terms of a movement from utopianism to hedonism via nihilism. By *utopianism,* I meant, simply put, the whole system of beliefs and practices informed by the communist ideal. By *hedonism,* I had in mind the increasingly openly acknowledged and guilt-free pursuit of wealth and pleasure that was set in motion by the initiation of economic reforms in the late 1970s. With the term *nihilism,* I designated the erosion of belief in communism that paved the way to hedonism. By the late 1970s, there could be little doubt that utopianism had largely ended up in nihilism. Nor was there much doubt that nihilism had in turn some-how contributed to the burst of hedonism. The really tough question had to do with the relation between utopianism and hedonism: is this relation best understood predominantly in terms of continuity or break? I came down in favor of continuity, and among my most important reasons for doing so was the realization that, despite its ascetic appearance, Maoist utopianism was actually the sublimation of hedonism—a sublimation that was made necessary by conditions of dire poverty and made possible, and given direction, by belief in a communist future. By the same token, the breakout of hedonism in post-Mao China was nothing but the desubli-mation of the original utopianism—the undoing of the original sublima-tion—thanks at once to a significant reduction of poverty, with the realistic prospect of yet further reduction, and to the loss of belief in the commu-nist future. In the context of this trajectory, desublimation means, then, the descent of utopianism into hedonism via a combination of nihilism and improved material conditions.[4]

When I presented the above account of the dialectic of the Chinese revolution back in the early 1990s, I thought that China's problems had been greatly simplified—which is not to say improved—by the desubli-mation of utopianism into hedonism. On the basis of this assessment, I located the prospect of future crises almost entirely within the framework of the new hedonism—in terms of a possible "management crisis of hedo-nism," as I called it.[5] With the benefit of nearly twenty years of hindsight, it is now clear to me that I seriously underestimated potential contradic-tions between the economic and political imperatives of the order that was emerging, or, put another way, between the radically new organization of desires and the in part (though only in part) old organization of power relations. These contradictions have come to the fore since, in the form of the simultaneous intensification of propaganda drawing on slogans and practices reminiscent of the Mao era on the one hand, and the unimpeded growth of the hedonistic and consumerist ethos on the other. In view of this development, I now find it necessary to reopen the subject of desub-limation and couple it with the idea of resublimation—hence the subtitle of this essay.

DESUBLIMATION

But first I want to present three reasons why I think desublimation remains a useful concept for understanding the nature of the transition from Mao's China to the era of reform, despite the need for a more sophisticated treatment. First, the concept is that of an integral process that involves three distinct dimensions, epistemic, moral, and corporeal, so that through it we can grasp the unity of these distinct dimensions of the moral-political trajectory of post-Mao China. The *epistemic* dimension has to do with belief in the truth of communism as a moral-political system. The *moral* dimension is a matter of the stringency of that system's moral codes and practices, that is, the degree to which they require self-denial and self-sacrifice in favor of collective interests. The *corporeal* dimension pertains to the organization of desires, in ways that are more or less ascetic or hedonistic. The unity of these dimensions of desublimation—and of sublimation for that matter—lies in the fact that all living and effectual worldviews and moral beliefs are embodied in everyday corporeal practices (by no means the only practices, to be sure), which in turn must be informed by worldviews and moral beliefs, if only implicitly.

Second, the very concept of desublimation helps draw attention to the otherwise easily neglected corporeal dimension of phenomena that are all too often treated as if they were essentially moral and political. When we put the accent on this dimension, we think of the reorganization of desires, in post-Mao China, in increasingly hedonistic rather than ascetic ways. If we replace "hedonistic" with "self-regarding" and "ascetic" with "other-regarding" (or "collective-regarding"), we will be shifting our attention to the moral dimension of desublimation. On this dimension we are concerned directly not with the organization of desires (or relation with oneself) but with the organization of power relations (or relation with others). The organization of desires and the organization of power relations are closely related, of course, and it would be interesting to examine this relationship in the context of Mao's China and after. But undertaking this task (although I will not do it here) presupposes identifying the organization of desires as a distinct dimension in the first place. The concept of desublimation helps us do just that.

Third, and especially important for my purposes in this essay, by distinguishing the three dimensions of desublimation and yet taking careful note of their close relationship, we are able to spot contradictions in attempts to reverse desublimation in one or two but not all three dimensions. This is not to suggest that it would be wiser or more feasible to reverse desublimation comprehensively, in all three dimensions at once. As far as present-day China is concerned, a comprehensive reversal of desublimation is simply not in the cards, and this is (arguably) a good thing, too. What *is* being attempted, as we shall see, is a selective reversal of desublimation. To understand and assess this selective reversal, we cannot do without a clear distinction among the three dimensions of desublimation. Indeed, it is only on the basis of this distinction that we are able to understand what is going on as a *selective* reversal of desublimation.

DIMENSIONS OF DESUBLIMATION

Let me say a little more about each of the three dimensions of desublimation in order then to say something about why they tend to go together. By the *epistemic* dimension of desublimation I mean the decline of belief in the truth of communism as a system of action-guiding (and state-legitimating) ideals, ideals that used to make the sublimation of hedonism into utopianism possible. This decline is not a purely epistemic matter but an integral part of the process of desublimation: it is the devaluation not of an epistemic system as such but of the epistemic *basis* of what happens in the moral-political sphere.

By the *moral* dimension of desublimation, I have in mind the relaxation of state prescriptions of altruism, collectivism, and so on, on the one hand, and the reduction of behavior in keeping with such prescriptions, on the other.

Finally, by the *corporeal* dimension of desublimation I refer to the gradual replacement of the ascetic organization of desires with a more and more hedonistic one. This replacement goes hand in hand with the gradual withdrawal of negative moral and political judgment on the expression and satisfaction of desires, not least the desire for pleasure and consumer goods.

To see how the three dimensions of desublimation implicate one another, take the moral dimension, for example, and start with the antecedent process of sublimation. If people are to act on a moral code that enjoins altruism and collectivism, both of which involve a high degree of self-denial, they must be presented with a set of reasons for doing so, reasons to which they are able to give (epistemic) credence. In Mao's China, those reasons took the form of the whole belief system know as *communism*. At the same time, people must be able to control their own desires in order to act in altruistic ways: it is much easier for them to practice altruism or collectivism if they are also drawn to asceticism. Every member of a revolutionary collective "carries within himself a small traitor who wants to eat, drink, make love," as Elias Canetti colorfully puts it, and this hedonism, rather than any so-called egoism and individualism per se, is the archenemy of altruism and collectivism.[6] This explains why in Mao's time *asceticism* (*jianku pusu*) and altruism/collectivism were almost always preached in the same breath and—to bring in the epistemic dimension as well—almost always with some reference to communism. Now, once the belief system on which prescriptions of altruism and collectivism rest is weakened, and once asceticism ceases to be a regular feature of everyday life, the practice of altruism and collectivism begins to lose not only its rationale but also what we may call its corporeal condition of possibility. Thus unfolds the multidimensional process of desublimation.

That we must see sublimation and desublimation in such comprehensive terms is because a certain way of organizing power relations (in terms of altruism and collectivism and, ultimately, of denial of self and obedience to authority) has a close affinity with a certain (ascetic) way of organizing desires and because both in turn must, short of relying exclusively on coercion, rest to some degree on belief in the truth of a certain (communist) doctrine. Thus it is that we tend to encounter sublimation in all three dimensions at once, and the same is true of desublimation.

Resublimation

It is one thing to suggest, as I have just done, that the three dimensions of desublimation—and of the antecedent process of sublimation—go naturally together. It would be something altogether different to say, however, that those who preside over the process of desublimation want it to occur in all three dimensions at once and to the same degree. As a matter of fact, there is every indication that they have been trying to prevent, halt, or slow down desublimation in its epistemic and moral dimensions while actively promoting desublimation in its corporeal (not least consumerist) dimension. What results from such attempts is an uneven process of desublimation that is rich in contradictions. This unevenness, or the effort to produce it, is dictated by the overriding need to maintain a semblance of public belief in the legitimacy of the political order, on the one hand, and by the almost equally pressing systemic need for heightened consumerism as part of the new economic order, on the other. At bottom, the contradictions that mark the uneven process of desublimation are contradictions between the political and economic imperatives of the brand-new type of society that has emerged, gradually but inexorably, since the start of the reforms.

How to keep these contradictions in check—it is impossible to resolve them without fundamentally changing the new social paradigm itself—is one of the toughest challenges for present-day Chinese politics. The fact, as I see it, is that desublimation had actually occurred quite evenly in all three dimensions, to a degree that was sufficient to give rise to the "moral vacuum" and "crisis of belief" I referred to at the outset. Thus, the relative evenness of desublimation was the problem, to begin with, and what I have called *uneven* desublimation, with all the contradictions it entails, has resulted from official attempts to tackle this problem. Maintaining the existing political system in the face of an increasingly even or comprehensive desublimation no longer seems a viable or safe option. The officially preferred state of affairs, it appears, is one that may be described in terms of a partial resublimation—*resublimation* in the sense of undoing some of the desublimation that has occurred or restoring some of the sublimation that has been lost, and *partial* because this resublimation applies only or chiefly to the epistemic and moral dimensions. This seems to have been attempted for some years now, with renewed momentum since the present leadership took over.

If an even process of desublimation is fraught with risks, not least political ones, the attempt to counter such risks through partial resublimation is in danger of looking like a farce. I have noted that the three dimensions of sublimation and desublimation have a natural tendency to go together. Thus, *partial* resublimation is something that goes against the grain. In the case of current attempts at partial resublimation, it should come as no surprise, given the omission of the corporeal dimension, if resublimation does not materialize in the epistemic and moral dimensions, either. Nor should it be a cause for surprise if this kind of selective resublimation does not make any but the most superficial sense to those generations of people who never went through the process of sublimation in the first place and cannot rely on their memory to understand what is going on in the current experiments with partial resublimation.

QUANDARIES

In these experiments, resublimation is taking the form of a revival, the bringing back of the substance or spirit of an earlier sublimation that has unraveled during the reforms. It is arguable, of course, that what is being revived is not so much the old system of belief and meaning as the old ethos of conformism and mass allegiance, together with the institutional means of creating and sustaining this ethos. The important thing for my purposes is that whatever is being revived depends for its meaning and possibility of internalization on the old social and political context, one of whose defining features was its future-oriented asceticism. That context is nothing less than the habitus that made sublimation in the epistemic and moral dimensions both necessary and possible and gave substance to those moral and political values that were part and parcel of this process of sublimation. There is little doubt that that context itself is not being brought back, and this is clear from the absence of the corporeal dimension from the current attempt at resublimation. For those who never lived in that context, what the current partial resublimation is reviving are mere discourses, discourses that bear little relation to a habitus, a concrete way of life. Just imagine what sense it makes to try and make the younger generations understand and act on the moral-political imperative "Serve the people," a dictum that used to be meaningfully embedded only in an ascetic, anticonsumerist form of life, which is itself in turn (we must not forget) an integral part of a totalitarian state.

What about those who went through the original process of sublimation and can draw on their memory to understand what is being revived? Major difficulties stand in the way of their *reinternalizing* the old values now. Obviously, the attempt at resublimation is taking place in a social and political context that is very different from the original one in which those ideals used to make some kind of sense by being integrated with their everyday, ascetic, and state-controlled existence. It could even be argued that those ideals were but ways of making a virtue of the necessity of a materially impoverished life as organized in a particular, totalitarian fashion. Now that that kind of life is no longer either a necessity or an expression of virtuousness, any attempt to bring back the old moral and political values without reintroducing the asceticism and the comprehensive state control that formed their necessary background is likely to strike those who used to *live by* those values as pure propaganda. Those who have memories of the old values are of course able to go through the (discursive) motions, with a little updating here and there, but they can no longer embody those values, since the context of those values is a thing of the past, and most of them have no desire to return to that context.

Mao's Legacy

None of this is contradicted by the seemingly widespread nostalgia for the Mao era. The main objects of nostalgia, the sort of things many people seem to hark back to with approval, are certain features of the Mao era—such as a guaranteed livelihood, relative equality of income, and low incidence of monetary corruption—that are often exaggerated or taken out of context in response to the perceived lack of these features in the reform period. The nostalgia appears to be real, up to a point, but there is little evidence to suggest a widespread desire to return *wholesale* to the Mao era. Many of those who remember Mao with fondness are no keener than anyone else to pick up ascetic values again, still less to go back to the ways of the totalitarian state. It is their sense of being left out or left behind, and unfairly so, rather than any principled objection to the new way of life in itself, that breeds resentment and nostalgia. One should not be surprised if this kind of selective nostalgia is found among the worse-off, especially among those who have joined the ranks of the worse-off since the reforms. Among the better-off, however, such nostalgia carries a rather different meaning, bespeaking the desire to have the best of both worlds or else expressing a measure of dissatisfaction with one's own (relative) place in a new social order that they otherwise prefer to the Maoist one.

Partial Resublimation

As long as the desire for a wholesale return to the Mao era is lacking, there is an obvious limit to how much can be accomplished by heightened attempts in the media (e.g., TV dramatization or redramatization of wartime and peacetime "revolutionary" heroes or events) to construct memory for those who lack the experience presupposed by resublimation and to reconstruct the memory of those whose recall of the Maoist past is too negative to serve as an aid to resublimation. To be sure, the old experience of poverty, hardship, and struggle is recaptured to some degree in the media representation of revolutionary deeds and personalities in the past.

And implicit in that representation is a revalorization of those ascetic and combative values that served as the vehicle for sublimating the unfortunate experience of poverty into the willed pursuit of an ascetic existence for the sake of posterity's eventual enjoyment of material and spiritual plenitude in a communist society. What is missing is any relevant similarity between that past experience and people's experience today. Equally missing, by the same token, is any connection between the old values—values that used to sublimate that experience—and a present experience that clearly does not call for the same kind or degree of sublimation. In the absence of such a connection, the implicit revalorization is only of disembodied values, values that have outlived their usefulness and can no longer inform everyday, corporeal practices. Memory can be created and re-created through media representation, up to a point, but what such representation cannot by itself create is the relevance of such memory for the present-day context, still less that context itself.

In this way, *partial* resublimation can easily end up as resublimation *out of context*. If such resublimation is unlikely to give a new lease on life to old moral and political values, what can it possibly accomplish? One of the things it can do, perhaps even effectively, is to keep the public space of belief and meaning occupied and send a "hands-off" signal to all alternative sources of belief and meaning that might otherwise expand and compete with the official one. In view of the internalization requirement for any system of belief and meaning, some may regard the increased levels of official propaganda as amounting to little more than going through the motions—and this on the part of initiators and recipients alike. Yet these motions are by no means idle, for they succeed in the external dimension of political management despite lack of success in the internal one. The result of this combination of success and lack of success is, predictably, the vacuum of belief and meaning that is so often talked about.

It could be that those who are presiding over the project of partial resublimation are not unaware of the likely outcome of their efforts. Should this be the case, it is not inconceivable that current ideological operations not only tend to perpetuate the vacuum that they are supposed to fill but are designed to achieve this *second*-best result.

There is even a sense in which this second-best outcome appears to dissolve, or at any rate render harmless, the contradictions between the intensified propaganda of socialist values (resublimation) and the increasingly entrenched reality of hedonism and consumerism (continued desublimation). It is the latter, after all, where the real action takes place and that does the real work of legitimation—of sorts—in that the Communist Party's ability to maintain popular acceptance depends more than anything else on uninterrupted economic growth and ever-rising standards of living. While the idealistic-sounding propaganda on its own commands little attention and even less credence, it is nevertheless the only discourse in terms of which the economic achievements of the reform, and the material basis of legitimacy, are publicly interpreted. And as long as the real goods are delivered, few have the incentive to subject the interpretation to serious challenge, and many have indeed come to believe it, if only half-heartedly, at least to the extent of seeing the Communist Party as the only political agent capable of leading the China it has created and presiding over its continuing prosperity and stability, for all the corruption and distributive injustice.

It may seem that such skewed legitimation is innocuous, with both parties to the process getting what they want. Indeed it is, from the narrow point of view of politics, as long as the economy keeps growing at the requisite pace and something is done and seen to be done about the gross distributive injustice and staggering relative poverty that are raising mass resentment close to the boiling point. But success at this kind of legitimation—supposing it can last—is one thing, and internalization of its constitutive values is quite another. So we have an ambiguous and volatile state of affairs: the political authority of the Communist Party is more or less happily taken for granted, and yet the values that ostensibly underwrite the party's distinctive claim to that authority and are ostensibly meant to inform the ethical and moral life of China's new breed of wealth- and pleasure-seeking subjects fall on cynical ears. If this diagnosis is roughly correct, we are in for a protracted moral crisis, a crisis of disjunction, of legitimacy without internalization of its ostensibly constitutive values. It would take extraordinary moral imagination and political ingenuity, and much else, to steer China out of this crisis toward a new conjunction of values and reality.

Notes

1. See Ci Jiwei, *Dialectic of the Chinese Revolution: From Utopianism to Hedonism* (Stanford: Stanford University Press, 1994).

2. An earlier attempt can be found in my article "The Moral Crisis in Post-Mao China: Prolegomenon to a Philosophical Analysis," *Diogenes* 56, no. 1 (2009): 19–25. See also my *Dialectic of the Chinese Revolution,* which contains much discussion of the moral crisis in an earlier phase, esp. in chap. 3.

3. I myself have pursued this line of analysis in "The Moral Crisis in Post-Mao China."

4. For a more detailed account of this process as well as the antecedent process of sublimation, see Ci, *Dialectic of the Chinese Revolution,* introduction and chap. 4.

5. Ibid., 241–42.

6. Elias Canetti, *Crowds and Power,* trans. Carol Steward (New York: Farrar Straus Giroux, 1984), 23.

10

China's Future

Suggestions from Petty Bourgeois Socialist
Theories and Some Chinese Practices

Cui Zhiyuan

How, in the final analysis, is one to comprehend today's China? This is a puzzling intellectual and moral question. On the one hand, when one looks at the coal mine incidents, the corruption, the increases in laid-off workers, and other such phenomena, one could say that social contradictions have become vary salient. If, on the other hand, one makes comparisons with other countries in the world, China's reforms have gained quite a number of successes. When I go to Russia for meetings, it is very hard to find a medium-grade restaurant in some big cities. All one sees are either handcarts selling cookies or other such snacks in the streets or luxury five-star hotels. This would seem to indicate that although inequalities of income and large regional differences have emerged in the course of China's reforms, the beneficiaries of China's reforms are, on the whole, more numerous than in Russia. It is very difficult to make a complete judgment of China, and the observations people make from different angles all hold a certain amount of validity. Hegel once said that truth is the entirety, whereas our observations are often partial. How should one comb out the threads of many different views that may be one-sided but that do make a certain amount of sense? This requires putting together a new conceptual framework that unifies the overall situation and resorting all the specific and partial observations. According to my personal reading, putting forward the concept of a "socialist market economy" is an exploration into, and a quest for, this new conceptual framework.

The theory and practice of a "socialist market economy" require abundant intellectual resources, as well as critical reference to humankind's existing theoretical achievements. I maintain that "petty bourgeois socialism" (or "liberal socialism") can become part of the intellectual resources of a "socialist market economy." We all know that Marx once conducted a profound critique of the "petty bourgeois socialism" advanced by J. S. Mill, Henry George, and P. J. Proudhon, in the belief that "petty bourgeois socialism" could not guide the proletarian revolution to success. This is undoubtedly correct. One of the eccentricities of historical dialectics, however, is that after the socialist revolution guided by Marxism has attained success, the proletariat cannot forever remain proletarian. Marx long ago pointed out that communism is not only designed to do away with the bourgeoisie but will also do away with the proletariat. Strictly speaking, a proletariat or working class, in the sense of one that simply sells labor power, should no longer exist in a socialist society. But clearly a society should not forever allow only a minority of people to get rich. "Comparatively well-off," or "common prosperity," may well be read as a "universalization of the petty bourgeoisie."

PETTY BOURGEOIS SOCIALISM

A specter is haunting China and the world—the specter of petty bourgeois socialism. Why? Both Marxism and socialism have lost their political and intellectual momentum worldwide. Disillusionment with neoliberalism is also growing. Petty bourgeois socialism can make some sense out of the current confusion in interpreting the institutional arrangements in today's China. Moreover, since socialism should not perpetuate the proletarian status of the working class, the universal petty bourgeoisie seems to be the promise of the future.[1] The central economic program of petty bourgeois socialism is to establish a "socialist market economy," especially through reforming and transforming the existing institutions of financial markets. The central political program of petty bourgeois socialism is to promote "economic and political democracy."

The leading thinkers in the rich tradition of petty bourgeois socialism are P. J. Proudhon, F. Lassalle, J. S. Mill, Silvio Gesell, Fernand Braudel, James Meade, James Joyce, Charles Sabel, Fei Xiaotong, and Roberto M. Unger.

The notion of the "petty bourgeoisie" used in this essay includes peasants. This is the main difference between this argument and the notion of "middle classes" used in the current Chinese discourses. But the concept of petty bourgeois socialism can be associated with the current Chinese effort to build "Xiao Kang society."

PROUDHON AND CHINA'S LANDOWNERSHIP SYSTEM

Pierre-Joseph Proudhon has challenged Locke's theory that "private property in land originated in first occupancy" by emphasizing that population growth makes it impossible for everyone to have private property in land:

> For, since every man, from the fact of his existence, has the right of occupation, and, in order to live, must have material for cultivation on which he may labor; and since, on the other hand, the number of occupants varies continually with the births and deaths,—it follows that the quantity of material which each laborer may claim varies with the number of occupants; consequently, that occupation is always subordinate to population. Finally, inasmuch as possession, in right, can never remain fixed, it is impossible, in fact, that it can ever become property. . . . All have an equal right of occupancy. The amount occupied being measured, not by the will, but by the variable conditions of space and number, property cannot exist.[2]

Proudhon's point is that if private property in land implies indefinite control of the owner, then it is incompatible with population change. Therefore, private property in land, understood as a universal[3] right applying to everyone, cannot exist.[4] In other words, if private landownership implies indefinite control on the part of the owner, it cannot adjust to population change; therefore private landownership cannot be a universal right for everyone. If private landownership adjusts to population change, it cannot be private property in the sense of owners' indefinite control. It is remarkable that today's land ownership in China testifies to this insight of Proudhon.

China's rural land is *not* owned by the state or by individuals. Rather, it is owned by the village collective. The current system is called the "household contract responsibility system for rural land lease" (in place for thirty years). How much land lease a family gets is in accordance with its size, and every member of the village, regardless of age or gender, gets an equal share. The land was leased out to the family by the village authority[5] for five years in the early 1980s, and the length of land lease was extended to fifteen years in 1984 and extended further to thirty years in 1993. Because the size of a family changes over time with in-and-out marriages and births and deaths, the village collective usually makes a small adjustment of the land lease every three years and a thorough adjustment every five years.

It is a mistake on the part of many Western leftists to assume that China has "restored" the "capitalist productive relations in the countryside" after abandoning the people's communes. China's rural landownership system is a Proudhonian version of petty bourgeois socialism, with all of its promises and contradictions.

The Chinese government is in the process of creating land contract law, trying to consolidate the household contract responsibility system while achieving economy of scale and speeding up urbanization. It is a great experiment of petty bourgeois socialism in that one of the core ideas of petty bourgeois socialism is to realize socialized production without depriving peasants.

John Stuart Mill and the Genealogy of the "Modern Enterprise System"

"Modern enterprise system" is the most often used phrase in contemporary Chinese discourse of economic reform. However, few have noticed that petty bourgeois socialism is at the heart of the genealogy of the "modern enterprise system." In fact, a petty bourgeois socialist, John Stuart Mill,[6] was the key figure in bringing one of the main features of the "modern enterprise system"—limited liability for shareholders—into existence.

It was due to concern for the development of the workers' cooperatives of his time that John Stuart Mill started to study the issue of limited liability. He first analyzed the so-called *en commandité* form of partnership. This special form of partnership had many proponents in England, the Christian Socialists perhaps the most prominent among them. In this form of organization the active partners were subject to unlimited liability, in keeping with the idea of tying liability to responsibility, while the "sleeping" partners were subjected to limited liability, since they were not responsible for running the business. John Stuart Mill advocated this form of partnership because it would allow workers to form associations to "carry on the business [with] which they were acquainted" and also allow the "rich to lend to the poor." Mill argued: "No man can consistently condemn these partnerships without being prepared to maintain that it is desirable that no one should carry on business with borrowed capital. In other words, that the profits of the business should be wholly monopolized by those who have had time to accumulate, or the good fortune to inherit capital, a proposition, in the present state of commerce and industry, evidently absurd."[7]

In 1850, Mill testified before the Select Committee on Investments for the Savings of the Middle and Working Classes of the British Parliament. He proposed to establish the corporate regime with generalized limited liability for shareholders, because this would induce the wealthy to lend more freely in support of projects by the poor. The poor would also benefit by having the opportunity to invest their savings in producers' or consumers' cooperatives. As a result of the efforts of Mill and others, the British Parliament passed the 1855 Act of General Limited Liability for Corporations.

This genealogy of limited liability has almost been forgotten by contemporary economists. The point of retelling this forgotten chapter of economic history is to highlight the fact that the "modern enterprise system" is not necessarily capitalist. If shareholders have only "limited liability," this implies that they are not taking the full risks "private owners" are supposed to take; therefore they should not enjoy all the profits of the enterprises.[8] In other words, the shareholders are not the only risk-bearing group. The employee's firm-specific human capital also runs a risk. Moreover, shareholders can diversify their shareholding through a portfolio of different firms' shares, but a single worker cannot work for several firms at the same time. In this light, it can be argued that employees' human capital runs a higher risk due to lack of diversification. This opens the door for our understanding of the widespread institutional innovation in China's rural industry—the "shareholding-cooperative system."

JAMES MEADE AND THE CHINESE "SHAREHOLDING-COOPERATIVE SYSTEM"

James E. Meade, the 1977 Nobel laureate in economics, is one of the founders of modern gross national product (GNP) accounting. As a student of Keynes, Meade was inspired by the tradition of petty bourgeois socialism.[9] He always called his program "liberal socialism." Meade's program aims to combine the best features of liberalism and socialism. It has two main components in its institutional design: the "labor-capital partnership" and the "social dividend."

The Labor-Capital Partnership

In Meade's design, outside shareholders own capital share certificates and inside workers own labor share certificates. The operational mechanism of the program is roughly as follows:

> There is a labor-capital partnership, whereby the workers and those who provide risk capital jointly manage the concern as partners. The capitalists own capital shares in the business, which are comparable to ordinary shares in a capitalist company. The worker partners own labor shares in the partnership; these labor shares are entitled to the same rate of dividend as the capital shares, but they are attached to each individual worker partner and are cancelled when he or she leaves the partnership. If any part of the partnership's income is not distributed in dividends but is used to develop the business, new capital shares, equal in value to their sacrificed dividends, are issued to all existing holders of labor as well as capital shares. These partnership arrangements greatly reduce the areas of conflict of interest between workers and capitalists, since any decision that will improve the situation of one group by raising the rate of dividend on its shares will automatically raise the rate of dividend on the shares of the other group.

In addition to this benefit of aligning the interests of outside shareholders and those of insider workers, Meade's labor-capital partnership has the other main advantage of introducing flexibility into the labor market. The current social democracy in the Western European style suffers from a major problem: the high wage of workers on the job is maintained at the cost of rigidity of the labor market, thus implying an inefficient reduction of output and a level of employment below potential full employment. When the labor-capital partnership uses a labor share certificate to replace a fixed-wage arrangement, a degree of flexibility is introduced into the labor market, which formerly was characterized by downward rigidity of wages.

It is important for "progressive" forces in China and other post-communist countries not to imitate social-democratic policies pursued in

Western Europe, where the social-democratic parties have long lost their radical inspiration. Instead of challenging and reforming the institutions of the existing forms of market economy and representative democracy, the social-democratic program merely seeks to moderate the social consequences of structural divisions and hierarchies. We need more radical institutional innovations like the labor-capital partnership to make up for the deficiencies of conventional social-democratic policies. The flexibility in labor markets is just one case that illustrates this general point.

The Social Dividend

The second feature of Meade's program of "liberal socialism" is the "social dividend": every citizen is paid a tax-free social dividend according to the citizen's age and family status, but without any other conditions. Two basic reasons for instituting the social dividend are: (1) promotion of equality by providing everyone with the same basic unconditional income; (2) reduction of risks by providing some part of income that is unaffected by variations required by flexibility in the labor market. The intuitive core of the idea of the social dividend lies in the attempt to replace the demand for job tenure with an enhancement of the resources and capabilities of the individual citizen.

One of the advantages of the social dividend over the conventional social-democratic policy of "conditional benefit" is that the former improves the incentives of the recipient for low-earning jobs. This may look counterintuitive at first sight, because an "unconditional social dividend" seems to reduce the incentive to accept low-paying jobs more than a conditional benefit (based on unemployment or illness) would. However, intuition is wrong in this case. Meade argues against intuition with the following simple example: "A recipient of a Social Dividend of 80 supplemented by a Conditional Benefit of 20 will have an incentive to take outside earnings so long as those earnings after deduction of Income Tax are greater than 20; but if he or she had relied for the whole 100 on a Conditional Benefit, there would be no incentive to accept any outside earnings less than 100."[10]

THE "SHAREHOLDING-COOPERATIVE SYSTEM" IN CHINA

In their effort to create a proper ownership form for rural enterprises, the Chinese "peasant-workers" and their community governments have designed an ingenious solution: the "shareholding-cooperative system" (SCS).[11] It is similar to James Meade's "labor-capital partnership" in that both systems have labor shares and capital shares;[12] however, the Chinese SCS is distinct in that capital shares are mainly collective, in the sense of belonging to the representative of the community—township and village governments. Thus, the SCS in China's rural industry may serve to harmonize the interests of inside workers and outside members of the same community. To convey a sense of its working mechanism, I now describe briefly one of the earlier experiments with the SCS in rural China.

In one locality where I conducted preliminary field research in the summer of 1993, Zhoucun District of Zibo (Shangdong Province), the SCS was invented in 1982 as a response to the difficulties of dismantling the collective properties of the people's commune. The peasants found some collective properties (other than land) simply physically indivisible. They decided to issue shares to each "peasant-worker" on equal terms, instead of destroying the collective property (such as trucks) or selling it in pieces (as had happened in many other regions). Soon after, they realized (or conceded) that they should not divide up all collective property into individual shares to the current workforce, because the older generation of "peasant-workers" had left the enterprises and the local governments had made previous investments. Thus, they decided to keep some proportion of "collective shares" that would not go into individual labor shares. These collective shares are designed to be held by outside corporate bodies, such as local governmental agencies, other firms in and outside the locality, banks, and even universities and scientific research institutions. The following figure shows the flow of SCS profits in Zhoucun District:

After-tax profits of SCS firm
10 percent: workers' welfare fund
30 percent: firm development fund
60 percent: share fund (collective and individual shares)

Clearly, the development of the SCS is the joint product of two factors: (1) accumulated change of Chinese rural institutions (such as the dissolution of the commune) and (2) accidental solutions to the problem of the indivisibility of the property of people's communes. Therefore, the SCS has created an attitude of ambiguity among Chinese practitioners and China scholars as to how to evaluate the potential of this new form of property.

As Karl Polanyi once said: "The contemporaries did not comprehend the order for which they were preparing the way."[13]

As for James Meade's "social dividend," there is so far no Chinese experiment in a similar spirit. However, it is my belief that China can benefit from considering seriously Meade's program of "social dividend" in establishing its own social welfare system.

BRAUDEL, ANTI-MARKET CAPITALISM, AND REAL ESTATE IN CHINA

Most commentators in the West, from the Right as well as the Left, believe China is becoming increasingly "capitalist." But what is the meaning of the word *capitalism*? It is worth citing Fernand Braudel's struggle with this word:

> I have only used the word *capitalism* five or six times so far, and even then I could have avoided it. . . . Personally, after a long struggle, I gave up trying to get rid of this troublesome intruder. Capitalism . . . has been pursued relentlessly by historians and lexicologists. . . . But it was probably Louis Blanc, in his polemic with Bastiat, who gave it its new meaning when in 1850 he wrote: "What I call 'capitalism' [and he used quotation marks] that is to say the appropriation of capital by some to the exclusion of others." But the word still occurred only rarely. Proudhon occasionally uses it, correctly: "Land is still the fortress of capitalism," he writes . . . And he defines it very well: "Economic and social regime in which capital, the source of income, does not generally belong to those who make it work through their labor." Six years later however, in 1867, the word was still unknown to Marx.[14]

Most important, Braudel makes a crucial distinction between the "market economy" and "capitalism." According to him, "there are two types of exchange: one is down-to-earth, is based on competition, and is almost transparent; the other, a higher form, is sophisticated and domineering. Neither the same mechanisms nor the same agents govern these two types of activity, and the capitalist sphere is located in the higher form."[15] Braudel considers the market town as the typical case of the first type of exchange and the monopoly of long-distance trade and financial speculation as the model of the second type, that is, "capitalism," which is essentially "anti-market."

Braudel's distinction can make sense of the two types of real estate markets in China today. The first type is illustrated by He Gang City, Hei Long Jiang Province; the second type is illustrated by Bei Hai City, Guang Xi Province. In the case of He Gang City, where land speculation is prohibited by the local government, the real estate market becomes the engine of local economic growth. In contrast, in Bei Hai City, where real estate developers collude with the banks (borrow money from the banks to speculate in the land market), the result is that common people cannot afford to buy houses due to very high prices.[16] Petty bourgeois socialism must embrace the first type of market, while rejecting the second.

China versus Russia: Petty Bourgeois Socialism versus Oligarchy Capitalism

The Russian privatization program of 1992 "offered all citizens including children, for a nominal payment of 25 rubles, an opportunity to receive a voucher with a denomination of 10,000 rubles."[17] However, this happy starting point soon turned into a situation that produced oligarchy capitalism (in the sense of Braudel). The reasons are as follows:

(1) Russia allowed free trading in vouchers. According to the three main advisers to the Russian government, "tradability lets people convert vouchers to cash right away, which especially helps the poor who have great immediate consumption needs. . . . It vastly improves opportunities for potential large investors." Obviously, this produces reconcentration of wealth in the hands of the rich people, and this is the design of the program! No wonder the Russian prime minister Chernomyrdin said in December 1992 that the program of voucher privatization is comparable to Stalin's bloody collectivization of agriculture.

(2) Each firm can choose among three options in the Russian privatization. The most widely used option is so-called Option 2, in which workers and managers together can buy 51 percent of the voting shares at a nominal price of 1.7 times the July 1992 book value of assets, with vouchers and/or cash. Among the rest of the shares, 29 percent should be sold to the general public through

voucher auctions. However, workers are prevented from holding their shares as a block. They can only own their shares individually. This is the deliberate design of Anatoly Chubais, the head of the State Committee on the Management of State Property, in order to avoid any possible workers' control.[18] As a result, managers and big outside investors are eager to buy vouchers from workers, and workers are not resistant to selling them, even selling one voucher for a bottle of vodka.

(3) The Russian privatization did not rely on proper valuations of current state-owned firms' assets. No adjustment for inflation and "intangible assets" was made. Anatoly Chubais "simply declared that book value of the Russian companies as of July 1992, without any adjustment, would serve as the charter capital." This decision gives tremendous benefits to the new buyers of state assets (29 percent of the firm's share, as described in Option 2 above) through voucher auctions, as well as firm insiders, who can buy up to 51 percent of shares. Not surprisingly, the end result is the extremely low asset value of Russian industry: at the end of the voucher privatization scheme in June 1994, the aggregate value of Russian industry was under $12 billion. Even Anatoly Chubais's three main advisers were shocked: how could it be that "the equity of all of Russian industry, including oil, gas, some transportation and most of manufacturing, was less than that of Kellogg [a U.S. cereal company]?"[19]

JAMES MEADE'S TOPSY-TURVY STATE SHARE OWNERSHIP IN CHINA?

There are two stock exchanges in today's China, the Shanghai Stock Exchange (opened on December 19, 1990) and the Shenzhen Stock Exchange (opened in July 1991). The corporations listed in these two stock exchanges usually have three types of shares: state shares, legal-person shares, and individual shares.

First, *state shares:* these shares are held by governments (both central and local) and solely government-owned enterprises.

Second, *legal-person shares:* these shares are held by other stock companies, nonbank financial institutions, and other social institutions.

Third, *individual shares:* these shares are held and traded by individual citizens. They are called tradable A shares, since B shares are offered exclusively to foreign investors.

A typical Chinese corporation listed in the Shanghai or Shenzhen stock exchange usually includes the three types of shareholders listed above, that is, the state, legal persons, and individuals. Each holds about 30 percent of total outstanding shares.[20] By the end of July 1997, there were a total of 590 companies listed on the Shanghai and Shenzhen stock exchanges. However, only individual shares are allowed to trade on these two stock exchanges; state shares and legal-person shares may not be traded.

Right now, there is a heated policy debate on whether state shares should be traded on the stock exchanges. People who are against the trading of state shares mainly cite ideological reasons: they think trading in state shares amounts to "privatization"; those who are in favor of trading state shares argue that the large proportion of state shares in a given corporation still cannot prevent governmental officials from arbitrarily intervening in business decisions, since the state must appoint officials to sit on the board of directors.

Someone might think that the case of the state as shareholder is too special to offer any general theoretical insight. However, one of America's leading liberal thinkers, Louis Hartz, has written a definitive history of the "mixed corporation"—"mixed" in the sense that the state government is a shareholder among other private shareholders—in Pennsylvania between 1776 and 1860.[21] Upon reflection, it should not be surprising that states in the United States had to resort to shareholding as a means for their expenditure and industrial policy: it was not until February 1913 that the Sixteenth Amendment of the U.S. Constitution legalized the income tax (as not being against private property).[22]

The example of "mixed corporations" in U.S. history reminds us that the state as shareholder may not be so special or exceptional. For example, the UK nationalized its steel, electricity, railways, and coal industries after World War II, but the state in the UK was only a residual controller without being a residual claimant, for the state "did not receive for its own free use the profits . . . since this was offset by the payment of interest on the national debt issued to raise the compensation cost of the nationalization schemes. Thus, the state became the owner-manager but without the benefit of an increased income."[23]

James Meade proposes to reverse the UK nationalization process. What he calls "topsy turvy nationalization" essentially gives "residual claims" rights to the state as shareholder without granting control rights. Two major benefits of this "topsy turvy nationalization," according to Meade, are (1) that the government can use the proceeds of its shareholding to finance "social dividends," which will provide flexibility to the labor markets by granting a minimum income to everyone; and (2) that government can be separated from micromanaging business decisions for the companies it partly owns.

There is some resemblance between James Meade's vision and the Chinese emerging policy consensus on the state as a passive shareholder. Even the idea of "social dividend" can be partially seen in local practice: Shunde City in Guangdong Province has used the sale proceeds of government shares to finance its "social security fund." For this reason, I dub the prospect of passive state shares in China "topsy turvy state ownership." It raises deep theoretical questions about petty bourgeois socialism's vision of reforming the existing institutions of financial markets.

SILVIO GESELL: PETTY BOURGEOIS SOCIALISM'S FINANCIAL REFORMER

Keynes has an amazing statement in his *General Theory of Employment, Interest and Money:* "The future would learn more from Gesell than from Marx."[24] Silvio Gesell (1862–1930) was a German businessman and finance minister in the government of Gustav Landauer of the Räterrepublik of Bavaria in 1919. Gesell considered himself a disciple of Proudhon. According to Gesell, Proudhon's central insight was that money held competitive advantage over labor and goods. Proudhon tried to raise goods and labor to the level of money but failed. Since it is impossible to alter the nature of goods, Gesell proposed to alter the nature of money: "We must subject money to the loss to which goods are liable through the necessity of storage. Money is then no longer superior to goods; it makes no difference to anyone whether he possesses, or saves, money or goods. Money and goods are then perfect equivalents, Proudhon's problem is solved and the fetters that have prevented humanity from developing its full powers fall away."[25]

Concretely, Gesell proposes a "stamp script" or "stamp currency." Gesell's insight was that money as a medium of exchange should be considered a public service (just like public transportation) and, therefore, that a small user fee should be levied on it. In Gesell's time, stamps were the normal way to levy such a charge. Now the generalized use of computers in payment would make this procedure much easier to implement.

To give a vivid sense of how "stamp script" works in reality, let us look at the Austrian experiment in the 1930s. In 1932, Herr Unterguggenberger, mayor of the Austrian town of Worgl, decided to eliminate the 35 percent unemployment rate in his town. He issued 14,000 Austrian shillings' worth of "stamp script," covered by exactly the same amount of ordinary shillings deposited in a local bank. A stamp was needed each month (at 1 percent of the face value of the "stamp script") in order to make this "local currency" valid. Since the cost of the stamp was a user fee for holding this currency, everyone wanted to spend "stamp script" quickly and therefore automatically provided work for others. After two years, Worgl became the first Austrian city to achieve full employment.

Keynes specifically states his support for "stamp script": "Those reformers, who look for a remedy by creating an artificial carrying cost for money through the device of requiring legal-tender currency to be periodically stamped at a prescribed cost in order to retain its quality as money, have been on the right track, and the practical value of their proposal deserves consideration."[26]

At the most general philosophical level, Gesell's "stamp script" can be viewed as a reform effort to separate the two traditional functions of money—money as medium of exchange and money as store of value, since "stamp script" eliminates money's function as store of value. This separation helps to solve one of the major economic problems of recession: when money serves as both the medium of exchange and the store of value, anybody in a time of recession will save more and consume less, thereby exacerbating the recession.

Gesell's "stamp script" proposal is a telling case of petty bourgeois socialism's economic vision: instead of abolishing the market economy, we can create a market economy with more freedom and equal opportunity by reforming monetary institutions.

James Joyce and the Art of Petty Bourgeois Socialism

It is well known that James Joyce considered himself a "socialist artist."[27] But what kind of socialism? A hint of the answer can be found in *Ulysses:* when Bloom runs for municipal election, he declares: "I stand for the reform of municipal morals and the plain ten commandments. New world for old. Union of all, jew, moslem and gentile. Three acres and a cow for all children of nature. . . . Free money, free rent, free love and a free lay church in a free lay state."[28]

Obviously, Joyce's socialism is petty bourgeois socialism. More tellingly, Ezra Pound, a great Modernist poet and a promoter of Joyce's works, devoted a huge amount of time and energy to studying Gesell's financial reform proposal.[29] Also interestingly, the Soviet film director Sergei Eisenstein (1898–1948) met with Joyce in Paris and considered Joyce's *Ulysses* a great inspiration for his "dynamic montage.[30] In this context, we can understand deeply Walter Benjamin's "The Arcades Project"—a montage of the social life of perpetual transitions and juxtapositions.

The great Modernist writers, such as James Joyce and Robert Musil,[31] have articulated the petty bourgeois socialist sensibility. Institutional innovations and personal transformations always go together!

POST-FORDISM, FEI XIAOTONG, CHARLES SABEL, AND ROBERTO M. UNGER

There is a long tradition of petty bourgeois socialism in modern China. Fei Xiaotong is especially important in this tradition. Beginning in the 1930s, Fei Xiaotong became concerned with "rural industry" and "small township." Fei realized that "to improve the produce [of rural industry] is not only a matter of technical improvement but also a matter of social reorganization."[32] Writing his dissertation in London under Borislav Malinowski in the late 1930s, Fei argued that "the real nature of the communist movement [in China] was a peasant revolt due to their dissatisfaction with the land system. . . . It must be realized that a mere land reform in the form of reduction of rent and equalization of ownership does not promise a final solution of agrarian problems in China. Such a reform, however, is necessary and urgent because it is an indispensable step in relieving peasants."[33] More important, at that time (1938), Fei already pointed out: "Being a latecomer in the modern industrial world, China is in a position to avoid those errors which have been committed by her predecessors. In the village, we have seen how an experiment has been made in developing a small-scale factory on the principle of cooperation. It is designed to prevent the concentration of ownership of means of production in contrast with the capitalist industrial development in the West. In spite of all difficulties and even failures, such an

experiment is of great significance in the problem of the future development of rural industry in China."

It is important to note that Fei, like Proudhon, did not object to large-
scale industry per se:

> When the industrial revolution began, the major innovation was
> steam power, which caused the concentrated location of industry.
> Between steam engine and working machine, there must be a strap
> which connects them, so it was more economical to put these two
> machines close. . . . The use of electrical power could change the
> [concentrated] industrial location, [since] the distance between
> electrical power engine and working machine no longer needs to
> be short. . . . The invention of the internal combustion engine and
> its applications in transportation makes concentrated industrial
> location even more unnecessary. . . . If the new economic oppor-
> tunities opened by the new engines could not be shared by the
> majority of the [rural] people, it may have harmful effects on peo-
> ple's livelihood. The more [rural] people use these new engines
> and new technologies, the more likely that they will be used prop-
> erly. This is the reason why I do not advocate the Western capital-
> ism as a way to develop our new industries.[34]

Fei's concern can be connected to the theory of post-Fordism, or "flexible specialization." Theoretically, China's rural industry fits the definition of
flexible production. According to David Friedman, who applies the theory
of flexible specialization developed by Piore and Sabel[35] (1984) to the Japanese machine tool industry, "Mass production is the attempt to produce a
single good at the highest possible volume to reduce costs through economies of scale. Flexible production is the effort to make an ever-changing
range of goods to appeal to specialized needs and tastes with tailored
designs." In comparison to state enterprises in cities, China's rural enterprises face a very unstable market for their products, subject to fluctuations
due to economic and administrative shocks. Economic shocks come from
the fact that their products have never been included in central planning,
and central planning can be viewed as a mechanism that serves the function of "futures markets," that is, stabilizers of market demand. Administrative shocks come from the fact that the tight national credit policy in
1986 and 1989 had a disproportionately large impact on rural industry,

because some policy coalition in the central government still favors big state enterprises in cities, especially in bad economic times. Facing highly unstable markets, China's rural enterprises have developed various technological and organizational arrangements for flexible production. Their dictum is "a small ship can change direction easily." They usually produce multiple products and often change their product every one or two years. If we adopt the above-mentioned definition of mass production as producing a single good at the highest possible volume, China's rural enterprises are clearly engaged in flexible production.

The conventional wisdom is that mass production is the most efficient means of modern industrial production, because it can reduce costs through economies of scale. The innovative idea put forward by Piore and Sabel is that flexible specialization is more efficient than mass production under the condition of demand instability. The price shocks due to the oil crisis; the collapse of the Bretton Woods system, which stabilized international markets from 1944 to 1973; and the saturation of consumer-goods markets in the industrial countries—all these factors make it more and more difficult to expand mass production further. The way out is "flexible specialization," which is the "second industrial divide." According to Piore and Sabel, "flexible specialization is a strategy of permanent innovation: accommodation to ceaseless change, rather than an effort to control it. This strategy is based on flexible-multi-use-equipment; skilled workers; and the creation, through politics, of an industrial community that restricts competition to those favoring innovation. For these reasons, the spread of flexible specialization amounts to a revival of craft forms of production that were marginalized at the first industrial divide." As insightful as it is, this definition emphasizes too much the technology: multiuse, general-purpose, digitally controlled machines. Indeed, this definition may give people the impression that flexible specialization is impossible without computer-aided general-purpose machines.[36]

Chinese rural industry highlights the importance of the institutional, in contrast to the technological, foundations of flexible specialization.[37] The reason for Piore and Sabel's (over)emphasis on general-purpose technology is, I suspect, that they do not distinguish between fixed costs and avoidable costs. In other words, they adopt conventional microeconomics' distinction between fixed costs and variable costs. As they put it, "within the firm, the distinction between general and specialized resources is seen as a distinction between variable and fixed costs." However, as J. Maurice

Clark (1923) pointed out long ago, fixed cost is only one of the costs under the general heading "overhead costs." William Sharkey recently picked up Clark's theme to develop his theory of "efficient production when demand is uncertain." According to him, avoidable costs, like fixed costs, are independent of output. But "avoidable cost differs from the plant construction cost, or fixed costs, in that it can be avoided by taking a particular plant out of production. . . . The interaction of uncertain demand with fixed plus avoidable costs requires a determination of the optimum flexible capacity. The nature of the avoidable costs creates an incentive for smaller, more numerous plants that can be shut down when not needed in order to save on operating costs."

In other words, fixed cost is independent of both output and plant capacity; variable cost is not independent of output; and avoidable cost is independent of output, but not capacity.[38] By making the distinction between fixed cost and avoidable cost, we can open our eyes to many possible organizational innovations that reduce avoidable cost, rather than only focusing on technological innovations that reduce fixed costs. Viewed from this perspective, the scope for flexible specialization is much larger than previously perceived.

China's rural industry has often been criticized for lacking economy of scale. However, given the high demand instability caused by economic and administrative shocks, mentioned above, it is not rational to pursue economy of scale single-mindedly. In fact, Sharkey proves that "in a world of uncertainty there can be no optimum scale of plant or minimum efficient scale, although the same cost functions in a world of certainty clearly do imply a single optimum size of plant." China's township and village governments seem to understand this theorem; their decision to keep their enterprises relatively small is an institutional arrangement for reducing avoidable costs rather than a sign of ignorance about economies of scale.

Another type of avoidable costs is the fixed wage. It follows that a flexible payment system will reduce avoidable costs and thus increase flexibility of production. China's rural enterprises have done just that. Most of these enterprises use, at least partially, a piece rate and/or a "contract responsibility system," so that payment of wages is not totally independent of output. According to the survey by the State Statistical Bureau mentioned above, the closing rate of rural enterprises at a time of economic adversity (such as austerity in 1986 and 1989) is high, while the reopening rate is also high when times get better. This flexible means of adjustment between agricul-

ture and the rural industrial sector is made possible by community governments' policy of "supporting agriculture from the profits of rural industry"
(*Yi Gong Bu Nong*), which, among other things, establishes a common pool
for aiding adjustment in bad economic times. All this shows that flexible
specialization requires not only competition but cooperation at the level of
the whole community.

Fei's concern can also be connected to Roberto M. Unger's effort to
"rescue" petty commodity production in our time of post-Fordism. "Petty
commodity production" refers to the economy of small-scale, relatively
equal producers, operating through a mix of cooperative organization and
independent activity. Both the positive social sciences and Marxism consider "petty commodity production" to be doomed to failure, because it
precludes economies of scale in production and exchange vital to technological dynamism. Unger sees "petty commodity production" differently. He neither accepts nor rejects it in its unreconstructed form. Rather,
he tries to "rescue" petty commodity production by inventing new economic and political institutions. For example, we can satisfy the imperative of economies of scale by finding a "method of market organization
that makes it possible to pool capital, technologies and manpower without
distributing permanent and unqualified rights to their use." This solution
amounts to the new regime of property rights in Unger's programmatic
proposal, discussed below. We can invent new institutions rescuing from
the old dream of yeoman democracy and small-scale independent property the kernel of a practical alternative, open to economic and technological dynamics as well as to democratic ideals.[39]

Unger draws out the affirmative democratizing potential in that most
characteristic theme of modern legal analysis: the understanding of property as a "bundle of rights." He proposes dismembering the traditional
property right and vesting its component faculties in different kinds of
rights holders. Among these successors to the traditional owner will be
firms, workers, national and local governments, intermediate organizations, and social funds. He opposes the simple reversion of conventional
private ownership to state ownership and workers' cooperatives, because
this reversion merely redefines the identity of the owner without changing
the nature of "consolidated" property. He argues for a three-tier property
structure: the central capital fund, established by the central democratic
government, which makes ultimate decisions about social control of economic accumulation; various investment funds, established by the central

capital fund for capital allotment on a competitive basis; and primary capital takers, made up of teams of workers, engineers, and entrepreneurs.

We can appreciate Unger's ideas about "disintegrated property" from the standpoint of both the radical-leftist tradition and the liberal tradition. From the radical-leftist perspective, Unger's program is related to Proudhon's petty bourgeois radicalism. Proudhon was a forerunner of those who propose the theory of property as a "bundle of rights," and his classic work *What Is Property?* provides a thorough critique of "consolidated property." It is important to realize that, in its economic aspects, Unger's program amounts, in a sense, to a synthesis of Proudhonian, Lassallean, and Marxist thinking. From the petty bourgeois radicalism of Proudhon and Lassalle, he absorbs the importance of the idea of economic decentralization for both economic efficiency and political democracy; from the Marxist critique of petty bourgeois socialism, he comes to realize the inherent dilemmas and instability of petty commodity production. This realization prompts Unger to reverse petty bourgeois radicalism's traditional aversion to national politics. He develops proposals for decentralized cooperation between government and business. He connects these proposals with reforms designed to accelerate democratic politics through the rapid resolution of impasses among branches of governments to heighten and sustain the level of institutionalized political mobilization and to deepen and generalize the independent self-organization of civil society.

From the perspective of the liberal tradition, Unger's program represents an effort to take both economic decentralization and individual freedom one step further. In today's organized, corporatist "capitalist" economies, economic decentralization and innovation have been sacrificed to the protection of the vested interests of capital and labor in advanced industrial sectors. Unger's program remains more true to the liberal spirit of decentralized coordination and innovation than does the current practice of neoliberalism and social democracy. Conventional institutionally conservative liberalism takes absolute, unified property rights as the model for all other rights. By replacing absolute, consolidated property rights with a scheme for reallocation of the disintegrated elements of property among different types of rights holders, Unger both rejects and enriches the liberal tradition. He argues that the Left should reinterpret rather than abandon the language of rights. He goes beyond both Proudhon-Lassalle-Marx and the liberal tradition by reconstructing a system of rights, which includes four types of rights: immunity rights, market rights, destabilization rights, and solidarity rights. In this sense, we can understand why Unger sometimes names his program "superliberal" rather than antiliberal. Any reader of John Stuart Mill's *Autobiography* would recognize that "superliberalism"—realizing liberal aspirations by changing liberal institutional forms—recalls Mill's new thinking after his mental crisis.

Thus, we can view Unger's programmatic alternative as a synthesis of the petty bourgeois socialist tradition and the liberal tradition. This synthesis can be called "liberal socialism." The vision of "liberal socialism" will compete with Marxist, social democratic, and neoliberal visions in China and the world.

The petty bourgeoisie can only liberate itself after it liberates humankind as a whole![40]

Petty bourgeois socialists of all countries, unite!

NOTES

1. Marx and Engels famously predicted the disappearance of the petty bourgeoisie in their "Communist Manifesto": "In countries where modern civilization has become fully developed, a new class of petty bourgeois has been formed, fluctuating between proletariat and bourgeoisie, and ever renewing itself as supplementary part of bourgeois society. The individual members of this class, however, are being constantly hurled down into the proletariat by the action of competition, and, as Modern Industry develops, they even see the moment approaching when they will completely disappear as an independent section of modern society." See Robert C. Tucker, ed., *The Marx-Engels Reader* (New York: Norton and Co., 1972), 354–55. However, their prediction has not come true. According to Erik Olin Wright's recent study, the petty bourgeoisie has been increasing in number. See his *Class Counts: Comparative Studies in Class Analysis* (Cambridge: Cambridge University Press, 1997).

2. Joseph Proudhon, *What Is Property?* (Cambridge: Cambridge University Press, 1994), 82–83.

3. Drawing on H. L. A. Hart's distinction between "special rights" and "general rights," Jeremy Waldron makes a distinction between "general-right-based arguments for private property" and "special-right-based argument for private property." As he points out, Proudhon is successful in arguing against "general-right-based arguments for private property." See Waldron, *The Right to Private Property* (Oxford: Oxford University Press, 1988), 324.

4. The "Proudhon strategy" can be summarized in his own words: "Every argument which has been invented in behalf of property, whatever it may be, always and of necessity leads to equality, that is to the negation of property." See *What Is Property?* 66.

5. The "village" here mostly means the "natural village." In some cases, land leases are issued by the "administrative village"—an entity higher than a "natural village."

6. About Mill's socialist ideals after the 1848 Revolution, see Michael Levin, *The Condition of England Question: Carlyle, Mill and Engels* (New York: Macmillan, 1998).

7. Citied in *Collected Works of John Stuart Mill*, 8 vols. (Toronto: University of Toronto Press, 1967), 5: 462.

8. This was exactly one of the reasons Adam Smith was against limited liability for shareholders in his famous *The Wealth of Nations*.

9. There is an interesting theoretical connection between Keynes and Proudhon, via Silvio Gesell. See Dudley Dillard, "Keynes and Proudhon," *Journal of Economic History* (May 1942): 63–76.

10. James Meade, *Liberty, Equality and Efficiency* (New York: New York University Press, 1993), 152.

11. After three years of experiments in three areas in Shandong, Zhejiang, and Anhui provinces, the Chinese Ministry of Agriculture issued "The Temporary Regulations for Peasant's Shareholding-Cooperative Enterprises" in Feb. 1990. It indicates that this ownership form will become more and more important in Chinese rural enterprises.

12. It is important to notice that both systems differ significantly from the employee stock ownership plan (ESOP) in the United States. The ESOP promotes "worker participation in the firm's fortunes only in so far as a part of the worker's past pay has taken the form of compulsory savings rather than the receipt of freely disposable income, whereas Labor Share Certificates depend directly upon the employee's current supply of work and effort to the firm without any reference to past compulsory savings." See James E. Meade, *Alternative Systems of Business Organization and of Workers' Remuneration* (London: Allen and Unwin, 1980), 117.

13. In an article I wrote in Chinese in 1994, I argued that the SCS should be considered an institutional innovation. This article appears to have had an impact on the final decision of top authorities to allow the SCS to spread in rural China. See Cui Zhiyuan, "Zhidu Chuangxin He Di'erci Sixiang Jiefang," *Beijing Qingnian Bao*, July 24, 1994.

14. Fernand Braudel, *Civilization and Capitalism 15th–18th Century: The Wheels of Commerce*, 2 vols. (Berkeley: University of California Press, 1992), 2: 231, 237.

15. Fernand Braudel, *Afterthoughts on Material Civilization and Capitalism* (Baltimore, MD: Johns Hopkins University Press, 1994), 62.

16. For the details of these two types of real estate markets in China, see Wang Xiaoqiang, "Reports from He Long Jiang" (in Chinese), *Shi Jie*, no. 6 (2002).

17. Maxim Boycko, Andrei Shleifer, and Robert Vishny, *Privatizing Russia* (Cambridge, MA: MIT Press, 1995), 83.

18. Ibid., 79.

19. Ibid., 117.

20. The governmental regulation requires that tradable A shares should account for no less than 25 percent of a company's initial public offering.

21. Louis Hartz, *Economic Policy and Democratic Thought: Pennsylvania, 1776–1860* (Cambridge, MA: Harvard University Press, 1948).

22. See Robert Stanley, *Dimensions of Law in the Service of Order: The Origins of the Federal Income Tax 1861–1913* (New York: Oxford University Press, 1993).

23. James Meade, *Liberty, Equality and Efficiency* (New York: New York University Press, 1993), 95.

24. John M. Keynes, *General Theory of Employment, Interest and Money* (London: Macmillan, 1936), 234.

25. Silvio Gesell, *The Natural Economic Order* (Berlin: Frohman, 1929), 9.

26. Keynes, *General Theory of Employment*, 355.

27. In a letter to his brother, Joyce said: "It is a mistake for you to imagine that my political opinions are those of a universal lover: but they are those of a socialist artist." See *Letters of James Joyce*, ed. Richard Ellmann (New York: Faber and Faber, 1966), 2: 89.

28. James Joyce, *Ulysses* (New York: Random House, 1987), 803.

29. See Tim Redman, *Ezra Pound and Italian Fascism* (Cambridge: Cambridge University Press, 1991), esp. chap. 5, "The Discovery of Gesell."

30. Gosta Werner, "James Joyce and Sergey Eisenstein," *James Joyce Quarterly* (1990): 491–507.

31. Robert Musil seems to be under the influence of Gesell's theory of money too. Musil wrote in 1923: "During the recent period of revolution and confusion, a kind of natural economy involving every imaginable form of favoritism established itself everywhere. This point needs to be made, since many people seem to believe that abolishing money would abolish selfishness. But selfishness is as old and eternal as its opposite, social feelings." See Robert Musil, *Precision and Soul* (Chicago: University of Chicago Press, 1990), 181.

32. Fei Xiaotong, *Peasants' Life In China* (London: Macmillan, 1939), 283.

33. Ibid., 285.

34. This is my translation from Fei Xiaotong's book *Xiang Tu Chong Jian* [Rural reconstruction] (Shanghai: Guancha Publisher, 1948). The citation is from the section titled "Electricity and Internal Combustion Engine Make It Possible to Decentralize Modern Industrial Production" (in Chinese). However, this crucial section was missed in Margaret Park Redfield's English translation of the book (*China's Gentry*, intro. Robert Redfield [Chicago: University of Chicago Press, 1953]).

35. Michael Piore and Charles Sabel, *Second Industrial Divide* (New York: Basic Books, 1984).

36. Certainly, I do not deny the tremendous importance of general-purpose technology for flexible specialization. According to the data collected by the International Institute for Applied System Analysis in 1989, there are about eight hun-

dred "flexible manufacturing systems" (FMS) now in operation around the world. The FMS are used to produce a variable number of product varieties: "30% produce less than ten varieties, 44% between ten and 100, 22% between 100 and 1,000, . . . the remaining 4 per cent used to produce more than 1,000 product varieties." My intention is only to emphasize that flexible specialization is also possible in developing countries without many general-purpose machines.

37. In my view, only by studying institutional underpinnings can we understand why a specific flexible technology, such as the Jacquard loom, did or did not develop and spread.

38. This is my illustration, which is still imprecise. Strictly speaking, avoidable cost means that the cost function is not convex on the closed set X 0 and is convex only on the open set X 0.

39. Roberto M. Unger, *Politics,* ed. Cui Zhiyuan (London: Verso, 1997).

40. There is debate among historians about the political inclinations of the petty bourgeois in modern history. According to Arno Mayer, the petty bourgeois was a swing sector between the conservative and the radical forces and became increasingly conservative after 1871 See Arno Mayer, "The Lower Middle Class as Historical Problem," *Journal of Modern History* (Sept. 1975): 409–36. George Orwell famously depicts the petty bourgeois as following: "The real importance of this class is that they are the shock-absorbers of the bourgeoisies." See his *The Road to Wigan Pier* (London: Gollancz, 1937), 14. However, Richard Hamilton's important study of the social basis of German fascism shows that the highest level of support for Hitler came from the big bourgeoisie rather than the petty bourgeois. See his *Who Voted for Hitler* (Princeton: Princeton University Press, 1982). The petty bourgeois socialist program presented here can be viewed as a break from petty bourgeois conservatism and an innovation in the tradition of petty bourgeois radicalism.

11

Taking the China Model Seriously

One-Party Constitutionalism and Economic Development

Frank Fang

In the late twentieth century, few people in the West believed that China could experience an economic miracle. In the early twenty-first century, even fewer in the West believe that China can sustain its economic growth. Western logic is simple: no growth can take place without carrying out Western-style market reform, and no country can sustain its growth without developing a Western-style democracy. In fact, a growing number of people in the West believe that the problem of the Chinese government is not about how to sustain growth but about how to maintain its political survival.

In this chapter, I argue that the popular reasoning regarding economic takeoff is as mistaken as the popular reasoning regarding sustaining growth. By proposing a "property rights theory of the state," I demonstrate that Western democracy is not what is required for sustaining growth and that China's ongoing political reform will not only help uphold its growth momentum but also help maintain its political stability. The key conclusion of this essay is that China will continue to rise and that China's challenge to the West is neither economic nor military, but rather a political challenge on the "state-model" level.

There are six sections in this essay. The first section explains China's unique approach to economic growth. The second brings up the debate on whether democracy or the rule of law sustains growth. The third introduces a "property rights theory of the state" that is used in the fourth section to interpret China's political change in a nonconventional way. The fifth section goes beyond the democracy and rule-of-law approaches to explain growth by proposing a "three-tiered effort-based institutional analysis." The sixth section concludes with an emphasis on China's accountability crisis and the reasons why it will not throw the country into political turmoil.

To better understand China, we need new thinking and a new perspective on "old facts." Conventional theories cannot be disproven by facts; they can only be disproven by facts and new theories.

EXPLAINING CHINA'S ECONOMIC GROWTH: FROM SOURCES TO CAUSES

At the turn of the new century, the rise of China is an economic miracle by almost any observer's yardstick. Since many experts were busy forecasting China's collapse after 1989, the economic boom in China certainly took everyone by surprise. Yet even with the benefit of hindsight, explaining China's growth is still by no means easy.

After the rise of "new institutional economics" in the 1970s, the study of economic growth witnessed a major shift from technical focus to institutional focus and from economic factors to political factors. This paradigm shift is associated with five key contributors to the field: Douglass North, Mancur Olson, Robert Barro, Daron Acemoglu, and Dani Rodrik. While Rodrik's 2007 book *One Economics, Many Recipes* has helped refute the popular reasoning regarding economic takeoff, it, along with Douglass North's 2009 book *Violence and Social Orders* and Daron Acemoglu's studies,[1] nevertheless strengthens the problematic reasoning regarding sustaining growth.

"Economic growth" refers to increased output in goods and services on a per capita basis. To increase output, all a society needs to do is increase such input as land, labor, and capital. After the 1960s, orthodox growth theory became more sophisticated by looking at labor, capital, and a residual component called "total factor productivity," which could be determined by population structure, education, human capital, savings, capital accumulation, relative price of resources, geography and climate, economies of scale, trade, knowledge, technology, innovation, entrepreneurship, work methods, management, public infrastructure, and macroeconomic policies. In this long list of factors (including those put forward by the so-called new growth theory), the focus is still the same: input.

Yet, if all that is required for economic growth is simply input and investment, why have so many societies failed to grow? This is the question asked by Douglass North and Robert Thomas in their 1973 book, *The Rise of the Western World: A New Economic History*. This simple question turns out to be a landmark in the field's tidal change from investigating the "sources" of economic growth to investigating its "causes."

In 1982, pursuing a similar line of thought, Mancur Olson, in *The Rise and Decline of Nations: Economic Growth, Stagflation, and Social Rigidities*, further stated that "estimates of the sources of growth, however meticulous, subtle, and useful, do not tell us about the ultimate causes of growth. They do not tell us what incentives made the saving and investment occur, or what explained the innovations, or why there was more innovation and capital accumulation in one society or period than in another. They do not trace the sources of growth to their fundamental causes; they trace the water in the river to the streams and lakes from which it comes, but they do not explain the rain. Neither do they explain the silting up of the channels of economic progress—that is, what I shall call here the 'retardants' of growth."[2]

While North concentrates more on progrowth "productive causes," Olson focuses on antigrowth "distributional retardants." Both, as a result, contribute to the theoretical foundation for the more practical issue of shaping the right "growth policies" in developing countries. Following the "shock therapy" recommended by Jeffrey Sachs during the early 1990s,[3] the "Washington Consensus," a term coined by John Williamson in 1989, details policy prescriptions constituting a standard reform package promoted for growth-hungry developing countries by Washington, D.C.–based international institutions. This neoliberal market-oriented package, summarized by Dani Rodrik as "stabilize, privatize, and liberalize," has unfortunately proved disappointing if not disastrous for the developing world. The Washington Consensus and its "second-generation" version,[4] therefore, became the "Washington confusion," at least to Rodrik.[5]

What went wrong with the Washington Consensus, according to Rodrik, is that its "one size fits all" best practices fail to account for local knowledge and needs and, most important, fail to account for identifying and prioritizing specific factors that prevent or impede growth.[6] While more recent research by Douglass North, Mancur Olson, and Daron Ace-moglu all points to the importance of market-augmented institutions and credible political commitment, the fact that China depends more on poli-cies opposite to the Washington Consensus's main recommendations for success reveals that there is a huge gap between abstract theories and con-crete policies. Indeed, if China had failed to grow or failed to grow as fast as it did, there would be no surprise for the West.

For China's rapid growth, what mattered was not the sudden removal of price and currency controls, the withdrawal of state subsidies, immedi-ate trade liberalization, or large-scale privatization of state-owned enter-prises. What actually happened in China was a gradual reform strategy that included the development of a dual-track price mechanism, the rural-household responsibility system, township-and-village enterprises, local-government fiscal-responsibility arrangements, and special economic zones that encourage foreign investment. It is a low-cost reform-on-the-margin approach that best minimizes opposition to changes and best max-imizes ongoing mass support.

The lesson from China is that market-supporting institutions are not going to work as expected if people and the government are not market ready. What is important, in reality, is the market-oriented goal rather than the market-oriented shock. For example, high levels of protectionism, lit-tle privatization, export-led strategy and extensive industrial policies plan-ning, strong government involvement, and lax fiscal and financial policies are more the rule than the exception in various stages of China's growth. Market reforms in specific areas are only called for when development pri-orities evolve and shift. Essentially, growth is not a concept but an opera-tion, and the market is not a government-free institution.[7]

Rodrik correctly points out that there is no single mapping between the market and the set of nonmarket institutions required to sustain it, yet he fails to provide a logical link between this statement and the conclu-sion that Western democracy, or the "participatory political system," is the most effective mechanism for processing and aggregating local knowledge and is therefore the only "meta-institution" for building good institutions and sustaining economic growth.[8] Equally problematic is the fact that the statement "Democracy sustains economic growth" is simply not true, as is convincingly demonstrated by massive empirical evidence from studies by Robert Barro, Adam Przeworski, and José Tavares.[9] Barro's findings sug-gest that increases in political rights initially increase growth but tend to retard growth once a moderate level of democracy has been attained: "One cannot conclude from this evidence that more or less democracy is a critical element for economic growth."[10]

SUSTAINING GROWTH: OPEN ACCESS TO ECONOMIC AND POLITICAL COMPETITION?

The "meta-institution" problem nevertheless is picked up by Douglass North in his ambitious *Violence and Social Orders: A Conceptual Framework for Interpreting Recorded Human History,* coauthored with John Wallis and Barry Weingast and published in 2009. Earlier, in *Understanding the Process of Economic Change* (2005), North asserts that "there is no set formula for achieving economic development. No economic model can capture the intricacies of economic growth in a particular society. While the sources of productivity growth are well known, the process of economic growth is going to vary with every society, reflecting the diverse cultural heritages and the equally diverse geographic, physical, and economic settings."[11] In *Violence and Social Orders,* the "set formula for achieving economic development" appears to have eventually been found.

According to North and his coauthors, the "natural state" and the "open access society" are two basic forms of social order in which violence control is the central problem; the degree of open access to political-economic organizations, characterized by impersonality and perpetuality, defines various social orders and their level of social development. The key message of their "social orders framework" can be summarized by its "open access logic": open access in political-economic competitions drives social development; societies are different simply because they are different in how they provide political-economic access to different social groups.

Open access logic, if it is correct, has to rely solely on the simple fact that all rich countries, measured by per capita income, are indeed open in providing access to political-economic competition. At first glance, this seems true in all twenty-three Western countries in the cited top thirty economies.[12] The challenge, however, is to explain why the other seven (Qatar, United Arab Emirates, Kuwait, Brunei, Singapore, Hong Kong, and Macao) are rich yet not politically open. There are three ways to explain this away: first, find a nonsocial factor like oil or any other natural resource to account for high per capita income; second, claim to have no available data in the study; third, argue for a closely matched pattern, not a completely harmonized correlation.

As it turns out, surprisingly, North and his coauthors appeal to all three of these arguments. Even more shocking is the fact that they fail to further explain why, if oil contributes to high national income, other oil-rich countries are not as rich. "The resource curse" or "the paradox of plenty" is a well-known matter of debate,[13] and one should certainly be very careful to use oil as part of an argument without proving otherwise. And if there are no available data, is it not obvious even to nonexperts that "the other seven" are not at all politically open in the early twenty-first century? Furthermore, if the small size of "the other seven" is used as an argument, one needs to explain why other small economies have not become as rich. Yet North and his coauthors choose to ignore relevant empirical evidence (as provided by Robert Barro and Adam Przeworski) and instead put up a "protective belt" around their elegant theoretical "core." Their attempt to hide or avoid facts, however, is clearly an embrace of "selection bias," which can only result in a faulty foundation for their theory.

Interestingly, open economic competition with a stable social order is the "common denominator" not only for "the other seven" but also for the other twenty-three Western countries in the top-thirty list. Why does the open access framework use a "noncommon denominator" instead of a "common denominator" to explain economic success? Why does it choose to ignore what seems to be obvious, especially when further considering the role of the "common denominator" in the recent experience of emerging markets (including China)? The only plausible answer is that open political competition or democracy is a value that is more important than any fact in their eyes and that giving thought to the "common denominator" will inevitably destroy the whole open access framework. Simply put, their logic is: "It is true because we like it, and we know most people like it."

It is not a coincidence that the seven rich economies with less open political access happen to be non-Western and that the twenty-three countries with more open political access happen to be Western (with the exception of Japan). This simple fact should force us to question ourselves: Is democracy truly a causal intervening variable, or is it just a noncausal intervening variable that expresses something else that actually leads to economic development? Is it possible that something else (e.g., religion and/or a more contractual-oriented culture)[14] causes Western countries to move to the rule of law and development first (to be imitated by latecomers) and that "something else" is expressed by the widespread political-economic open access in these countries? Put it differently: is it because open access leads to development, or is it because a more contractual-oriented culture leads to the rule of law and development that are expressed by Western-style open access?

Another simple fact is that adopting democracy does not really cause economic development for most latecomers.[15] What we should ask ourselves is whether democracy is unconditionally good for growth. Is adopting democracy or sustaining democracy only a unique cultural-historical experience, or is it truly universally feasible?

When Douglass North won the 1993 Nobel prize in economics, the institutional framework he developed in *Institutions, Institutional Change and Economic Performance* (1990) was one of the key contributive factors. This is a well-balanced framework that incorporates formal rules, informal rules, and organizations for explaining institutional change and economic development. In the open access framework, however, the key factor of informal rules is removed. Formal institutions and organizations are now providing the whole explanation.

The role of informal rules can be ignored if we assume that we are all the same as human beings. A "we are all the same" approach can reduce a three-level model of "human nature–cultural characteristics–individual uniqueness" into a single-level model of "human nature." Such is the ambition of the open access framework, its subtitle "A Conceptual Framework for Interpreting Recorded Human History."

The cost of the "Euro-American focus" is giving up a well-balanced institutional framework in North's earlier works and creating tension between the 1990 formal framework and the 2009 substantive framework: "Impersonally defined access (rights) to form organizations is a central part of open access societies" (North et al., *Violence*, 7). Yet impersonal characteristics may be highly cultural. The discussion of impersonal characteristics in a noncultural context demonstrates a regretful shift of attention from "formal rules–informal rules–organizations" to "formal rules–organizations" in explaining institutional changes. In fact, informal rules play a key role in explaining why various social orders progress or regress in different directions. Impersonality is not only modern but also cultural; it expands markets, reduces precontracting costs, yet also raises postcontracting costs and develops lawsuit commercial culture. The choice of social order is not only political but also cultural. As a result, "a deep understanding of change must go beyond broad generalizations to a specific understanding of the cultural heritage of that particular society" (North et al., *Violence,* 271)—a maxim that remains lip service in their book and is not actually integrated into its framework.

The solution should be obvious. By mistakenly subscribing to the outcome approach, the open access framework provides an argument for the "end of history" thesis because it tells us that open access social order is the ideal society perfected by open political-economic competition, although it indicates that historical determinism is not what it suggests.

While the nearly two dozen Western countries in the top-thirty list confirm that developed societies always have developed economies and developed polities, such a "confirmation fact" may divert our attention away from other countries that pose a challenge to the preconceived idea of open access. When an "unconfirmation fact" is put before our eyes, it is instantly clear that what is necessary is not to explain developed societies by open access. Explaining open access (especially political access), or explaining how open access performs differently in specific countries, or explaining why open access happens in specific countries at specific times, becomes more relevant.

In other words, the more pertinent questions are: What causes open access in some countries and not in others? Is it really due to pure, non-cultural political choices, such that a society's development is controlled by random chances? If the performance of an open access arrangement depends on overall open access structure, what role does culture play in the performance of open access during transition? If culture is relevant, will societies in transition eventually enjoy the ideal type of open access performance? If culture is irrelevant, why and how long does it take for the performance of open access to conform to the ideal type? Is there only one model of developed polities?

North and his coauthors' "idea of an equilibrium set" (*Violence,* 141) appears to be a new version of the neoclassical "complete competition" in politics. Here institutional analysis is unfortunately downgraded into noninstitutional idealistic interpretation. What has been turned "on their heads" (140) is not the logic of collective actions and rent-seeking, but the rigorous and realistic logic of the balanced ideas in North's earlier work. In the end, open political competition becomes the universal remedy for all social-order problems. Such a "total solution idea" (instead of a "part of the problem idea") eventually fails to understand how political competition is fundamentally different from economic competition.

A "PROPERTY RIGHTS THEORY OF THE STATE"

The dilemma of the open access framework is that if democracy is defined as open access in "political-economic competition" rather than "contested elections" (as it is by Joseph Schumpeter and Adam Przeworski),[16] then one must follow North and his coauthors and use a problematic-outcome approach to explain growth. But when democracy is defined as "contested elections," history tells us that, to many latecomers, the initial outcome of democracy may have a mixed result of growth and violence[17] and that the spread of democracy might not be accompanied by the triumph of free markets, the rule of law, and the separation of powers.[18] When the double balance of politics and economics is depicted as a social tendency, history shows that the double imbalance, or the relative independence of politics and economics, is more the norm than the exception. North and his coauthors' "competition worship" comes from a "normative urge" stemming from parochial Western experiences, not from broader historical facts.

In a comment on Dani Rodrik's 2007 book *One Economics, Many Recipes,* Adam Przeworski points out that "if there is no single mapping between the market and the set of non-market institutions required to sustain it, then identifying the institutions that are compatible with sustained growth calls for a different methodology than Rodrik, and everyone else, uses."[19] But if the methodology employed by Rodrik, North and his coauthors, and everyone else arrived at the same problematic conclusion, that only democracy sustains growth, where is the way out? Should we just go back to Douglass North's previous approach that focuses on property rights and the rule of law?

What I am suggesting here is a new perspective on the state and a new way of explaining growth, both of which aim at understanding China's economic rise and political future.

Following Aristotle, the typology of the state has long been known as monarchy, aristocracy, and democracy, in which the "number of rulers" criteria is used to differentiate all types of states. Following Robert Nozick in his 1974 *Anarchy, State, and Utopia* and Yoram Barzel in his 2001 *A Theory of the State,* I propose to use "ownership," or "property rights," as a new criterion to identify different types of states. Where I go one step further than both Nozick and Barzel is in recognizing that not only is the state designing property rights for its people, but it is also taken explicitly as a form or object of "property rights" by the ruler or rulers.

The state is therefore viewed as a special "firm" or "organization" that can be owned. It can be owned by a monarch, some oligarchs, a dictator, a political party, or the people (through many political parties). Hence, a state can be a monarchy, oligarchy, autocracy (dictatorship), dominant-party rulership (or "partyocracy"), or democracy. Note that the criterion here is not the "number of owners." The key is to shift the focus from "number" to "entity," which can be a person, a family, a certain number of people, or a political party. The idea of "entity" is to emphasize the degree of an entity's impersonality and the degree of its perpetuality.

Under this "property rights perspective," monarchy is not only a monarch but also the family behind a monarch. And more important, a dominant-party rulership is now differentiated from a dictatorship. I define dominant-party rulership ("partyocracy") as a dominant single-party system that has term limits strictly enforced for its leadership transition. Therefore, if a state is controlled by a dominant party without term limits for its succession of leadership, it is still a dictatorship (such as in North Korean and Cuba). Term limits differentiate dominant-party rulership from dictatorship because term limits are a key step toward the constitutionalization of a government. Term limits increase the degree of impersonality of a dominant party, which in turn enhances the degree of perpetuality of a dominant party.

The importance of impersonality and perpetuality can only be fully understood when the state is viewed from a "property rights" perspective. It is the institutional features of an organization that "eternalize" the life span of a ruler, and it is the "term-limit device" that solves, to a great extent, the "gene pool" problem embedded in both monarchy and dictatorship. In monarchy, the "gene pool" problem is the "family gene pool," or the chance to have a qualified heir. In dictatorship, the "gene pool" problem is similar, except that the legitimacy of family rulership is weakened. The "gene pool" problem threatens the continuity and the stability of ruling, which is the "institutionally destructive factor" in both monarchy and dictatorship. When the institutionalization of "term limits" is enforced, it makes absolutely no sense to still categorize a "partyocracy" government as a dictatorship or as post-totalitarianism. This is in fact a big problem in the "democracy-autocracy dichotomy" of Western political theory. (A recent example is George B. N. Ayittey, who recklessly listed China's president Hu Jintao as one of "The World's 23 Worst Dictators" in the July–August 2010 issue of *Foreign Policy.*)

According to this "property rights theory of the state," the Communist Party of China (CPC), beginning from 2002, is a dominant-party ruler-ship, not a dictatorship. The implication of the CPC's term-limits institu-tion in 2002 is far-reaching and is still underestimated or neglected. When compared with monarchy, term limits in dominant-party rulership make "leadership succession" far less problematic than in monarchy, as is clearly demonstrated by the well-known "dynastic cycles" in China's imperial his-tory. Compared with dictatorship, term limits in dominant-party ruler-ship make its "leadership succession" far less complicated, as is also clearly demonstrated by the CPC's internal political struggles from 1921 to 1989. Even more important is the fact that "term limits" create an institutional momentum that pushes the CPC toward greater possibility for further constitutionalization and democratic accountability, as will be discussed later in this chapter.

One other important aspect of the "property rights theory of the state" is related to how the understanding of Western democracy can be changed and why Francis Fukuyama's "end of history" perspective is in fact mistaken.[20]

To truly understand "contested elections" or "open access in politi-cal competition," it is necessary to see it not only as the critical force that sustains liberal democracy but also as the driver that diverts individual rationality from social rationality. The fundamental differences between economic competition and political competition are usually seen by econ-omists from the perspective of a buyer-seller relation. Market competition is seen as continuous, and political competition is intermittent; market competition usually allows several competitors, and political competition has an all-or-none feature; market competition better defines the buyer's benefit, while political competition has more uncertainty in binding prom-ises and pledges; and market and political decisions have very different external effects.[21]

What is added to this perspective by a "property rights theory of the state" is the recognition that while, in a dominant-party rulership, it is only nominal to say that the state is owned by its people, in a democracy this statement is more substantive, in that people get to decide who will be elected and in that it is indeed more "real" to say "the state is publicly owned." Yet the fact that "the state is publicly owned" means that the property rights structure for political competition is totally different from the structure for market competition. In market competition, you compete for what you own, or agents compete for what their principals own. In political competition, you typically compete for what the public owns, in which everyone is only entitled to a small and negligible proportion.

Indeed, in democracy, the state becomes a "common good," a term used by economists to describe something characterized by "subtractability and nonexcludability." Subtractability and nonexcludability means open access and unrestricted demand that can cause problems of congestion or overuse, leading to the worsening of the common property resource. This is the well-known "tragedy of the commons,"[22] which can also be explained by the prisoner's dilemma or the logic of collective actions.[23]

Representative democracy (constitutional or liberal democracy) is like a "common property regime" (a term used by 2009 Nobel laureate Elinor Ostrom),[24] where the "property" is not some small-scale natural resource but the monopolistic power to use violence and to tax. Open access sustains the "common property regime" on the one hand; it leads to congestion, overuse, and the worsening of state power on the other.

How can individual rationality (in the prisoner's dilemma) and concentrated cost benefits (in the logic of collective actions) lead to the worsening of state power? When state power is commonly owned rather than privately owned, the most important thing in human nature is to show a different tendency toward responsibility and time preference. Even though equal open access in political competition has some "moral high ground" attached to it, the theory of public choice tells us that a political actor in the public domain is still a private actor in an economic sense and that equal open access doesn't make open access have equal value for everyone. The moral disguise of open access, unfortunately, ends right here. What's at work is a lack of responsibility and a high "time preference"[25] (both define short-termism) when open access logic is put into a broader "commonly owned property" background.

The commonly owned state opens free equal access to competition for government power. The nature of subtractability and nonexcludability dictates that there is not only a congestion (oversupply) of opportunistic power-hungry politicians but also a high "time preference" or short-term impulse for these politicians to extract the value of state power for themselves and for those who elect them, both of which are reinforced by contested elections, limited terms, and constrained power. Maximizing reelection is the driver, but maximizing the use of power becomes more relevant when reelection is out of the picture.[26] Democratic short-termism is particularly acute in such issues as mounting budget deficits, high public debts, unfair intergenerational treatment, political hypocrisy, and law-evading corruption, which in turn leads to the degeneration of civilization, including rising levels of crime, the erosion of morality, growth of the megastate (state regulations and employment), oversupply of fiat money or inflation, intellectual stultification, general malaise, declining savings rates, declining family values, falling fertility rates (loss of value in children), high interest rates, high tax rates, and high military spending.[27]

This may be seen as an "extremely radical" view of democracy by many liberals or conservatives. Yet this "attack" is not from the "left" side; it is coming from the "right" side that values both individual "property rights" and "social rationality," but it is different from the antiliberal perspectives of Leo Strauss and Alasdair MacIntyre.[28] Yet it is not "radical" at all if one further looks at the "public debt crisis" in Iceland and Greece and potentially in many more Western countries, including Spain, Portugal, Italy, Ireland, Britain, Japan, and even the United States. Ironically, part of this "debt of democracy" has had to be financed by China's nearly three trillion dollars in foreign reserves.

In open access to political competition, Gresham's law ("Bad money drives out good") becomes "Individual rationality drives out social rationality." Individual rationality is encouraged due to the individual's concentrated benefit and dispersed cost, while social rationality is discouraged due to the individual's dispersed benefit and concentrated cost.[29] The logic of the "tragedy of the commons" is so strong and inherent that even a forceful procedural mechanism for accountability can't stop it. Where responsibility is out, accountability can't easily be in. Short-termism spawns opportunism and moral hazard; law evasion shores up legal complexity. Accountability therefore has to be enforced through a litigation-prone culture, with transaction costs shooting higher in a contractual society that is supposed to save transaction costs. This is the tragedy of open access, or the "tragedy of commonly owned democracy."

The financial crisis after 2008 and the sovereign debt crisis in 2010 are demonstrations of how public-owned logic is transformed into irresponsible public deficits and public debt policies. If the social crisis in the West were not viewed from a "property rights perspective," one would find it hard to understand why the accountability mechanism in democracy, which the West is so proud of, could possibly fail to solve its public debt problem, which will soon worsen due to higher welfare expenditures for its increasingly aging population.

ONE-PARTY CONSTITUTIONALIZATION AND THE "CHINA MODEL"

Putting democracy under a "property rights perspective" will inevitably challenge Francis Fukuyama's "end of history" thesis. The fact is, both absolute monarchy and dictatorship are simply not going away, and China's dominant-party rulership is consolidating, while many new democracies are in deep trouble, and many old democracies are in crisis. *The Logic of Political Survival,* by Bruce Bueno de Mesquita, and *The Clash of Civilizations and the Remaking of World Order,* by Samuel Huntington, can help shed some light on this reality.[30] One can hate the reality, but one can't deny the facts (if one tries to deny the facts, the people will know). There is simply no "end of history" and no historical determinism. Each and every form of "property rights" of the state has its own problems. There is simply no "good democracy" in any abstract sense; we know new democracies in the Third World are bad, and the "tragedy of commonly owned democracy" in the West should not be taken lightly either. The argument that "democracy is relatively less worse" is in fact wrong in countries like Iraq, Haiti, Kyrgyzstan, and many more.

The rise of China is indeed one of the most noticeable events in the new century. It ignites the imagination of people like Joshua Ramo, former senior editor of *Time* magazine and a partner at Kissinger Associates, who coined the term "Beijing Consensus" in 2004 to describe the "China Model." The Beijing Consensus represents an alternative economic development model to the Washington Consensus, each symbolizing quite different political orientations. The three guidelines of the Beijing Consensus (a commitment to innovation and constant experimentation, the sustainability of the economic system and an even distribution of wealth, and a policy of self-determination), however, are full of journalistic emptiness and wishful thinking, especially "an even distribution of wealth." From the Beijing Consensus, one simply cannot gain any fundamental understanding of China's rise.

What backs up the "China Model" from within is what I call "one-party constitutionalization," which is the political foundation for China's "reform and open policy," characterized by the institution of term limits for

China's leadership transition and the potential for further constitutionalization. As stated above, the importance of the institutionalization of term limits has to be understood in contrast with China's "dynastic cycles" and the CPC's political history.

On the surface, what has happened in China over the last thirty years is no more than a policy shift toward "marketization, liberalization, privatization, and globalization." In fact, if one does not look at the institutional background, one would almost confuse this shift with the Washington Consensus. The focus here, nevertheless, is not on the four "-izations," but on the so-called Chinese characteristics. As discussed in the first section, what has happened in China is a "low-cost gradual-reform approach" in the Chinese way, which is "soft" both in political and in market reform, especially when compared with Eastern European countries. The point here is that there has been never a lack of a "good policy shift" in the long political history of China, yet there has always been a lack of corresponding "institutional foundations" for a "good policy shift" to consolidate and sustain changes. Here lies the key to understanding China's future.

The most important change in modern China, though it is frequently underestimated, is the transformation from "family rulership" to "party rulership," or from family-based autocracy to party-based meritocracy. This transformation and other related changes (most importantly term limits) will put an end to the "dynastic cycle" that crippled the Chinese empire for the last two thousand years. As an elite-based revolutionary "vanguard" imported from Russia in 1921, the CPC radically transformed China's political landscape by instituting a stern ideology that far outweighed that of the Kuomintang. Compared with the corrupt ideology of the two failed peasants' uprisings at the end of the Ming and Qing dynasties, the CPC ideology proved highly successful in mass motivation, discipline enforcement (reining in the culture of "weak relational sanction"), and transaction-cost reduction.

Under the auspices of party politics, the rules of the game, the expectations of game playing, and the action plans and behavior patterns of players are all institutionally different from those under dynastic family politics. The succession system, the "gene pool," term structure, and power-exercising schemes are some key aspects of this institutional change. But the institutional change from "family rulership" to "party rulership" has been so taken for granted that its far-reaching implications are mostly ignored or unrecognized.

In the current regime under the CPC, the long-practiced hereditary succession in dynastic politics came to an end. This is common sense, plain and simple. Yet party politics with succession (with term limits) had been institutionally transformed from a genetics-driven to a merit-driven arrangement. The logic here is that the merit-driven arrangement would inevitably evolve from reliance on revolutionary credentials, for first-generation leaders, to reliance on regime-building credentials, for later-generation leaders. In other words, dynastic politics appealed to the "mandate of heaven" and genetics for legitimacy; party politics appealed to the "mandate of merit" and performance for legitimacy. The genetics factor is gone, the patronage factor still helps, and the merit factor is of overwhelming importance.

The "mandate of merit" is one of two aspects in the new succession game; the other is the succession process. In contrast to dynastic succession, there is now no more baby emperor, ailing emperor, or old and incompetent emperor. There is also no more worry about succession fights among the emperor's sons and brothers, or manipulation due to favoritism by eunuchs, ministers, the empress, the empress dowager, relatives of the empress, and the emperor's sisters. Deng Xiaoping successfully employed a mechanism similar to the "retired emperor" or the "grand emperor" (*Taishang Huang*) to smooth the succession process. After Deng retired, he kept the title "chairman of the Central Military Commission" (CMC). When he gave up that position in 1989, he could still manage to "rule from behind the curtain" due to strong revolutionary and state-building credentials.

As the leader of a nonrevolutionary generation, Jiang Zemin did not enjoy Deng's informal authority. But he still followed in Deng's footsteps by holding the title chairman of the Central Military Commission from 2002 and 2005, for the leadership transition to Hu Jintao. The transition from Jiang to Hu was often hailed as "the first orderly and institutionalized transition of power in the history of the People's Republic of China." This smooth succession that required no death or purge of an incumbent had in fact been institutionally built into the merit-driven arrangement, which evolved from reliance on revolutionary merit to reliance on regime-building merit, from individual authority to norm formation, from the cult of personality to consensus building, and from strong-man politics to collective leadership.

The merit-based logic puts the legacy of nepotism and credential requirements into a delicate balance. On one hand, blood ties, school ties, regional identities, bureaucratic affiliations, and patron-client ties still matter. The "Shanghai Gang," the "Princelings' Party" (*Taizidang*), "the Qinghua Clique," the "fellow provincials" (*Tongxiang*), the "Chinese Communist Youth League (CCYL) officials" (*Tuanpai*), the "personal secretary clusters" (*Mishuqun*), and the "student returnees from overseas" (*Haiguipai*) also play a part in leadership selection. On the other hand, educational background, experience, skills, and performance are increasingly important in elite recruitment.

The autocratic legacy as a manifestation of cultural inertia went away with the passing of the revolutionary leaders. As merit-based logic matured, collective leadership took hold, and there was no more paramount leader and no more "core" in the party leadership. Power sharing, regional representation, and diversification of political connections became the trend. Rules of "regional representation" on the Central Committee were instituted to ensure that all provinces have two full members in the central leadership.

The voting mechanism is also at work. The most emotion-stirring sideshow is the practice of "plurality-at-large bloc voting," or "multiple-winner approval voting" (*Cha'e Xuanju,* or simply "elections with more candidates than seats"), adopted after the Thirteenth Party Congress in 1987. This rule is for electing both the Party Congress and the Central Committee. When the number of candidates is 12.5 percent more than the available seats, candidates chosen by favoritism rather than by merit now face a serious threat of elimination, since large-scale vote buying is practically impossible. Voting as a way of expressing objection is also becoming aggressive. In 2003, for example, one-tenth of delegates voted against Jiang Zemin staying on as the chairman of the Central Military Commission.

The narrow dynastic family "gene pool" was quietly replaced by a much wider range of party elites. Smooth succession and top-level political stability were institutionally installed by rule building and the elimination of clashing inheritances, manipulation of dynastic favoritism, and personal overindulgence. The "mandate of merit" therefore leads to regime legitimacy, as there is increasingly reliance on both leadership performance and institutional rules. Performance legitimacy and institutional legitimacy in turn stabilize leadership succession. Fragile, dynastic "hereditary succession" was radically replaced by more orderly "meritocratic succession."

Several critical institutional developments underscore orderly "meritocratic succession." First is "age limits" for leadership positions. The 1997

Politburo regulations stipulate that, except in extraordinary circumstances, all top leaders in both the party and government must retire by age seventy. All ministers of the State Council, provincial chiefs, and top military officers must retire by age sixty-five, their deputies at age sixty-three.

The immediate effect of this rule is a relatively young Politburo. One other important result is a new two-tiered hierarchy within the Politburo: the Politburo Standing Committee, with senior members, and a group of other regular Politburo members with junior status. This two-tiered arrangement can be seen as an innovation intended to institutionalize a process of promotion for a future orderly "meritocratic succession."[31] Leadership positions are now also subject to "term and year limits." Top party and government terms are limited to five years, and no more than two terms are allowed. According to new rules in 2006, there is also a fifteen-year limit for holding different positions with the same rank.

These "rule-of-law" or constitutional elements of "appointment limits" on age, term, and year have been so taken for granted in the West that their innovative institutional nature was ignored by almost all Western observers. In contrast, the live-and-let-die "tiger fight" culture persisted throughout China's history because no institutional mechanism under "family rulership" could internalize political competition into self-reinforcing cooperation. When the prospect of ruling was defined by lifetime tenure, political competition would externalize into brutal contestation or internalize into suspicious cooperation. The emperor had to be vigilant: potential rivals surfaced within and outside of his court. The ministers had to avoid being framed as part of a scheme to rebel. Such a subtle relationship existed even between Mao Zedong and Zhou Enlai.

Deng Xiaoping's greatest political wisdom was the will to institutionally put an end to this "life-term" tradition. Clearly, family rulership could not install a "term limits" mechanism on the emperor due to the unchallenged political culture and "commitment problems."[32] Only under party rulership ("partyocracy") could such innovation be made possible in China. The merit-based succession that replaced heredity-based succession has evolved from relying more on individual-heroic nation-building credentials to relying more on widely distributed state-building credentials.

The Chinese culture of reciprocal meritocracy enabled China to choose the "economy first" approach and install the term-based mechanism in due time (compared with the former Soviet Union). The innovations of "term limits" and "intraparty elections" miraculously maintain the

Chinese family-centered, interdependent-oriented, and harmony-minded national psychology—and at the same time draw on virtues from Western individual-centered, self-dependent-oriented, and contest-minded cultural psychology. The party is like a big family, membership is open to the whole society, and consultative cooperation is cherished. In short, after the orderly 2002 "meritocratic succession," the CPC is now characterized by "impersonality, term limits, open membership, and institutionalization."

However, if this "rule of the game" change is not viewed from a historical-institutional and paradigm-shift perspective, it may not be all that clear to common sense or conventional wisdom. Term-based party rulership eliminates the following uncertainties that existed under "family rulership": the leader's lifespan, the leader's ability due to aging, the limitation of successor selection, the successor's ability, the successor's support system, and the successor's lifespan. The reason Mao's rule had autocratic traits was exactly because the term limits mechanism had not been installed, which in turn made "meritocratic succession" impossible. The two most important characteristics of autocracy are absolute power and a life term. Constitutional monarchy transforms autocracy by limiting absolute power. Chinese reformed meritocracy transforms autocracy by installing term limits, which in turn also limit absolute power. Once put under the microscope of institutional examination, it is all common sense. But only a paradigm shift of institutional analysis can make the murky water crystal clear.

The implications of China's "rule of the game" change are much more far-reaching than has been recognized. As political competition internalized into self-reinforcing cooperation under party rulership, the advantages in policy-making efficiency, succession cost savings, and talent retention over Western-style electoral democracy are all hard to deny. Most important, party elites may now be much more confident in China's own political institutions and less weak-minded in resisting Western democracy, especially as they gain more understanding of how Western democracy actually evolves and works.

In any case, the current Chinese regime is no longer the stereotypical autocracy, dictatorship, or guardianship, as discussed in Robert Dahl's *Democracy and Its Critics*. In fact, the "Mao era" was only a transition period before the institutional logic of the transformation from "family politics" to "party politics" ran its full course. It is simply a myth that Chinese communist leaders are ineffective, incompetent, politically rigid, narrow minded, and shortsighted. It is also wishful thinking that a vicious power struggle is going on among various factions, especially among the top contenders of the fourth generation, thus leading to a major internal crisis.[33] Those who stick with the autocracy mental model are going to be disappointed if they expect a traumatic political crisis in future China. And the most disappointed of all will be those who expect China's "coming collapse."

In short, strong and stable top leadership effectively keeps under control the deep-seated fear of disorder in both the bureaucracy and society. The Chinese usually call their failing governments "corrupt and incapable" (*Fubai Wuneng*). The theory for the current regime is that it is "corrupt but capable" (*Fubai Youneng*); that is, the government is capable of handling corruption due to the institutional change of "meritocratic succession."

Applying Western "vertical experience" to China and predicting democratization are symptoms of cultural-historical naivete. There is simply no "China puzzle": if everything in China is so bad, why is China still rising and the government not collapsing? The "China puzzle" exists when we conceptualize the Western experience and use context-sensitive ideas to view China, only to find that China refuses to conform to our abstractions. A seeming "bad" may not be really "bad" when put into China's own cultural-historical context, much as when cultural anthropologist Richard A. Shweder argues that those who suffer are not inherent victims if we "think through cultures."[34] But psychological law dictates that it is easier for one to maintain one's cognitive mental process when seeing something that conflicts with it. Hence, there is always something wrong with reality, while in fact what's wrong is one's mental model.

In summary, the importance of institutional change from "family rulership" to reformed "party rulership" cannot be emphasized enough. The "China Model" can only be understood in terms of China's "partyocracy." "Meritocratic succession" is the most critical step for the CPC's survival; it is also an important first step before the CPC can further constitutionalize its ruling.

INSTITUTIONS AND GROWTH: A "THREE-TIERED EFFORT-BASED INSTITUTIONAL ANALYSIS"

If China's political change provides a solid foundation for consolidating its market-oriented policy shift, what does it suggest about its growth and its economic prospects? If focusing on democracy or regime types for explaining growth is a dead end, does China's experience prove that "marketization under the rule of law" is the only right approach to explaining growth?

The answer is no. While the democracy approach cannot explain why so many new democracies fail to grow and why some rich economies are not democratic, the rule-of-law approach fails to explain why so many advanced economies stagnate. Most important, the rule-of-law approach fails to explain why China can grow without a Western-style rule of law.[35] The presence or absence of the "rule of law" and "open access in economic competition" may cause or impede economic growth, especially in the long term. But there are other ways of providing property rights arrangements and stable expectations like those that are provided by the rule of law. In China's case, these could be "hidden rules," administrative "hard rules," and informal "soft rules," which are all different from Western formal legal rules.

If Przeworski's notion that "identifying the institutions that are compatible with sustained growth calls for a different methodology" is indeed true, what a "property rights theory of the state" can offer is a change of methodology from focusing on either regime type or the rule of law. The change I am suggesting here is looking at some specific types of institutions that promote or prohibit growth and examining how well these institutions are supported by different regimes. This alternative perspective on economic growth can be called "three-tiered effort-based institutional analysis."

A desirable theory of economic growth has to answer a series of questions on several levels: What are the common factors that are present in developed countries and absent in underdeveloped countries? Within a developed or a rapidly developing country where these common factors are present, why does the economy grow faster during certain times, and why does the economy grow faster in certain areas? To be sure, a desirable theory of economic growth has to look at both the presence and the absence of the causes of growth, as well as the presence and the absence of the retardants of growth; it also has to deal with the aspects of time, place, and duration (short term, intermediate term, and long term). These are the essential elements for the "theoretical structure" of a growth theory that are not fully present in existing explanations.

In reference to this "theoretical structure," *Institutions, Institutional Change and Economic Performance,* by Douglass North, as mentioned earlier, actually provides a good reference point, where institutions, organizations, culture, and ideology are all well integrated.[36] We may start from the most fundamental level by using the "cake analogy." Human production or economic growth is like making a cake. Individual efforts can be directed to making a cake, dividing or stealing a cake, and simply destroying a cake. We can summarize all these activities into "productive efforts" (making), "distributional efforts" (dividing or stealing), and "destructive efforts" (destroying). From the perspective that "only the institution matters in shaping human behavior," it is the institution that promotes "productive efforts," restrains "distributional efforts," and controls "destructive efforts" that jointly determines the level of economic growth.[37] Marketization, the rule of law, informal rules, and democracy all become factors that affect the degree of these three types of human efforts.

The state is at the center of providing the institutional framework for promoting "productive efforts," restraining "distributional efforts," and controlling "destructive efforts." It is here where economics meets politics. This is why an integrated theory of economics and politics requires a solid theory of the state (see the third section, above). The key here is that from the "property rights perspective," none of the state models can provide institutions that can successfully deal with the three types of efforts all at the same time. In other words, institutions are not designed just for growth, but are created for self-interest or distributional advantages,[38] and that's why focusing on regime types for explaining growth is doomed to failure.

In contrast with the vertical and stage-based open access framework, "effort-based institutional analysis" provides a horizontal structure that is positive and empirical in nature, with normative or ethical content squeezed to a minimum. To be more explicit, "effort-based institutional analysis" does not attempt to fit human history into a stage-based artificial construct that somehow suggests some progressive direction one way or another. It does not attempt to give any normative guidance as for what counts as "development," for it strives to avoid confusions between pro-market practices and pro–"market fundamentalism," and between pro-democracy and pro–"democracy fundamentalism." Ultimately, it strives to keep away from some "theoretical trap" inherent in stage-based frameworks, which usually must make compromises because of potential conflicts between theory and reality. Too frequently, a stage-based framework fails to refrain from "torturing the reality to confess" so as to fit reality neatly into a predetermined theoretical configuration.

A theory of institutions for promoting "productive efforts," restraining "distributional efforts," and controlling "destructive efforts" can at best be used to explain long-term economic growth. It does put both the presence and the absence of causes of growth ("productive efforts"), as well as the presence and the absence of retardants of growth ("distributional efforts" and "destructive efforts"), under examination. For institutions promoting "productive efforts," it looks at "organizational efficiency" (efficiency from incentive-sensitive organizational rearrangement), market-allocative efficiency (efficiency from free-market resource allocation), "adaptive efficiency" (efficiency from intentional learning of how institutions affect growth),[39] and "inducive efficiency." Open access for economic competition is indeed part of institutionalized "productive efforts."

"Inducive efficiency" is the overall result of how the three types of efforts are induced by institutions. Growth is not just about incentives (constrained free contracting with clearly defined rights); not just about institutions that favor reducing the gap between social and private rates of return (conformity between individual return and individual efforts); not just about achieving "organizational efficiency," "allocative efficiency" and "adaptive efficiency." It is also about how institutions and their enforcement direct individual incentives toward more productive efforts and at the same time channel individual incentives toward less destructive and distributional efforts. Therefore, it not only looks at the conformity between individual return and individual efforts but also examines the direction of individual efforts and their combined results under specific institutional settings. Hence, even if institutions for promoting "productive efforts" appear to be similar in certain economies, their economic performance could be very different due to their different institutions for restraining "distributional efforts" and controlling "destructive efforts."

For institutions restraining "distributional efforts," what comes into the landscape is Olson's theory of "distributional coalitions," Buchanan's theory of "rent-seeking and public choice," and Caplan's theory of "irrational voters."[40] It is here that we find the open access framework highly problematic in asserting that open access in political competition will only bring good results. Open access logic fails to account for the "logic of collective actions" (rational ignorance and rational action/inaction due to concentrated/dispersed costs/benefits), the "logic of collective decisions" (rational manipulation, decisions/external costs), and the "logic of collective belief" (rational bias) in understanding open political competitions. That's also why open access logic fails to explain why within those countries with an "open access social order," there is variation in economic performance due to different institutional structures for constraining "distributional efforts." This is a good case of a stage-based framework twisting the reality to fit it neatly into a predetermined theoretical construction.

For institutions controlling "destructive efforts," the fact is that it is much easier to destroy than to construct. But the point is not about destructive efforts; it's about how destructive efforts are culturally and politically institutionalized. The case of China's "dynastic cycles" (with productive rise, distributional paying, and destructive fall cycling through its imperial history) and the case of America's "democracy promotion" and overseas military overreaching make it clear how institutionalized "destructive efforts" can be harmful to long-term growth.

As for short-term and intermediate-term explanations for growth, "effort-based institutional analysis" further scrutinizes relative change in inputs and relative change in prices (in addition to relative change in institutions). This is the place where "effort-based institutional analysis" changes into "three-tiered effort-based institutional analysis."

Relative change in inputs is the area where neoclassical economics is at its best.[41] Relative change in prices refers to the dynamics of input and output prices, which involves comparative and competitive advantages in labor, resources, technology, the natural environment, demand, transaction costs, rates (interest, inflation, and exchanges), rents, and taxes. Relative change in inputs may be comprehensive in scope, and relative change in prices may be persuasive in explaining growth dynamics,[42] but they do not deal with incentives, efficiency, or justice (e.g., the use of slaves) comprehensively; hence, they only explain short-term and intermediate-term growth. It is the relative change of institutions (both formal and informal) that explains long-term economic growth.

Put together, this is a "structured effort-based institutional analysis" that conceptually explains economic growth for a specific time, place, and duration through capturing the relative changes in inputs, prices, and institutions that account for the presence and absence of the sources, advantages, causes, and retardants of economic growth.

Development, in this perspective, is not about "open access" to political-economic competition. Development is about an incremental and joint effort for the relative changes in inputs, prices, and institutions that are conducive to economic growth. It is an open process without clear-cut stages. One economy may have more favorable conditions for relative change in inputs, while the other may have better conditions for relative change in prices; one economy may have more constructive institutions for promoting "productive efforts," while the other may have more successful institutions for restraining "distributional efforts" or controlling "destructive efforts." There is no guarantee that today's developed economies won't fall behind tomorrow or that today's developing economies can't catch up with and exceed developed economies tomorrow. What this "three-tiered effort-based institutional analysis" calls for is location-, time-, institution-, and culture-specific "growth analysis."

China's Social Crisis and the Prospect for Democratic Accountability

In light of the "property rights theory of the state" and "three-tiered effort-based institutional analysis," the rise of China in the new century is a breakaway from the "dynastic cycles" in China's imperial past, a history characterized by institutionally determined "productive rise, distributional paying, and destructive fall." The "family gene pool" problem discussed in the third section, above, is what causes the dynastic "destructive fall."

By putting an end to the internal "class struggle" (1949–1976, after the "war century" of 1839–1949), creating a high level of national security in a relatively peaceful international environment, and reforming the dynastic family-based polity into a party-based political system, the current Chinese regime has been extremely successful in laying down a solid foundation for China's social economic development, which institutionally discourages politics-related and war-related "destructive efforts" (see the fourth section, above). After 140 years of social turmoil (1839–1978), China is back on track for social prosperity. Those who personally experienced the turnaround psychology in 1978 and 1992 will not have any problem expecting more to come after the first thirty years of economic boom (1978–2007).

By dismantling its planned economy, opening the door to private entrepreneurs, and inviting participation from the international community, the Chinese government has been equally successful in promoting organizational efficiency (the family responsibility system, SOE corporatization), allocative efficiency (a greater degree of free entry to formerly monopolized sectors, a greater degree of free-market pricing on products, labor, and capital), and adaptive efficiency (improved enforcement of business laws and property rights protection), which institutionally encourages organization-based, allocation-based, and ownership-based "productive efforts."

Through implementing the tax-sharing system, opening the party's and the government's doors to private actors, and strengthening the new "socialist authoritarianism" ideology of the "three bulwarks" against foreign and domestic political pressures, the central government has been particularly successful in gaining greater fiscal and political power. In this regard, the 1989 democratic movement became a historic watershed as both sides showed their "hold cards," and the party was repositioned to abandon the "state ownership doctrine" of the old ideology and shifted to boost the "legitimacy function" of the new "three bulwarks" ideology. In the sense that the 1989 tragedy (the Tiananmen Square crackdown) shifted the nation's attention from political strife to stable social economic development, it is not a bad omen for the Chinese people.

On the other hand, by devolving authority to local officials, phasing out the "discipline function" of its ideological control (not to mention that lenient party discipline often replaces severe law punishment), and continuing its negligence regarding the negative aspects of traditional culture, the Chinese government has fallen short of building a functional system that draws an adequate line between government functions and market functions. In the process of reform and decentralization, the government continues to regulate what should be further deregulated, and worse, it fails to regulate what should be regulated. This reflects the fact that the booming economy pushes government agents toward an incentive-based culture (rather than a service-based culture), a culture that echoes its connections-and-power-oriented tradition and weak "relational control." Such a social environment fails to institutionally discourage "destructive efforts" related to crime, social unrest, environmental degradation, and the degeneration of social mores (drug abuse, prostitution, addictive gambling) and fails to build enough disincentives to institutionally discourage "distributional efforts" related to power abuse, corruption, budget-based overheating, local protectionism, health care distortion, and violations of intellectual property rights.[43] All of these stem mostly from the "proxy rights" nature of central-local relations, reflecting the fact that the "property rights" of the state are on the central government level rather than on the local level.

Overall, "distributional efforts" are institutionally rising along with "productive efforts," but "productive efforts" outweigh "distributional efforts," and positive institutional developments for restraining "destructive efforts" outweigh negative institutional developments for inducing "destructive efforts." We see this mixed but upbeat picture in the 1990s as well as at the beginning of the new century, with all the similar factors working in the background. The fact that China did not melt down and still manages to enjoy encouraging growth in the beginning of the new century suggests that the seemingly weakened central government is in fact adding power by degrees, financially, organizationally, and militarily, while scaling back in magnitude and scoping down the playing field. The central government is in firm control, and there is simply no sign that it will lose its grip.

As discussed earlier, the installation of term limits and an institutionalized leadership succession mechanism are major steps toward one-party constitutionalization. This process, however, has yet to move more aggressively to decentralized social control, horizontal checks and balances, and vertical elections (except unrealistic multiparty contestation), all of which are essential for bringing government power under control.[44] The agent-principal relation game is played between the central and local governments in terms of monitoring costs and the price of getting caught. The central government simply cannot rein in local governments without more control mechanisms.

If "state property rights control" and the collective nature of the central government in a "partyocracy" enjoy a greater degree of responsibility and accountability, the "proxy rights" nature of central-local relations makes the local government more vulnerable to the accountability crisis. This is why most of China's pressing social problems are seen on the local level. China's accountability crisis can only be fixed by democratic accountability. The symptom of "good economic growth with bad local governance" means that the central government is too busy focusing on creating a bigger pie and bolstering the legitimacy of its political position—while at the same time failing to combat forces that work against making the pie bigger. This political strategy mirrors the one embraced for economic development: setting priorities, getting the business going, and then dealing with associated problems later. In the government's words: "Problems arising from reform will be solved in the process of further reform."

By appealing more to an after-the-fact "fire-alarm" mechanism rather than a before-the-fact "police-patrol" system, its social-crisis management remains passive rather than proactive, and the official image remains predatory rather than accountable. "Antirule psychology" leads to the "weak enforcement of rules," and the "weak enforcement of rules" in turn shores up "antirule psychology." This mutually reinforcing circle is the Chinese "cultural trap" that is responsible for most of the current problems discussed above. Even though the party has the strongest legitimacy motivation, the most powerful moral incentive, and the political clout necessary to get China out of this "cultural trap," the task remains challenging. The good news is that a "first push" by a strong central government does make a difference. Lessons to be learned mainly center on building the "authority of institutions" in transforming civic culture, whether Hong Kong–style anticorruption institutions or Singapore-style authoritarian measures. It will not take too long for the central government to realize that its current solutions lack the "shock and awe" effect. The central government is strong, yet it needs to be stronger and tougher to get China out of the "cultural trap." Top-down democratic accountability is also needed to get things going.

A constitutional order cannot be fully established without "spontaneous compliance" by the government.[45] China's leadership succession provides an encouraging case that exemplifies a self-reinforcing process for "spontaneous compliance." It is an institutional equilibrium that reflects a state of evenly distributed power in the new generation of leadership. The "reform and open" era also witnessed a positive spread of "rule by law" from political elites to all other social groups. In this regard, the participation of international stakeholders contributed to China's progress in terms of forcing the Chinese government to comply with nonhidden rules.

In fact, the accountability crisis in China will also drive the Chinese government toward more active management for its political survival, which in turn will boost the prospects for its democratic accountability. No government likes accountability unless it is compelled. No rule of law is possible without the government's self-interested compliance. People in the West usually do not take "the Chinese way" seriously enough, yet in terms of a "state model," there is a real "Chinese way." A one-party constitutional order is both realistic for the Chinese people and desirable for the government in China's current political setting.

From the perspective of the "property rights theory of the state," the China Model is a political model that will challenge Western democracy in the new century. For institutions that promote "productive efforts," the China Model is catching up with the Western model. For institutions that restrain "distributional efforts," the China Model still faces problems from its legacy and its new experiments. Yet for institutions that control "destructive efforts," the China Model conquers the "gene pool" crisis from its past and avoids the "tragedy of commonly owned democracy" that distresses so many new and advanced democracies in the rest of the world today.

NOTES

1. Daron Acemoglu, Simon Johnson, and James Robinson, "Institutions as the Fundamental Cause of Long-Run Growth," in *Handbook of Economic Growth,* ed. Philippe Aghion and Steven N. Durlauf (Amsterdam: Elsevier, 2005).

2. Mancur Olson, *The Rise and Decline of Nations: Economic Growth, Stagflation, and Social Rigidities* (New Haven, CT: Yale University Press, 1982), 4.

3. Grzegorz W. Kolodko, *From Shock to Therapy: The Political Economy of Postsocialist Transformation* (Oxford: Oxford University Press, 2000).

4. Pedro-Paul Kuczynski and John Williamson, eds., *After the Washington Consensus: Restarting Growth and Reform in Latin America* (Washington, DC: Institute for International Economics, 2003).

5. Dani Rodrik, "Goodbye Washington Consensus, Hello Washington Confusion?" *Journal of Economic Literature* 44 (Dec. 2006): 973–87.

6. Dani Rodrik, *One Economics, Many Recipes: Globalization, Institutions, and Economic Growth* (Princeton: Princeton University Press, 2007), chap. 1.

7. Karl Polanyi, *The Great Transformation: The Political and Economic Origins of Our Time* (1944; Boston: Beacon Press, 2001).

8. Rodrik, *One Economics,* chap. 5.

9. Robert J. Barro, "Democracy and Growth," *Journal of Economic Growth* (Mar. 1996): 1–27; Robert J. Barro, *Determinants of Economic Growth: A Cross-Country Empirical Study* (Cambridge, MA: MIT Press, 1997); Robert J. Barro, "Rule of Law, Democracy and Economic Performance," in *Index of Economic Freedom 2000,* ed. Heritage Foundation (Washington, DC: Heritage Foundation, 2000); Robert J. Barro and Xavier Sala-i-Martin, *Economic Growth,* 2nd ed. (Cambridge, MA: MIT Press, 2003); Adam Przeworski, Michael E. Alvarez, Jose Antonio Cheibub, and Fernando Limongi, *Democracy and Development: Political Institutions and Well-Being in the World, 1950–1990* (Cambridge: Cambridge University Press, 2000); Adam Przeworski, "Democracy and Economic Development," in *The Evolution of Political Knowledge,* ed. Edward D. Mansfield and Richard Sisson (Columbus: Ohio State University Press, 2004); José Tavares and Romain Wacziarg, "How Democracy Affects Growth," *European Economic Review* 45 (2001): 1341–78. See also A. Przeworski and F. Limongi, "Political Regimes and Economic Growth," *Journal of Economic Perspectives* 7 (1993): 1002–37; L. Sirowy and A. Inkeles, "The Effects of Democracy on Economic Growth and Inequality: A Review," *Studies in Comparative International Development* 25 (1990): 126–57; Uk

Heo and Alexander C. Tan, "Democracy and Economic Growth: A Causal Analysis," *Comparative Politics* 33, no. 4 (July 2001): 463–73.

10. Barro, *Determinants of Economic Growth,* 61.

11. Douglass C. North, *Understanding the Process of Economic Change* (Princeton: Princeton University Press, 2005), 165.

12. Douglass C. North, John Joseph Wallis, and Barry R. Weingast, *Violence and Social Orders: A Conceptual Framework for Interpreting Recorded Human History* (Cambridge: Cambridge University Press, 2009), 4 (hereafter cited in the text).

13. Daniel Lederman and William F. Maloney, *Natural Resources: Neither Curse nor Destiny* (New York: World Bank Publications, 2006).

14. Another related explanation is the well-known Weber thesis in *The Protestant Ethic and the Spirit of Capitalism.* Also, according to Fu Zhengyuan's *Autocratic Tradition and Chinese Politics:* "The ties between lord and vassals under Western feudalism were based on mutual obligations and, hence, were more contractual and voluntary, whereas under the Zhou system the relation was more hierarchical and one-directional, stressing the authority of the king versus the obligation of the vassals. Western feudalism developed into a system separate from kinship, whereas Zhou feudalism was essentially based on kinship and regulated by patrimonial norms. Western feudalism had a separate religious authority and a hierarchy independent of the political system, whereas Chinese traditional political system never tolerated an autonomous church independent from the authority of the state. Western feudalism contained seeds of pluralism, whereas Chinese feudalism was impregnated with monistic autocracy from its very inception." See Fu Zhengyuan, *Autocratic Tradition and Chinese Politics* (Cambridge: Cambridge University Press, 1994), 24.

15. Fareed Zakaria, *The Future of Freedom: Illiberal Democracy at Home and Abroad* (New York: W. W. Norton and Company, 2003). This book provides additional evidence to that provided by Robert Barro and Adam Przeworski.

16. See Przeworski et al., *Democracy and Development.*

17. Jack L. Snyder, *From Voting to Violence: Democratization and Nationalist Conflict* (New York: W. W. Norton and Company, 2000); L. Weinberg: *The Democratic Experience and Political Violence* (New York: Routledge, 2001).

18. Zakaria, *Future of Freedom.*

19. Henry Farrell, ed., "One Economics, Many Recipes: A Crooked Timber Seminar on Dani Rodrik's Book," 2007, 25, http://www.henryfarrell.net/rodrik.pdf.

20. Francis Fukuyama, *End of History and the Last Man* (New York: Free Press, 1992).

21. James M. Buchanan, "Keynesian Economics in Democratic Politics," in *Collected Works of James M. Buchanan,* 20 vols. (Indianapolis: Liberty Fund, 2000), 8: 98–99.

22. Garrett Hardin, "The Tragedy of the Commons," *Science* 162, no. 3859 (Dec. 13, 1968), 1243–48.

23. The Prisoner's Dilemma is a well-known problem in game theory that can be traced to research by Merrill Flood, Melvin Dresher, and Albert Tucker in the 1950s. The logic of collective action is attributed to Mancur Olson.

24. Elinor Ostrom, *Governing the Commons: The Evolution of Institutions for Collective Action* (Cambridge: Cambridge University Press, 1990); Elinor Ostrom, ed., *Rules, Games, and Common-Pool Resources* (Ann Arbor: University of Michigan Press, 1994); Elinor Ostrom, ed., *The Drama of the Commons* (Washington, DC: National Academies Press, 2002); Niles Dolsak and Elinor Ostrom, eds., *The Commons in the New Millennium: Challenges and Adaptation* (Cambridge, MA: MIT Press, 2003); Elinor Ostrom, *Understanding Institutional Diversity* (Princeton: Princeton University Press, 2005).

25. Hans-Hermann Hoppe, *Democracy: The God that Failed; The Economics and Politics of Monarchy, Democracy, and Natural Order* (New Brunswick: Transaction Publishers, 2001). Austrian School founder Carl Menger was one of the first to analyze "time preference."

26. Adam Przeworski, *Democracy, Accountability, and Representation* (Cambridge: Cambridge University Press, 1999).

27. Hoppe, *Democracy*. Hoppe even goes on to radically claim that "it is economically and ethically advantageous to choose monarchy over democracy" (xx) and that what should be preferred is the "natural order" (or anarcho-capitalism, ordered anarchy, private property anarchism, auto-government, private law society, pure capitalism) (xxi). Hoppe also states that "among the factors influencing time preference one can distinguish between external, biological, personal, and social or institutional ones" (3).

28. Stephen Holmes, *The Anatomy of Antiliberalism* (Cambridge, MA: Harvard University Press, 1993).

29. Problems in "the logic of collective belief" are also added to problems in "the logic of collective actions." See Bryan Caplan, *The Myth of the Rational Voter: Why Democracies Choose Bad Policies* (Princeton: Princeton University Press, 2007).

30. Bruce Bueno de Mesquita, Alastair Smith, Randolph M. Siverson, and James D. Morrow, *The Logic of Political Survival* (Cambridge, MA: MIT Press, 2003). Part of the discussion in this section is drawn from Frank Fang, *China Fever: Fascination, Fear, and the World's Next Superpower* (Berkeley: Stonebridge Press, 2007), chap. 5.

31. H. Lyman Miller, "China's Leadership Transition," http://media.hoover.org/documents/clm5_lm.pdf#search=%22Politburo%20with%20new%20people%20in%20effect%20creates%20a%20new%2C%20two-tiered%20hierarchy%20at%20the%20top%200f%20the%20party%22.

32. "Commitment problems" dictate that groups with political power cannot commit to not using their power to change the distribution of resources in their favor; or, in a narrower notion, that those with power cannot commit to their promises that benefit other social groups. Refer to Acemoglu, Johnson, and Robinson, "Institutions as the Fundamental Cause."

33. Li Cheng, "China's Political Succession: Four Myths in the U.S.," http://iicas .org/english/Krsten_24_05_01.htm.

34. Richard A. Shweder, *Why Do Men Barbecue? Recipes for Cultural Psychology* (Cambridge, MA: Harvard University Press, 2003).

35. Donald C. Clarke, "Economic Development and the Rights Hypothesis: The China Problem," *American Journal of Comparative Law* 51 (2003): 89–111. I follow Clarke in this essay to use "a reformulation of the Rights Hypothesis that retains the emphasis on security of property but substantially downgrades the importance of a formal legal system that provides effective enforcement of contract rights."

36. A good reference in cultural psychology can be found in Richard Nisbett's *The Geography of Thoughts* (New York: Free Press, 2004).

37. I developed this analysis in *China Fever* and updated it in the Chinese edition entitled *China Fever: The World's Next Superpower* (Beijing: Xinhua Press, 2009). Similar but less institutional ideas can be found in W. J. Baumol, "Entrepreneurship: Productive, Unproductive, and Destructive," *Journal of Political Economy* 98 (1990): part 1, 893–921. Here *institution* is defined as "formal rules and informal constraints" (Douglass North), which is also compatible with the idea that different social actors may have various impacts on institutional changes.

38. Jack Knight, *Institutions and Social Conflict* (Cambridge: Cambridge University Press, 1992).

39. Douglass C. North, *Institutions, Institutional Change and Economic Performance* (Cambridge: Cambridge University Press, 1990); North, *Understanding the Process of Economic Change.*

40. Olson, *Rise and Decline of Nations;* James M. Buchanan and Gordon Tullock, *The Calculus of Consent* (Indianapolis: Liberty Fund, 1962); James M. Buchanan, *The Logical Foundations of Constitutional Liberty,* vol. 1 of *Collected Works;* Caplan, *Myth of the Rational Voter.*

41. C. Mantzavinos, *Individuals, Institutions, and Markets* (Cambridge: Cambridge University Press, 2001); Daron Acemoglu, *Introduction to Modern Economic Growth* (Princeton: Princeton University Press, 2009).

42. Relative change of input relates to "total factor productivity," which includes not only land, labor, and capital but also other factors that contribute to the relative change of prices: industry structure, innovation, population structure, education, human capital, knowledge, technology, entrepreneurship, savings, capital accumulation, public infrastructure, economies of scale, trade, organization structure, management, and macroeconomic policies.

43. Minxin Pei, *China's Trapped Transition: The Limits of Developmental Autocracy* (Cambridge, MA: Harvard University Press, 2006). Part of the discussion in this section is drawn from Fang, *China Fever,* chap. 5.

44. Jeffrey Sachs, Wing Thye Woo, and Yang Xiaokai, "Economic Reforms and Constitutional Transition," *Annals of Economics and Finance* 1, no. 2 (Nov.

2000): 435–91. The only thing that appears unrealistic now in China is "multiparty contestation."

45. Adam Przeworski, *Democracy and the Market: Political and Economic Reforms in Eastern Europe and Latin America* (Cambridge: Cambridge University Press, 1991); José María Maravall and Adam Przeworski, *Democracy and the Rule of Law* (Cambridge: Cambridge University Press, 2003).

12

Why Is State Effectiveness Essential for Democracy?

Asian Examples

Wang Shaoguang

In the late 1980s and early 1990s, when the "third wave" of democratization began, many were very optimistic about the future of the unfolding "worldwide democratic revolution." Now, a decade later, the optimism has somehow faded away. Among nearly one hundred countries that appeared to be moving away from authoritarian rule in the early 1990s, over a dozen have suffered "democratic breakdown" or "democratic reversals," and most transition states are stuck in what Thomas Carothers calls the "gray zone."[1]

Why are so many third-wave transition countries in trouble? Or more generally, what are the conditions under which democracies can survive and function? The standard answer to this question normally points to three key variables as the preconditions for a successful venture into stable democracy, namely, a relatively high level of economic development,[2] a vibrant civil society,[3] and a strong civic culture.[4] There is no doubt that these are in fact attributes that characterize the old and stable democracies but are generally lacking in most of the transition countries. However, they are by no means the only things that are absent in the majority of third-wave countries. Another thing those countries are commonly wanting is a coherent, functioning state.

In most countries that once belonged to the former Soviet Union and the former Yugoslavia, no national state institutions existed before they began transition; throughout much of sub-Saharan Africa, states exist but are largely incoherent, nonfunctional, and unstable; most Latin American countries entered democratic transition with "a deep legacy of persistently poor performance of state institutions";[5] elsewhere in the third world, transition away from authoritarian rule often unfolded in the context of extremely weak state structures. Interestingly, almost all of the countries with nonperforming states are stuck in the "gray zone." It is in those third-wave countries where state building did not appear to be a major challenge that democratic progress seems to have made the most headway. These are primarily countries in Southern and Central Europe, though there are also a few in South America and East Asia.[6]

Based on this observation, a growing number of democracy activists and scholars have come to conclude that the presence of an effective state is a prerequisite for democracy.[7] However, the exact linkages between state effectiveness and democracy have not yet been systematically explored. This essay is designed to fill this vacuum. It is organized as follows. The first section tries to reconceptualize democracy. While most define democracy as a type of political regime, the discussion here emphasizes that it is also a form of public authority. As such, it needs to acquire what Michael Mann calls "infrastructural power."[8] Dealing with the concept of state effectiveness, the second section attempts to identify the nuts and bolts of an effective modern state. By doing so, it is intended to provide a framework for comparing state effectiveness across countries. The third section endeavors to answer the central question of the essay: why democracy cannot work and last without an effective state. Based upon the insight that an effective state is a prerequisite of a high-quality and sustainable democracy, the fourth section advances six hypotheses concerning conducive or adverse circumstances for democratic transition and consolidation. The fifth section uses five Asian cases to test these hypotheses. The upshot of the arguments presented in the first five sections is that democracy is unlikely to flourish where it is not based upon a solid infrastructure of state institutions. The final section explores the implications of this finding for China's political future.

DEMOCRACY

Democracy as a Type of Regime

Democracy is one type of political regime. What distinguishes democracy from various types of nondemocratic regimes is that democracy enables people to manage power relations and thus control rulers, while other regime types do not.[9] As a device for managing power relations, democracy at a minimum must meet two criteria at once, namely what Dahl calls "inclusiveness" and "public contestation."[10] The former refers to participation, or more precisely, the right for virtually all adults to vote and contest for office. The latter refers to opposition rights, or creating institutionalized channels for meaningful opposition by those who are adversely affected by government policies. A political system cannot be called democratic unless both inclusive participation and political competition are present. Only when contestation and participation are combined is it realistic for people to curtail domination. Then the system can be called democratic.

Democracy as a Form of Governance

Most scholars define democracy only as a type of regime. We think it is necessary to emphasize that democracy is also a form of state governance. Democracy differs from other forms of regimes in its distinctive way of governance, but as Bagehot points out,[11] every political system must gain authority and then use authority. In other words, "authority has to exist before it can be limited."[12] If a government cannot perform basic state functions, no matter how democratic its form, the people of the country would not benefit from it. In this sense, "the issues pertaining to the state are logically prior to those concerning the political regime."[13] Without an effective state, no democracy is meaningful.[14]

The separation between regime type and state allows us to conceptualize democracy as a compound of democratic institutions and state institutions.[15] The former refers to institutions that revolve around four stages of democratic representation: prevoting, voting, postvoting, and the interelection period. More specifically, democratic institutions include bundles of rights and obligations associated with citizenship, methods of organizing interests, an electoral system, arrangements for dividing and supervising powers, and so on. The central distinctive task of democratic institutions is to limit power. As for state institutions, we will deal with them in the following section. Suffice it to say here that the main purpose of state institutions is to furnish the government with authority and thereby enable it to govern.

In the literature, democratization has often been defined as the process of regime change, which involves the emergence of institutionalized contestation and the expansion of participation in contestation to groups that have been excluded from political life. The conceptualization of democracy as both a type of regime and a form of governance sheds new light on the real meaning of democratization. From this perspective, democratization consists of two separate processes: a process of transition from a nondemocratic regime to a more or less democratic one, as well as a process of state-building or rebuilding.[16] Similarly, the concept of consolidation of democracy needs to be reconsidered. In addition to "routinizing" democratic practices and internalizing democratic values,[17] a consolidated democracy must also be able to effectively govern the full territory over which it claims sovereignty. Thus, state (re)building should be an indispensable undertaking throughout democratization and consolidation. It is ill advised for third-wave countries to damage or weaken essential state capacities during their transition. Wherever and whenever the efficacy of the state is in doubt, a crisis of governance is likely to emerge; if not settled in due course, the crisis of governance may eventually give rise to the crisis of democracy.

STATE EFFECTIVENESS

Because state effectiveness is so vital to democratic transition and consolidation, we devote this section to examining the topic.

What is the state? The state may be defined, in the Weberian sense, as a set of institutions that monopolize the legitimate use of force and rule making within a given territory. The monopolization of physical force is the very foundation on which the state's existence rests, which endows the state with power to make authoritative binding decisions and to perform other functions. Without power, a state cannot be effective.

Power, of course, has many faces. Following Michael Mann, we believe it useful to distinguish two types of state power: despotic and infrastructural. The former refers to the power state elites can exercise "without routine negotiation with civil society groups."[18] State despotic power is measured by its intrusiveness or extensiveness. While such power is broad and sometimes unlimited in nondemocratic settings, it is more constrained, albeit in varying degrees, in democratic systems. Infrastructural power, on the other hand, is measured by its effectiveness. According to Mann's definition, "infrastructural power refers to the capacity of the state actually to penetrate civil society, and to implement logistically political decisions throughout the realm."[19] Infrastructurally, most powerful states are found in today's Western democracies, where the state's capacity to penetrate everyday life surpasses that of any historical or contemporary third world state. States in other times and other places may be intrusive and ruthless, but they often encounter enormous difficulties in penetrating people's social and economic life. State infrastructural power in Western democracies, however, is so pervasive that their citizens cannot even find a "hiding place from the infrastructural reach of the modern state."[20]

Despotic power and infrastructural power are analytically two independent dimensions of state power. While the former defines the nature of the state (or regime type), the latter conditions state capacity and effectiveness. Democratization by definition will weaken state despotic power, but it would be unwise to bring collateral damage to state infrastructural power in the process. A less intrusive state does not entail a less effective state. One can even argue that democracy probably needs more infrastructural power to function effectively, efficiently, and sustainably than other forms of government.

Where state infrastructural power is deficient, efforts must be made to build essential state institutions and capabilities. In the literature about the state, "state-building" is often vaguely defined as a process in which the state accumulates power. In our understanding, state-building involves accumulating only infrastructural power, not despotic power.

The above discussion leads to two fundamental questions of this chapter: What specific infrastructural power does a state have to possess to be effective? Why is an effective state a prerequisite of sustainable democracy? Despite growing evidence that state effectiveness underpins democracy, to our knowledge, these questions have not been systematically examined. The rest of this section tries to answer the first question and leaves the second to the next section.

Given the broad and growing scope of state activities, state effectiveness obviously is a complex and multidimensional phenomenon. No single index seems able to capture all aspects of state effectiveness. There are six critical functions we believe effective states should have capacities to perform.[21]

The Capacity to Monopolize the Legitimate Use of Violence (Coercive Capacity)

By Weber's definition, the basic test of the existence of a state is whether or not its national government can lay claim to a monopoly of force in the territory under its jurisdiction. Obviously, the monopoly of force is a "means" rather than an "end" for the state. Its end is to counter external threats to the sovereignty and internal threats to social order. To achieve this goal, all states must build up and deploy armed forces and police forces, the former primarily to defend against possible foreign invasion and the latter to prevent and punish deviant conduct and repress social unrest. Clearly, if the territory of a country is carved up by foreign forces, its government cannot claim to be an effective state. Similarly, if several internal rival groups coexist in a country and all possess organized violence, none would be in a position to establish permanent control of the contested territory. Wherever such a situation is present, we may call it "statelessness."

Here we want to emphasize the importance of developing a professional, resourceful, dedicated, disciplined, and uniformed police. Repressive regimes are often called "police states." This is actually a misnomer. In fact, the ratio of policemen to population tends to be low in so-called police states, while it is much higher in so-called free countries.[22]

The Capacity to Extract Resources (Extractive Capacity)

State monopoly of physical force does not come cheap. In order to establish a monopoly, states need to "extract from the population a share of the yearly product of its economic activities."[23] As early as the sixteenth century, when the modern nation-state just began to emerge, Jean Bodin already realized that "financial means are the nerves of the state."[24]

In the last century or so, the scope of state operations has expanded considerably. It is the availability of resources that permits the state to carry out its new tasks. To finance bigger governments, states need to explore more productive extractive devices. In the past, states raised revenue mainly through such mechanisms as military or colonial ventures, the sale of offices, tax farming, monopolies, donations, and even drawing on state elites' private wealth.[25] Now "the regular, unobtrusive levying of taxes on various phases and aspects of the modernized economic process" has largely replaced those less efficient instruments.[26] As a result, in Western democracies, government spending typically increased by three- to fivefold, if not more, in the twentieth century.[27] At present, it commonly accounts for one-third to one-half of the gross domestic product (GDP) in those countries.

Elsewhere, state extractive capacity varies greatly from country to country and generally is much weaker. Nevertheless, an effective state has to be fiscally viable. A state that is unable to generate sufficient resources for realizing its policy goals cannot be effective.

The Capacity to Shape National Identity (Assimilative Capacity)

Backed by extractive capacity, coercive capacity is the most basic aspect of state power. But it would be extremely costly to maintain domestic peace by coercion alone. For any political system to operate effectively, there must exist some shared identities. This is especially true in diverse societies.

In the early phases of state development in the West, and in the third world today, the state is one among many autonomous power centers that compete for people's loyalty. Thus, the construction of state coercive and extractive capacities must be followed by rationalization of authority and nation building. The former refers to the centralization of political power, involving the replacement of traditional familial, local, religious, and ethnic authorities by a single, secular, national authority. The latter means "internal homogenization,"[28] involving the transformation of "peoples' commitment and loyalty from smaller tribes, villages, or petty principalities to the larger central political system, creating a common national culture of loyalty and commitment."[29] The breakup of the Soviet Union, Yugoslavia, and Czechoslovakia and ethnic conflicts in Indonesia, Sri Lanka, and many African countries vividly demonstrate that the absence of national identity could be a powerful centrifugal force.

It is true that multiethnic and multicultural states normally have greater difficulties in winning and maintaining the allegiance of diverse population. But this observation should not lead us to the conclusion that ethnic, cultural, religious, or linguistic identity is primordially given and that thereby any effort to shape a national identity in such diverse societies is doomed to failure. Since almost all nations started out as very diverse culturally, linguistically, religiously, or ethnically, the presence of strong national identity in some but not others suggests that identity is amendable. In other words, the formation of national identity is best understood as an outcome of purposeful state efforts to overcome heterogeneity in the society, although some exogenous historical accidents may also affect the outcome. If a society is fragmented, where opportunistic politicians can use the strategy of exacerbating minuscule differences to pursue their personal interests, "it is more likely a consequence of institutional failure rather than a cause of it."[30] Wherever states are unable to mold national identity, they are unlikely to be effective, because a great deal more resources and energy would have to be diverted to fighting centrifugal forces.

The Capacity to Regulate the Society and the Economy (Regulatory Capacity)

The regulative capacity is defined as the ability of the state to change and subordinate the behavior of individuals and groups away from their own inclination and in favor of the behavior prescribed by the state.

Regulations are necessary because modern societies are full of hazards engendered from industrialization, commercialization, urbanization, and asymmetrical distribution of power and information. To protect people and nature, the state needs to regulate not only such clearly deviant social activities as murder and assault but also many aspects of economic and social life, including, among other things, weights and measures, contracts, industrial R&D, road construction, public utilities, food and drug quality, garbage collection, mail delivery, labor-management relations, working conditions, safety standards, the relief of destitution, consumer protection, protection of the environment and natural resources, health, education, sports, marriage, promotion of the arts, and even parental responsibility.

It is by no means easy for the state to regulate the society and economy. To facilitate effective regulation, for instance, the state must collect and store a massive amount of information about everyone living and working in the country. In developed countries, this is not a problem anymore. Birth, schooling, marriage, divorce, occupation, income, ownership of house and automobile, honor, misconduct, exit from and entry into the country, and death are all constantly under state watch. Nothing seems able to escape state screening. In the developing world, however, even statistics on such basic items as population size and distribution are often deficient, not to mention information about mobile tax bases or practices of food handling. For countries that are not capable of monitoring the whereabouts and behavior of their populations, it is unrealistic to expect their states to possess much regulative capacity.

In today's world, well-ordered societies, whether democratic or not, are highly regulated. Where governments lack adequate regulative capacity, again whether democratic or not, people typically have to put up with frequent industrial accidents and environmental disasters, untreated water, broken drainage systems, chaotic traffic, appalling work conditions, tense labor-management relations, shoddy consumer products, horrendous medical services, and the like. The contrast between the two types of countries clearly points to the significance of the regulative capacity for any modern state.

The Capacity to Maintain the Internal Coherence of State Institutions (Steering Capacity)

The state relies upon bureaucracy to perform the above functions. To be effective, the state has to make the bureaucracy professionalized and meritocratic so that its recruits have technical talent and the requisite training to be competent for the tasks assigned to them. Just as important from the perspective of the state is maintaining the internal coherence of bureaucratic institutions. The modern bureaucracy is a complex and sophisticated organization made up of multiple minute organs. Though all the activities of the bureaucracy are supposed to be ultimately sanctioned by and directed from a single center, there is a danger of the coherence of the system being undercut by the inertia and departmentalism of bureaucratic agencies and the particularism and corruption of individual bureaucrats.

It is often the case that political executives' policy-making efforts are thwarted by the bureaucracy not so much because it intends deliberately to sabotage political leaders as because large organizations tend to proceed from inertia and to persist in their routine unless stopped. In addition, bureaucrats and their organizations tend to believe that they understand the policy area in question better than political executives. A more acute problem with bureaucracy, however, is that each agency "seeks to maximize the state resources it commands, and to assign priority to its own concerns over all others."[31] This kind of desire may motivate bureaucratic agencies intentionally to hinder or block the collection of vital information for centralized decision making and to engage in pointless competition against each other. As a result, the ultimate authority of the state may find it difficult, if not impossible, to enforce its policy agenda and to prevent its agents from deserting their strictly implementary role. The corporate coherence of the state then becomes a casualty of "bureaucratic free enterprise."[32]

The most detrimental problems with the bureaucracy, especially among third world countries, are particularism and corruption. Rather than dehumanizing administrative processes, as expected by Max Weber,[33] officials who practice particularism allow love, hatred, and other personal factors to affect their decisions made in the name of the state. Corrupt officials also give preferentiality to people related to them in the execution of state directives, not out of emotion, but out of careful calculation of potential gains and risks. Despite the differences in motive, both particularism and corruption impair the impartiality of public administration, breed distrust of public authorities, set off political alienation, and in extreme cases even lead to system breakdowns.

A well-functioning state is supposed to operate as a machine "propelled by energy and directed by information flowing from a single center in the service of a plurality of coordinated tasks."[34] Where government institutions do not mesh with each other and particularism and corruption are rampant, intrastate and state-society conflicts are bound to increase, thus undercutting the ability of the whole system to control the flow of tax resources and to achieve other policy goals.

The Capacity to Distribute Resources (Redistributive Capacity)

The distributive capacity refers to the authoritative redistribution of scarce resources among different social groups. The purpose of redistribution is to provide the least fortunate members of society with economic security, as well as to reduce inequality in income and wealth distribution. Urbanization, high literacy levels, and the demonstration effect of Western welfare states have all increased the volume and intensity of pressures on governments everywhere to mitigate social risks and narrow the gaps between the "haves" and the "have-nots" through some form of redistribution. Some contend that since the welfare state is primarily a Western luxury that only rich countries can afford, the effectiveness of a state should not be measured by its distributive capacity. To the extent that inequality often increases the probability of political instability,[35] the distributive capacity in effect is one that helps to maintain domestic public order and enhance its legitimacy. Given the importance of public order and legitimacy for any regime, the instrumental value of redistribution should not be underestimated.

The first two sets of the abovementioned functions are those that define any state, including premodern states. Even premodern states were characterized by the creation of regular armies and a taxation system.[36] The other four functions are features of the modern nation-state, which adds "routine, formalized, rationalized institutions" of wider scope not only over its citizens but also to a very large extent over all actions taking place in the areas of its jurisdiction. If a state is capable of performing all of these functions well, we call it an effective state.[37] If a state is only capable of performing some of these functions, we call it less effective. When a state is unable to perform any of these functions, it can legitimately be called a failed state.

WHY IS AN EFFECTIVE STATE A PREREQUISITE OF SUSTAINABLE DEMOCRACY?

Having defined both "democracy" and "state effectiveness," we now turn to the relationship between the two. There may be a wide range of necessary conditions for democracy to work and last. We argue that the existence of an effective state is one of those necessary conditions and probably the most important one. Without an effective state, there can be no democracy. This point, of course, is by no means novel. Several scholars have called attention to the role of the state in recent years.[38] What we would like to add to the literature is theoretical explanations about how the operation of democracy is contingent on the viability and effectiveness of state institutions.

For a democracy to work and last, there must exist an effective state that is capable of performing the following tasks.

Defining the Political Community within Which Democracy Operates

A democracy presupposes a well-defined territorial-social unit, for, as pointed out by Robert Dahl, democratic methods "cannot solve the problem of the proper scope and domain of democratic units."[39] The majority principle, for instance, will not work unless we know exactly the boundary of the whole political community. Only when the vast majority of people "have no doubt or mental reservations as to which political community they belong to"[40] is it possible for them to organize their life in a democratic fashion.

Conversely, if large segments of the population in a territorial-social unit refuse to accept the unit as an appropriate entity to make legitimate decisions and desire to create their own independent states or to merge with other states, democratic procedure can neither work nor solve the problem of identity. Here the key challenge is to cultivate strong identification with the territorial-social unit. In Western Europe, the process of nation building was generally guided by coercive governments, which used a wide range of instruments to repress and eliminate multilingualism and multiculturalism in their territories. The resultant nation-states defined the political communities within which democratization could take place.[41] Although these methods are not acceptable by today's moral standards, the lesson from the first wave of democratization is that nation building should precede democratization.

Protecting Citizens' Basic Rights

For democracy to exist, all citizens must enjoy such basic civil rights as freedom of expression, the freedom to form and join organizations, the right to vote, and so on. During the Cold War era and soon after, it was widely believed that only by limiting the power of the state could personal liberties be secured. By now, however, the inadequacy of this notion of rights has become evident, because people in Russia and many other transition countries still do not enjoy many real liberties even after dictatorship has ended, dissidents have been released from jails, and censorship has been removed. The governments in these countries are simply too disorganized and weak to enforce their own laws. What has happened in these countries makes excruciatingly clear that liberties can be threatened just as thoroughly by state incapacity as by repressive state apparatus. This observation leads Stephen Holmes to conclude that "liberal rights depend essentially on the competent exercise of a certain kind of legitimate public power." State power is needed to guard property rights, to prevent harm, to repress force, to contain fraud, and above all to extend protection to the vulnerable. Viewed from this angle, rather than being a threat to personal freedoms, a liberal state is "the largest and most reliable human rights organization," and "a non-performing state cannot be a liberal state."[42]

Creating and Maintaining a Rule-Based Polity

The "rule of law" means the predominance of law over discretionary authority. A state based on the rule of law is not necessarily democratic (e.g., Singapore), but a high-quality democracy must be ruled by law rather than by arbitrary decisions of a ruler or his agents. In a democracy, laws constitute not only a tool to control the masses but also an instrument to constrain officials and bureaucrats.

In essence, laws are rules governing human behavior in a given society. Democracy is a rule-intensive polity. In addition to the legal provision of civil rights, there must be rules with regard to citizenship, elections, the distribution of power, the relationship between different branches of government, and so on. The guidance provided by these rules enables political actors to coordinate their behavior, thus helping reduce uncertainty and create order in human interactions. Without a set of elaborate, clear, and noncontingent rules, it is hard to imagine how democracy can function. However, it is unrealistic to expect rules to be self-enforceable. The threat of state sanction is imperative to ensure compliance.

Vitalizing Civil Society

Civil society plays a crucial role in checking, monitoring, and restraining the exercise of state power and in holding the state accountable to the people.[43] However, the state-society relationship is one of "mutual empowerment" or "synergy," rather than a zero-sum relationship. The two are interrelated in many ways:

1. At best, civil society can act as a counterweight to the Leviathan of state power. However, it can never provide a substitute for the organized public institutions of the state.
2. When civil society acts as a counterweight to state power, it should check and limit the despotic but not the infrastructural power of the state.
3. It makes sense for civil society to target the state as an object of its efforts only when the state is an effective one. If the state is incapable of solving any economic and social problems, there is no point in dealing with it.
4. Only robust state institutions can provide an arena in which civil society can operate. A crisis of the state more often than not leads to a degeneration of civil society rather than to its revival. Conversely, when the state is relatively strong and resilient, civil society is more likely to thrive.[44] This is so because "just as modern markets depend on economic decisions being nested in a predictable institu-

tional framework, likewise 'civic engagement' flourishes more easily among private citizens and organized groups when they have a competent public sector as an interlocutor."[45]

5. Civil society can improve the ability of the state to govern. When civil society and the state both are relatively strong, the vibrancy of the former itself may make citizens more respectful and hence obedient to the latter. In Robert Putnam's words, "civic associations are powerfully associated with effective public institutions . . . strong society, strong state."[46]

If the above remarks are correct, one may conclude, as Peter Evans does, that "a sustained efflorescence of civil society may well depend on the simultaneous construction of robust, competent organizational counterparts within the state. . . . A move toward less capable and involved states will make it more difficult for civic associations to achieve their goals, thereby diminishing incentives for civic engagement."[47]

Meeting Peoples' Basic Demands

For three reasons, a democracy, especially a premature one, has to deliver some basic public goods and services in order to survive. First, many people embrace democracy not for the sake of democracy, but as a solution for the crisis their country faces, including political as well as social and economic crises. Second, democratization is likely to heighten political and social citizenship, which may give rise to the pressure for uniformity of treatment, the reduction of social risks, higher living standards, a better quality of life, and a greater degree of equality. Third, democracy itself offers people more freedoms, opportunities, and power to push for policy changes.

If a democratic system proves unable to provide such essential public goods and services as external security, domestic order, justice, basic education, prevention of epidemic diseases, compensations for those hurt by market swings, and alleviation of gross inequality, its poor performance will make people increasingly more frustrated, thus eventually leading to a legitimacy crisis and probably the breakdown of democracy.[48] This danger tends to increase as the brief "honeymoon period" of democratization passes and "the memories of authoritarian failure fade."[49]

Only a state with strong capacities is able to perform well in generating social well-being. That is why both Linz and Stepan and Przeworski consider the efficacy and effectiveness of the state key to democratic legitimacy and stability.

In summary, if a democracy is to work and to last, the state must be able to define the community in which it operates, protect citizens' basic rights, create and maintain a rule-based polity, vitalize civil society, and meet peoples' basic demands. Only an effective state can perform those tasks. Without these capacities, there can be no democratic governance.

How Does State Effectiveness Affect Democratic Consolidation?

Based upon the insight that an effective state is a prerequisite of sustainable democracy, we intend in this section to derive some propositions concerning conducive or adverse circumstances for democratic consolidation. Most have been put forward before by others, but their underlying assumptions and logics are not necessarily identical with ours. For us, the key intervening variable that affects the outcome of democratic consolidation is the degree of state effectiveness, measured by the six capacities discussed in the second section. The higher the degree of state effectiveness, the less difficult democratic consolidation becomes. Conversely, where state infrastuctural power is deficient, democracy is less likely to function well and survive.

Proposition 1: There may not be any specific preconditions for democratization, but an effective state is a prerequisite to democratic consolidation. The third wave demonstrates that democratization can occur anywhere, including such "unlikely and unexpected places" as Albania and Mauritania, but consolidated and stable democracies are much harder to find because many third-wave countries do not have effective governments.

Proposition 2: Democratic consolidation is more likely to be successful where state and regime were distinguished from one another under the old regime. Under certain types of regimes (e.g., regimes ruled by a strongman or a hegemonic party), there is in effect no distinction between the regime and the state. Consequently, when democratization begins, the state apparatus is likely to collapse along with the old regime. The resultant statelessness may make democratic consolidation extremely difficult, if not entirely impossible.

Proposition 3: The more disruptive the transition process is, the more difficult it is to consolidate democracy. As far as democratic consolidation is concerned, incumbent-initiated transitions (Spain, Korea, and Taiwan) are preferable to opposition-led transitions (the Philippines); orderly and peaceful transitions are preferable (the former Czechoslovakia) to ones preceded by revolutionary wars, ethnic wars, or widespread riots (Indonesia). Put differently, where a state remains intact during the process of regime transition, it may help the new regime to consolidate; where transition undermines state cohesion and institutional hierarchy, it is more difficult for the new regime to consolidate.

Proposition 4: The more heterogeneous a society is, the more difficult it is to consolidate democracy. It is far more difficult for the people in a multiethnic and multicultural society to consider themselves members of the same community. When a large proportion of the population does not want to be part of the community upon which the state is founded, the issue of crafting democratic norms, practices, and institutions becomes secondary to what Linz and Stepan call "the problem of stateness." The presence of the stateness problem may damage the prospects of democratic consolidation in two ways. First, to solve the stateness problem, the new democratizing regime will have to make a great effort to nurture national identity, which will inevitably divert tremendous amounts of scarce resources and precious energy from its effort to consolidate democracy.[50] Second, "some ways of dealing with the problems of stateness are inherently incompatible with democracy."[51]

Proposition 5: The larger state size is, the more difficult it is to consolidate democracy. The larger a society, the more likely it is to encompass many religious, racial, ethnic, and linguistic groupings, which increases the difficulty of governance. In addition to the heterogeneity problem, larger countries are also likely to encounter considerable problems of vertical integration and horizontal coordination, which further lowers the effectiveness of the state.

Proposition 6: Stable democracy is more likely to appear in old than in new states. The longer a country has existed, the more likely it has been successful in crafting state loyalty. On the contrary, new states are very likely to run into the challenges of nation building, unless only one nation with nearly cultural uniformity exists in each of them. It would be logically and empirically impossible for a new state to consolidate democracy before it solves the problem of national identity.

ASIAN DEMOCRACIES

From data about five third-wave Asian democracies (Indonesia, the Philippines, Thailand, South Korea, and Taiwan), we can derive two broad observations. First, the factors identified in propositions 2 through 6 do affect state effectiveness. Second, the degree of state effectiveness does have a bearing on the quality of democracy.

The Determinants of State Effectiveness

Compared to Organisation for Economic Co-operation and Development (OECD) countries, all the five Asian democracies listed here are experiencing some sort of governance crisis, made evident by their much lower scores with regard to the indexes of political stability, government effectiveness, regulatory quality, the rule of law, and control of corruption. Yet among them, Indonesia has suffered the most acute governance crisis. This is by no means surprising. Indonesia is a relatively young nation-state, which did not take form as an independent political entity until the late 1940s. With nearly 220 million people, Indonesia is the fourth most populous nation in the world. Unlike China, India, and the United States, however, Indonesia is an archipelagic state of 14,000 islands, spanning more than 5,000 kilometers from Sumatra to West Irian, and its population consists of 490 ethnic groups and speaks 250 distinct languages. Adding to its noncontiguous nature are religious divisions between Muslims (who account for almost 90 percent of Indonesians) and non-Muslims (e.g., Protestants, Catholics, Hindus, and Buddhists, among other religious groups) on the one hand, and divisions among Muslims on the other.

The extreme heterogeneity of the Indonesian population makes governance a tremendously difficult task. Prior to 1998, Suharto tried to maintain unity in this highly diverse country by force. The collapse of the Suharto military dictatorship, coupled with the imminent independence of nearby East Timor, has spurred strong centrifugal tensions throughout the country. Demoralized and internally split, the military now finds it hard to maintain the country's territorial integrity. Just formally separated from the military in 1999–2000, the Indonesian police force is even less disciplined and capable of enforcing law and order. With only 150,000 personnel, a much smaller proportion than in most nations, they have no experience in dealing with insurgencies, regional conflicts, and other forms of intercommunal enmity. No wonder even the most optimistic observers describe the political situation as chaotic. Many believe that Indonesia has already become a stateless society, and some even underscore the possible disintegration of the Indonesian state.

The Philippines is also a large archipelagic state. With more than 80 million people, it stands as the fourteenth most populous nation in the world. The archipelago consists of around 7,100 islands (among which about 1,000 are inhabited) stretching over 1,100 miles. Due to the archipelago's noncontiguous nature, people's regional affinities are often stronger than their national identity. This is especially true among the Muslim population concentrated in Mindanao and the Sulu and Tawi-Tawi archipelago in the southern Philippines. In addition to religious rifts, the unequal distribution of resources drives a wedge between the country's middle and upper classes, on the one hand, and its underclass, on the other.

The wretched poverty, gross inequality, and religious hostility have been the sources of political instability in the Philippines. Since the late 1960s, there have been at least four major insurgent movements in operation with the aim of seeking Islamic rule in their region or overthrowing the Philippine government through guerrilla warfare (e.g., New People's Army, Bangsa Moro Army, Moro Islamic Liberation Front, and Abu Sayyaf). Structurally more ominous are the over five hundred private armies scattered in the provinces. In many cases, their rule over local areas has gone unchallenged for decades, effectively undermining the government's monopoly of the means of physical violence and authoritative, binding rule making.

The long-lasting insurgencies are not the only sign of the governance crisis. The incapacity of the Philippine state also manifests itself in its wavering on major policy issues, inept public administration, a persistently weak economy, some of the world's worst pollution, rampant corruption at every level of government, and recurrent incidences of kidnapping.

With a longer history and a smaller and more homogeneous population, Thailand is relatively easier to govern. However, the Thai state faces its own set of problems, chief among which are glaring inequality and epidemic corruption. On both accounts, Thailand is on a par with the Philippines. Thai politics is notorious for the role money plays in it. Vote buying is extensive, especially in the countryside and poor regions. Once they have gotten into office after spending huge sums, politicians tend to do everything to recoup their investments and make hefty profits. Political corruption erodes the corporate coherence of the Thai government, making it weak, inept, and factious.

Compared with the three Southeast Asian countries, South Korea and Taiwan have some advantages in meeting state (re)building challenges. First, they are much smaller. Taiwan's population is just one-tenth of Indonesia's. Second, their populations' composition is much simpler. Korea's population is one of the most ethnically and linguistically homogenous in the world. Third, and perhaps more important, their democratic transitions, initiated by incumbents of the old regimes, were relatively gradual and peaceful, thus avoiding the destruction of state institutions. Of course, neither Korea nor Taiwan is free of social conflicts. While regional antagonism (the eastern and northern parts of the country vs. the western and southern parts) and the class divide (between big business and organized labor) to a large extent define Korea's political landscape, the most conflict-ridden issue in Taiwan concerns peoples' political identity: whether they prefer the island being permanently separated from China or eventually unifying with China. Without an effective mechanism for interest intermediation, disputing parties in both systems resort to all kinds of maneuvers to undermine one another, which not only causes endless policy gridlocks but also enfeebles state institutions.

The Governance Crisis and the Democracy Crisis

By procedural standards, Indonesia, the Philippines, Thailand, South Korea, and Taiwan can proudly claim to be legitimate members of the world democratic club. Elections are competitive, the press is free, citizens enjoy extensive personal liberties, new political parties are thriving, the formal division of power among different branches of government has been institutionalized, and except for Thailand the military has largely withdrawn from politics. This is why these Asian democracies all receive relatively high "polity scores."

Yet the fulfillment of the formal, procedural conditions of democracy does not necessarily make a polity truly accountable to the people. This is revealed by the relatively low scores the five political systems obtain when we use the World Bank's "voice and accountability index" and the Economist Intelligence Unit's "democracy index" to assess quality of democracy.

To be accountable, a political system must be capable of getting things done. A weak state may not be able to deliver public goods, even if it is willing to do so. This ostensibly intricate theoretical proposition is actually quite obvious to many ordinary people living under the five systems. After experiencing the exhilaration of political opening, they expected to reap the fruits of democracy, such as prosperity, stability, and good governance. But many of them soon found their hopes dashed by incessant political skirmishing, persistent policy gridlock, recurring political scandals, endemic corruption, blatant bureaucratic ineptness, a languishing economy, widening income gaps, a deteriorating environment, rising violent crime, escalating ethnic and religious warfare, and intensifying regional insurgencies. Since "democracy" has not resulted in significant political and economic gains for large segments of the population, the distractions offered by free elections, party competition, and the separation of powers have gradually lost their novelty. Protracted governance crises have led many to believe that the more things change, the more they remain the same, if not growing worse. "Democracy" gives them extensive personal liberties but little political participation outside elections; election may allow them to topple corrupt politicians but cannot stop corrupt politicians from returning to power. Given that for the most part only rich people backed by wealth can afford to run for office, it is natural for many to conclude that "democracy" is just a tool for a handful of people, who are rich and powerful, to seek personal gain.

When a significant proportion of the population in a country casts doubt on the utility as well as the intrinsic value of its democratic regime, a governance crisis could lead to a democracy crisis. Nowhere in Asia is democratic crisis more prominent than in Thailand, where the military deposed Prime Minister Thaksin Shinawatra in a nonviolent coup and reasserted its traditional self-defined role as the "arbiter" of Thai politics in September 2006. Rather than resisting the coup, an overwhelming majority of people in Thailand actually supported the generals' actions. This was so because, even before the removal of Thaksin, Thai democracy had already been in severe crisis, owing to a succession of elected but do-nothing or exceedingly corrupt regimes since 1992.

Unlike Thailand, the Philippines faces no imminent danger of a military junta taking power. However, the threat of new coups has been a chronic feature of Philippine politics. Since the fall of Ferdinand Marcos in 1986, civilian rule has been challenged by more than a few military coup attempts. What is worse, in a country once famous for "people power," the people have become so disillusioned with the political system that they no longer surge to the street to protest such a clear-cut case of electoral fraud as President Gloria Macapagal Arroyo's. While people dislike Arroyo, whose overall performance rating is the lowest among the country's five most recent presidents, many of them have come to realize that the two previous popular revolts (in 1986 and 2001) led to no improvement in the quality of their lives. They are afraid that whoever replaces her will probably be as bad, if not worse.

In Indonesia, the political momentum sparked in 1998, when Suharto was ousted as president, is also all but dead. On the surface, the country has introduced a wide range of democratic reforms since 1998, such as lifting long-time restrictions on the press and nongovernmental organizations (NGOs), allowing new parties to emerge, and holding free elections. If one looks beneath the veneer, however, one sees that much-touted political reforms are not as meaningful as they first appear. For one thing, political and economic power in most parts of Indonesia remains in the hands of those tied to the Suharto regime. For another, democratization has yet to bring tangible benefits to ordinary Indonesians: unemployment has remained high, crime has worsened, and elected politicians at all levels are as corrupt as Suharto's cronies. As recent public opinion polls reveal, most Indonesians believe that conditions were better under Suharto's New Order. Besides, the country's new democracy is widely seen as having failed to cope with the massive challenges the nation is facing, including political and economic instability, social unrest, terrorism, natural disasters, and above all the separatist movement in Aceh and Irian Jaya.

Compared with Thailand, Indonesia, and the Philippines, the democracies in South Korea and Taiwan are in much better shape. In fact, they have been widely recognized as two of the most successful third-wave democracies not just in the region but in the whole world. However, even these two political systems are in serious trouble. First, both the South Korean president and the Taiwanese president face strong domestic challenges. People's cynicism toward the two leaders has grown to universal proportions, so that their approval ratings have plummeted to all-time lows. More important, both systems have long been paralyzed by endemic corruption, incessant partisan strife, enduring legislative gridlock, unaccountable bureaucracies, and recurring political scandals. Unlike their counterparts elsewhere, people in South Korea and Taiwan experienced a variant of soft authoritarianism that was seemingly less corrupt and more efficacious in delivering economic prosperity and social stability. Given this historical legacy, people's expectations about the performance of new democratic regimes tend to be higher. This explains why the levels of popular satisfaction with the overall performance of democratic institutions have been relatively low in both places. Were the political turmoil to last, citizens' distrust of democratic institutions could reach a crisis level.

IMPLICATIONS FOR CHINA

The central argument of this essay is that, without an effective state, there can be no stable democracy. Since an effective state is a prerequisite for democracy, it would be folly for China to follow the conventional "third-wave" wisdom and conceive of pursuing democracy as a matter of weakening state institutions. Of course, during the democratic transition, the ways state power is being exercised must change, but state power itself should not be enfeebled. Rather than single-mindedly trying to restrain state power, democratic reformers should make more efforts to build national state institutions where none existed before and to strengthen state capacities where they are weak.

There are four additional reasons for China to embrace the rebuilding of the state as the nation's top priority.

First, most Chinese desire their government to become more capable of performing essential state functions effectively and efficiently because state incapacitation has done a great deal of harm to their socioeconomic well-being.[52]

Second, where state effectiveness is lacking, it cannot be supplied through the practice of democracy itself.[53] Specific efforts must be made to strengthen state capacities.

Third, precisely because democratization would allow more social forces to take part in competition for political power, a functioning and stable democracy is possible only in the presence of a set of effective state institutions that can keep the nation's business moving forward despite political uncertainty set off by liberalization and democratization.

Finally, democratization may unleash forces that are likely to put enormous pressures on the system. For instance, popular respect for government may plummet in a new political environment; rising expectations may overload the government, exceeding its capacity to respond; the demise of the previously dominant party may leave both the state and the society disorganized, thus creating an institutional vacuum; and pressures for greater uniformity (a result of expanded citizenship) may expose and exacerbate previously suppressed regional, ethnic, class, and religious tensions, triggering territorial disintegration.

None of this is to say, of course, that a crisis of governance constitutes an excuse to embrace an iron-fisted state. While an effective state is a necessary condition of stable democracy, it is by no means sufficient.

The best strategy for China is democratic state rebuilding—namely, strengthening essential state governing capacities while institutionalizing "inclusive participation" and "public contestation," two basic features of a democracy, as described by Robert Dahl. In China today, socioeconomic polarization; urbanization; and increases in literacy, education, and media exposure have conspired to give rise to enhanced aspirations for participation in decision making. If groups within society cannot find institutional channels through which they can express their needs and interests, their repressed discontent could erupt in violence. To let off some of the steam, the state must gradually incorporate social groups that have acquired political consciousness during the process of transition and guide their participation in ways that foster political integration.

In this sense, institutionalized participation constitutes not only a device to mitigate the domination of the state but also a safety valve by means of which the state can reduce state-society tensions. In the long run, as the variety and complexity of interests being articulated increase, the time will come for the country to replace its monopolistic structure of interest aggregation with a competitive one.

NOTES

1. Thomas Carothers, "The End of the Transition Paradigm," *Journal of Democracy* 13 (2002): 5–21.

2. See Seymour Martin Lipset, "Some Social Requisites of Democracy: Economic Development and Political Legitimacy," *American Political Science Review* 53 (1959): 69–105; Francis Fukuyama, "Capitalism and Democracy: The Missing Link," *Dialogue* 2 (1993): 2–7; Robert Barro, "Determinants of Democracy," *Journal of Political Economy* 107 (1999): 158–83; Adam Przeworski et al., *Democracy and Development: Political Institutions and Well-Being in the World* (Cambridge: Cambridge University Press, 2000).

3. Robert D. Putnam, *Making Democracy Work: Civic Traditions in Modern Italy* (Princeton: Princeton University Press, 1993); Juan J. Linz and Alfred C. Stepan, *Problems of Democratic Transition and Consolidation in Southern Europe,*

South America, and Post-Communist Europe (Baltimore, MD: Johns Hopkins University Press, 1996).

4. Gabriel Almond and Sidney Verla, *The Civil Culture: Political Attitudes and Democracy in Five Nations* (Princeton: Princeton University Press, 1963); Ronald Inglehart, *Modernization and Postmodernization: Culture Economics, and Political Change in Forty-Three Societies* (Princeton: Princeton University Press, 1997); Larry Diamond, *Developing Democracy toward Consolidation* (Baltimore, MD: Johns Hopkins University Press, 1999).

5. Carothers, "End of the Transition Paradigm."

6. Linz and Stepan, *Problems of Democratic Transition;* Carothers, "End of the Transition Paradigm."

7. Richard Rose and Doh Chull Shin, "Democratization Backward: The Problem of Third Wave Democracies," *British Journal of Political Science* 31 (2001): 331–54.

8. Michael Mann, *The Sources of Social Power: The Rise of Classes and Nation-States, 1760–1914* (Cambridge: Cambridge University Press, 1993), 59–61.

9. Ian Shapiro, "The State of Democratic Theory," in *Political Science: The State of the Discipline,* ed. Ira Katznelson and Helen Milner (Washington, DC: American Political Science Association, 2001).

10. Robert A. Dahl, *Polyarchy: Participation and Opposition* (New Haven, CT: Yale University Press, 1971), 4.

11. Walter Bagehot, *The English Constitution* (London: Oxford World Classics, 1949), 3–4.

12. Samuel P. Huntington, *Political Order in Changing Societies* (New Haven, CT: Yale University Press, 1968), 8.

13. Adam Przeworski et al., *Sustainable Democracy* (Cambridge: Cambridge University Press, 1995), 13.

14. Linz and Stepan, *Problems of Democratic Transition,* 17.

15. Rose and Shin, "Democratization Backward."

16. Ibid., 333.

17. Linz and Stepan, *Problems of Democratic Transition,* 5.

18. Mann, *Sources of Social Power,* 59.

19. Ibid., 114.

20. Ibid.

21. See Lucian W. Pye, *Aspects of Political Development* (Boston: Little, Brown and Co., 1966); Leonard Binder et al., *Crisis and Sequences in Political Development* (Princeton: Princeton University Press, 1971); Raymond Grew, ed., *Crises of Development in Europe and the United States* (Princeton: Princeton University Press, 1978).

22. Shi Tianjian, "State-Building and Democratization: Some Basic Theoretical Issues" (unpublished ms., Duke University).

23. Ginfranco Poggi, *The State: Its Nature, Development and Prospects* (Cambridge, UK: Polity Press, 1990), 66.

24. Cited in Jacek Kugler and William Domke, "Comparing the Strength of Nations," *Comparative Political Studies* 19 (1986): 45.

25. Gianfranco Poggi, *The Development of the Modern State: A Sociological Introduction* (Stanford: Stanford University Press, 1978), 97.

26. Poggi, *State*, 66.

27. Ibid., 109–10.

28. Charles Tilly, "Reflections on the History of European State-Making," in *The Formation of National States* in *Western Europe,* ed. Charles Tilly and Gabriel Ardant (Princeton: Princeton University Press, 1975), 661.

29. Gabriel Almond and G. Bingham Powell Jr., *Comparative Politics: A Development Approach* (Boston: Little, Brown and Co., 1966), 36.

30. Przeworski et al., *Sustainable Development*, 21.

31. Poggi, *State,* 30–31.

32. Gordon Tullock, *The Politics of Public Bureaucracy* (Cambridge, MA: Harvard University Press, 1965).

33. H. H. Gerth and C. Wright Mills, eds., *From Max Weber: Essays in Sociology* (New York: Oxford University Press, 1946), 215–16.

34. Poggi, *Development of the Modern State,* 78.

35. See Alberto Alesina et al., "Political Instability and Economic Growth," *Journal of Economic Growth* 1 (1996): 189–212; Alberto Alesina and Roberto Perotti, "Income Distribution, Political Instability, and Investment," *European Economic Review* 40 (1996): 1203–28.

36. Max Weber, *Economy and Society,* 2 vols. (Berkeley: University of California Press, 1978), 1: 54–56.

37. Mann, *Sources of Social Power,* 56.

38. See Guillermo O'Donnell, "Delegative Democracy?" working paper no. 21 (Chicago: University of Chicago, 1992); Przeworski et al., *Sustainable Democracy;* Linz and Stepan, *Problems of Democratic Transition;* Rose and Shin, "Democratization Backward."

39. Robert Dahl, *Democracy and Its Critics* (New Haven: Yale University Press, 1989), 207.

40. Dankwart Rustow, "Transition to Democracy: Towards a Dynamic Model," *Comparative Politics* 2 (1970): 351.

41. Linz and Stepan, *Problems of Democratic Transition,* 33–34.

42. Stephen Holmes, "What Russia Teaches Us Now," *American Prospect* 8, no. 33 (1997): 30–39.

43. Diamond, *Developing Democracy toward Consolidation,* 239.

44. See Naomi Chazan, "Engaging the State," in *State Power and Social Forces,* ed. Joel Migdal et al. (Cambridge: Cambridge University Press, 1994), 255–89; Vivienne Shue, "State Power and Social Organization," in Migdal et al., *State Power and Social Forces,* 65–88.

45. Peter Evans, "The Eclipse of the State?" *World Politics,* no. 50 (1997): 62–87.

46. Larry Diamond, "Rethinking Civil Society: Toward Democratic Consolidation," *Journal of Democracy* 5 (1994): 176.

47. Evans, "Eclipse of the State?" 85–87.

48. Linz and Stepan, *Problems of Democratic Transition,* 12–13.

49. Samuel P. Huntington, "Democracy's Third Wave?" in *The Global Resurgence of Democracy,* ed. Larry Diamond and Marc F. Plattner (Baltimore, MD: John Hopkins University Press, 1993), 10.

50. Taras Kuzio, et al., *State and Institution Building in Ukraine* (New York: St. Martin's Press, 1999), 6–7.

51. Linz and Stepan, *Problems of Democratic Transition,* 29.

52. Wang Shaoguang and Hu Angang, *The Chinese Economy in Crisis: State Capacity and Tax Reform* (Armonk, NY: Sharpe, 2001); Wang Shaoguang, "The Problem of State Weakness," *Journal of Democracy* 14 (2003): 36–42.

53. Rupert Emerson, "The Erosion of Democracy," *Journal of Asian Studies* 20 (1966): 7.

13

The Legitimacy of Proletarian Political Practice

On Marxist Political Philosophy

Cheng Guangyun

Recently, political philosophy has been proclaimed "first philosophy," which is an opportunity and a challenge for Marxist philosophy. I believe the study of Marxist philosophy is not a closed one but is open to the following. First, it is open to other political philosophies, exploring a critical and sustainable relation to classical political philosophy and modern political philosophy and improving the conversation between Marxist political philosophy and modern political philosophy (such as Western Marxism, neo-Marxism, and post-Marxism). Second, it is open to other political thought through a discussion from the angle of democratic politics of "socialism with Chinese characteristics," which means we perceive and evaluate other political ideas such as neoliberalism, New Leftism, and neoconservatism in terms of Marxist political philosophy. It is self-evident that the central theme of Marxist political philosophy, formed by the combination of Marxist political philosophy and the democratic politics of "socialism with Chinese characteristics," is the challenge to put theory into practice.

I believe that Marxist political philosophy is a kind of theoretical demonstration of the legitimacy of proletarian political practice. Therefore, Marxist political philosophy is neither textual research nor practical research. In its methodology, Marxist political philosophy should first and mainly focus upon logical argumentation. Here the so-called logic of argumentation is taken not in its narrow sense, but in a broad sense that has something to do with the creation of a theory involving argumentative structure and mode.

Marxist Philosophy

According to philosopher Leo Strauss, political philosophy as a discipline has a special meaning. Political philosophy is a branch of philosophy that investigates deeply and widely the issues of human political life. Facing the issues involved in the political field, it is impossible for us not to adopt the attitude of approving or opposing, choosing or refusing, and praising or condemning, all of which relates to the judgment of goodness and bad-ness, mercy and evil, justice and injustice. This presupposes all kinds of judgment standards that are explored by us to gain real knowledge of these standards. Therefore, political philosophy itself is not neutral; its purpose is to recognize not only the nature of political things but also the just or good social system.

Political philosophy is different from general political ideology and general political theory. Political ideology is a reflection or interpretation of political conceptions, which are the basic rules governing politics. Politi-cal theory is a reflection on the political situation and policy recommenda-tions, which will eventually resort to principles acknowledged by the public. All political philosophies embrace political ideology, political theory, and political doctrine; conversely, not all political thoughts, political theories, and political doctrines are political philosophy. In other words, the relation between political philosophy and general political ideology, political the-ory, and political doctrine is the same as the relation between knowledge and opinion. Political philosophy was political science originally. However, with the separation between philosophy and science, namely the authorita-tive establishment of modern natural science and the loss of authority by philosophy, the difference between nonscientific political philosophy and nonphilosophical political science appeared. It can be said that the relation between political philosophy and political science is the relation between value judgments and factual judgments. According to the Marxist point of view, however, value and fact can be unified.

Political philosophy has existed since ancient times. Ancient Chinese philosophies, especially Confucian philosophy and Legalist philosophy, are typical forms of political philosophy. Western political philosophy, so far, has experienced three basic forms: first, classical political philosophy, as represented by Plato and Aristotle; second, modern political philosophy, as represented by Hobbes, Locke, Hume, Smith, Mill, Rousseau, Kant, and Hegel; and third, contemporary political philosophy, as represented by Hayek, Rawls, and Strauss. Marxist political philosophy is a transitional system of political philosophy from modern to contemporary and has exerted a significant impact upon international communism and socialist political practice.

At present, political philosophy tends to claim the status "first philosophy." Under the influence of different kinds of political philosophy abroad, political philosophy in China has become a central issue in recent years and plays an important role in affecting a variety of political thought, such as Hayek's research in neoliberalism, Rawls's focus on left liberalism, and Strauss's commitment to neoconservatism. With the background of this academic thought, many philosophers and other scholars in the fields of the humanities and the social sciences turn to the study of political philosophy. It is both an opportunity and a challenge for the research of Marxist political philosophy. Meanwhile, building a democratic politics of "socialism with Chinese characteristics" has raised a number of problems that must be solved from the angle of political philosophy, which provides necessity, possibility, and reality for Marxist political philosophy studies. "Socialism with Chinese characteristics" is guided by Marxism, which implies that it should be actually based upon Marxist political philosophy (as well as political science) from the angle of the construction of democratic politics.

If we wish to improve our understanding of the development of foreign political philosophy and promote the study of Chinese political philosophy, we need the systematic study of Marxist theory, political philosophical dialogue with foreign countries, doctrinal clarification of the issues, and expounding of the standpoints of all political philosophies. All of these play an important role in building a special Marxist-oriented political philosophy with Chinese characteristics. The major problems of political philosophy are not political issues, but academic issues concerning the basic problems of political thought from the view of philosophy. The bias of Western scholars is that there is only political ideology but no political philosophy in China's mainland. The dividing line between political philosophy and political ideology consists in whether it resorts to human reason or logical argument. The study of Marxist political philosophy will promote our national political philosophy through the study of contemporary Chinese and foreign political philosophy.

How to understand political philosophy from the perspective of Marxism? How to understand Marxist political philosophy? How to understand Marxism from the perspective of political philosophy? Our analysis of Marxist political philosophy consists of all these questions.

First, understanding political philosophy according to Marxism means understanding from the perspective of historical materialism. This is the Marxist theory of political production and reproduction. Marx and Engels proposed several theories of production and reproduction in *The German Ideology*:[1] life production and reproduction includes the production of our own lives through work, the production of other lives and communicative forms through the fertility and the production of language ideas, the production of concepts and awareness through languages. Furthermore, Engels claimed two kinds of theories of production and reproduction in *The Origin of the Family, Private Property and the State*,[2] which hold that the direct production and reproduction of life include the production of tools and productive material through work and the production of human beings through family. This theory is nothing but the abbreviated form of the production theory mentioned above. Production implies concepts such as practice, labor, contracts, world objectification, and the objectified world. "World objectification" and the "objectified world" refer to the fact that the object-world is produced and reproduced by people through practicing, working, and communicating. This is the essence and the core of the Marxist conception of historical materialism. It is noticed that the production of the communicative form is also political production in a broad sense, which contains political production in a narrow sense. The Marxist conception of historical materialism explains political and cultural production from the perspective of material production, getting rid of its independent appearance: "Political and cultural production do not have their own history and development, which means people who develop their own material production and material communication not only change the reality but their thought and its product at the same time."[3] They also change their communication and the product of it—the social relationship between human society and the social essence (humanity). This is the basic Marxist understanding of political philosophy and the essential characteristic of Marxist political philosophy.

Second, Marxist political philosophy consists of three basic levels.

First, the level of political strategy (including military strategy) is reflected in the texts on proletarian revolution written by classical Marxist writers. Strictly speaking, this level is not political philosophy as such, but general political thought and political theory. However, some political conceptions undoubtedly have the status of political philosophy, which should be treated carefully but not divorced from specific context. The second level is embodied in the research of basic political issues by classical Marxist writers, such as in Marx's early writings on ethics and the law; Engels's research on equality and freedom in the *Anti-Dühring* (part 1, Philosophy); and the famous doctrines of class struggle, national doctrine, proletarian revolution, and the dictatorship of the proletariat. Strictly speaking, however, this level does not belong entirely to the category of political philosophy but partly to political science. But it should be noticed that Marxist political philosophy and political science are closely combined. Third, the most fundamental and important level is Marxist philosophy as political philosophy.

Finally, understanding Marxism from the perspective of political philosophy means understanding the conception of historical materialism from the perspective of political philosophy. Marxist political philosophy involves the theoretical argument for the legitimacy of proletarian political practice. The Marxist conception of historical materialism is a strictly logical and completely theoretical system. It contains two basic logics: one is the life theory, or the logic of practice, which means we could infer the legitimacy of the proletariat changing the world from proletarian living conditions; the other is the historical conception, or the natural logic, namely that the social laws deduced form the natural laws as the "iron laws" determine the legitimacy of proletarians changing the existing world. By comparison, the former is more original than the latter; they should supplement each other. However, they were usually separated in the historical process and the former was overwhelmed by the latter, which turns Marxism into dogmatism or doctrinaire pragmatism.

In addition, there is no doubt that Marxist political philosophy has important guiding significance in the construction of the democratic politics of "socialism with Chinese characteristics." The significance includes defense of the fundamental socialist political system by applying Marxist political philosophy; criticism of the existing political system; and most important, justification of the way to build the democratic politics of socialism with Chinese characteristics. Conversely, construction of the democratic politics of socialism with Chinese characteristics plays a basic role in enriching and developing Marxist political philosophy.

THE TWO LOGICS OF MARXISM

When we interpret the whole of Marxist philosophy as political philosophy, we have already defined Marxist political philosophy as the theoretical justification of the legitimacy of proletarian political practice. Now, we further explore the two basic logics of Marxist political philosophy: one is its life theory, or its logic of practice, which means we infer the legitimacy of the proletariat changing proletarian living conditions; the other is the historical conception, or the natural logic, deducing social laws from natural laws, understood as the "iron laws." This justifies the legitimacy of the proletariat and its vanguard, the Communist Party. The difference and connection, or the opposition and unity, between the two logics should be apprehended.

In a short text, the interview with Karl Marx by John Swinton, published in the *Sun,* Marx answered the question "What is being?" His answer was "struggle." This shows the logical premise of Marxist political philosophy: *I struggle, therefore I am.*

Marxism is Marx's innovation. Therefore, Marxism first reflects its creator's life situation. A person's life situation is composed of two aspects: first, objective living environment or experience; second, subjective attitude toward living environment or experience. Marx was a typical public intellectual. His identity as a human being determined his real situation and fate as a member of the lowest social sphere. Meanwhile, his identity as an intellectual determined his conceptions and his awareness of his mission as a senior member of the intelligentsia. This tension dominated Marx's character. As is well known, Marx completed a questionnaire drawn up by his eldest daughter, Jenny, like this: "What is your understanding about happiness?": "Struggle"; "What is your understanding about unhappiness?": "Surrender."[4] There is no doubt that there are only two ways to save people living at the bottom of society: struggle or surrender. Senior intellectuals, however, have no choice but to struggle.

The young Marx engaged in theoretical criticism and practical struggle with passion and reason. He wanted to discover the new world by criticizing the old world and all existent things rigorously, which means criticism that is not afraid of its conclusions and its conflict with various existing forces.[5] He wanted to combine theoretical criticism with practical struggle. However, he knew that once we moved from theoretical criticism into practical struggle, the move would not be limited to individual intellectuals who had to mobilize the masses to participate in the struggle. He held that the weapon of criticism cannot, of course, replace criticism of the weapon and that material force must be overthrown by material force; but theory also becomes a material force as soon as it controls the masses. Theory is capable of controlling the masses as soon as it persuades people, and it persuades people as soon as it is complete. To be complete means to grasp the nature of the matter. However, the nature of people is just people themselves.[6] Marx found the proletariat according to a strict logic that can be described as follows: philosophy takes the proletariat as its material weapon, so the proletariat takes philosophy as its spiritual weapon; the head of the emancipation is philosophy, its heart the proletariat.[7] All roads lead to Rome; Marx's comrade Engels found the proletariat in his real life. Engels pointed out that the proletariat is not only a class suffering pain but also one of humble economic status, propelling it forward invariably and forcing it to fight for its ultimate emancipation. The struggling proletariat can help itself.[8]

The thoughts of Marx and Engels, and the living conditions of the proletariat, define Marxism as the class-consciousness of the proletariat, which not only gives to Marxism its class basis but also enables the proletariat to gain self-consciousness. Marxism as a political philosophy was set up first in the Western industrial proletariat.

The proletariat is a suffering class, a special class status that contributes to its ability to fight. The struggle is the justification of the existence of proletariat. However, Marxism is consciousness of the proletarian class not only because it has aroused the struggling consciousness of the proletarian but also because it points out the practical approach to and the ideal objective of struggle.

"How do we fight?" The way of struggle is the second basic aspect of Marxist political philosophy.

The proletariat's living condition means that it cannot rely upon any other power but its own. It has neither "gun" nor "effective writer"; it has no wealth, knowledge, power, public opinion, and so on. It fights against the bourgeois and other social forces depending only upon its union and organization, uniting all forces that can be united as its collective power.

"Unity is power" is the basic way of proletarian struggle. As is well known, two sentences are inscribed on Marx's "epitaph": "Philosophers have only interpreted the world in various ways. However, the point is to change it" and "Working men of all countries, unite!"[9] The first sentence expresses the theme of "struggle," while the second expresses the theme of "unity."

It should be noted that as "scholar revolutionaries," Marx and Engels emphasized the proletarian union. Lenin, as a "professional revolutionary," emphasized particularly the "organization" of the proletarian party. Lenin once pointed out that when the proletariat fights for political power, there is no other weapon but organization.[10]

"Why do we fight?" The target of struggle is the third basic aspect of Marxist political philosophy.

From Plato's *Republic* to More's *Utopia,* communism as the common ideal of humankind has an ancient origin and a long development in the history of human society. It is people's glorious memory of the primitive system, the Romantic protest against the existing social system, and the happy vista of the future social system. However, the reason why the utopia of socialism is utopian is because it only concentrates on how human society "should be" and upon moral sympathy for the proletariat as a suffering class. However, Marx and Engels accomplished the move of communism from the utopian to the scientific level. Scientific socialism is a science because it provided an explanation of how human society "must be" and an economic understanding of the proletariat as a revolutionary class. Thus, Marxism points out the historical inevitability of realizing the communist ideal through the conception of historical materialism and points out the power of social reality, which realizes the communist ideal through the theory of surplus value. As a result, the communist ideal has become the faith of proletarian struggle through scientific justification.

"Communism is our ideal" is the basic theme of proletarian struggle. As we all know, the last two sentences of *The Internationale* are: "This is the final struggle. / Let us group together, and tomorrow / The Internationale / Will be the human race!" The expression of the first sentence is the "struggle" theme; the second expresses both the "unity" theme and the "ideal" topic.

The Marxist spirit of struggle presupposes a historical logic. Marx and Engels were both revolutionaries and scientists. Marx and Engels founded their revolutionary strategy on their scientific theory. Furthermore, struggle is the starting point of this construction in their strategy and theory.

They argue that the reason the theory is irresistibly attractive for socialists all over the world is that it combines the nature of revolution with the nature of strict science. And the combination is inherent and indivisible.[11]

In Marxism, "struggle" is a social practice. For Marxists, "practice, labor, communication, production, etc.," are the essence of being human. In this sense, we point out that the foundations of Marxist theory are life theory and practice theory. In *The German Ideology,* Marx and Engels stressed repeatedly that the first premise of all human history is, of course, the existence of living individuals. We must begin by defining the first premise of all human existence and therefore of all history. The premise is that people have to live in order to "create history."[12] In this book, Marx and Engels took human lives as the precondition to establish their basic theory. The logic here is that people's lives depend upon their living conditions, which require people to produce and reproduce continuously themselves, others, and all social conditions. True understanding of human society and history derives from the practice of human life and a series of objective activities. Marx established the theory of historical materialism, the social organic system, and the "natural" history process from the perspective of human life and a series of objective activities including practice, labor, communication, production, and reproduction.

There are two basic study paths in Marxism: one is research, and the other is narrative. The first expresses the "life theory" and "practice theory." Marx established the struggle position, the revolutionary strategy, and the scientific theory by examining humanity's life conditions, especially the situation of proletariat. The second expresses "the historical conception" and "the natural conception." It seems that Marxism establishes the proletarian struggle position because it expresses the scientific truth of natural law and the historical law of human society.

Marxism originally focuses upon "life theory and practice theory," while afterward it embraces "the history conception" and "the natural conception," which leads to dogmatic and deterministic Marxism. From the standpoint of dogmatic and deterministic Marxism, there is only the "iron law" people should obey and the truth that people should sacrifice themselves to it. Because of obliviousness toward the people's living conditions, people are mere tools for realizing the ideal, the means of achieving the target but not the target itself.

In short, there are two logical arguments in Marxist political philosophy. The first is that bad living conditions force proletarian struggle; poor resources force the proletariat to unite, organize, and associate. Only when universal and inevitable historical ideals are founded will the proletariat mobilize others widely and effectively to change the world. The second is that there is an objective natural and social law unchanged by human will, which leads to the inevitable historical trend of the extinction of the existing world and the victory of ideal society. Those who know the law will represent the direction of the historical development; those who represent the direction of the historical development will exercise the leadership. The two logical arguments can be combined occasionally but are strictly unrelated. For example, we could define the proletariat according to poverty, while we could also define the proletariat according to historical advance. There is a kind of relation between the two definitions. However, the legitimacy of the leadership of the Communist Party cannot be justified by the relation above because its logic is not strict and needs to be clarified.

LIVING CONDITIONS AS THE STARTING POINT

Marx made theoretical arguments for the legitimacy of proletarian political practice during his whole life. The development of socialism from a utopian to a scientific view is the foundation of Marxist political philosophy.

Utopian socialism is an ancient thought system and reflects the human pursuit of social justice. Modern utopian socialism is the production and outgrowth of the Industrial Revolution and the capitalist social system. It is manifested in two aspects: its critique of existing capitalism and its utopian nature, which refers to the future of socialism. Utopian socialism has the idealist historical conception as its philosophical foundation. Its explanation of human social history is a moral one. Depending upon this theory, it can prove that socialism should replace capitalism exclusively when one demonstrates the badness of capitalism and the goodness of socialism. In this way, the problem of achieving socialism will depend on the conscience of the bourgeoisie and the social experiment of reformism to change education and the environment.

Although the early views of Marx and Engels are still confined to utopian socialism, in my opinion, they contain the seeds of scientific socialism. Marx defined communism in *Economic and Philosophic Manuscripts of 1844*. There, Marx develops what is useful in the "alienation of labor" and "private assets" and discards what is not germane to "communism." "Naturalism" and "humanism" are the earliest expressions of the "practical materialism" theory. "The conflict between man and nature" and "the conflict between man and man" are the earliest expressions of historical materialism's productive force, production relations (economic basis), and superstructure. The theory of "alienation" embraces the seeds of the residual value theory.

Generally, Marx and Engels's early arguments on socialism are about "life theory and practice theory." In *The German Ideology* Marx and Engels take "real individuals," "living existing individuals," "individuals in reality," "individuals engaged in practical activities," and "individuals who are real, visible through the experience and developing in certain conditions," as their premise and starting point to describe communism again. They believe that, in fact, all the problems for practical materialists, namely communists, consist in making the existing world revolutionary and fighting against and changing the existing world. Furthermore, they point out that what we call communism is the real movement that transforms the present state of things. The conditions of the movement result from actual premises in existence.[13]

In the mature stage of Marx and Engels's thought, the argument of "life theory and practice theory" turns into "the history conception" and makes "the natural conception" supplementary. There is a subtle relationship between the two forms of argument. On the one hand, the latter is derived historically and logically from the former. In *The German Ideology* Marx and Engels first pay close attention to the "real individual," then to the "material living condition" of the "real individual" and the "production" of the "material living condition," which implies the classical historical conception of materialism. On the other hand, in the mature theory, the logic of "life and practice theory" is replaced by the logic of "history and natural conception." From the *Manifesto of the Communist Party* to *On Capital*, Marx and Engels raised the development of socialism from the utopian to a scientific level. Engels points this out clearly: because of Marx's "two greatest discoveries—the historical conception of materialism and the secret of capitalist production, . . . socialism turns to be scientific."[14]

The historical conception of materialism exposes the law of social history, which justifies the objectivity and the necessity of replacing capitalism with socialism. The representative work that expressed the legitimacy of the above justification is the *Manifesto of the Communist Party*. The *Manifesto* demonstrates the legitimacy of replacing capitalism with socialism through grand-historical narrative logic. The theory of surplus value exposes the secret that capitalists exploit workers, justifying reasonably the necessity and the possibility of the proletarian revolution overthrowing the bourgeoisie, which is articulated in *On Capital*. It would be better to define *On Capital* as a work of political philosophy rather than an economic work. This work does not expound the methods of enhancing national wealth but expresses the reasons for "expropriating expropriators" and demonstrates the legitimacy of the proletariat overthrowing the bourgeoisie.

The historical conception of materialism and the surplus value theory are the basic logics of scientific socialism. Both endorse the "history conception" and abandon the argumentative form of "life theory and practice theory," but they preserve and develop the basic elements of those two theories. Engels even used the argument of "natural conception" as a supplement to Marx's "historical conception" argument. In this way, the argument of socialism seems not to take human living practice as its premise or starting point; rather, it takes natural laws existing independent of human consciousness and the "iron law," which is not up to human will, as its premise or starting point. Scientific socialism is a new thought system; it takes the historical conception of materialism as its philosophical foundation. It is a "deterministic" way of explaining human social history. According to it, the transition from capitalism to socialism is necessary. Therefore, the problem of realizing socialism consists in arousing the consciousness of the proletarian class.

Compared with utopian socialism, the argument form of scientific socialism is significantly changed. Marx and Engels changed their thought from the ideal to reality in their old age. On justifying socialism, the old Marx and Engels modified their argument obviously: through the "theory of stages" and the "theory of national conditions." In the *Critique of the Gotha Program*, Marx differentiated the "the first stage of the communist society" from "the higher stage of the communist society." The former stage stresses "the rights of the bourgeois" (e.g., "from each according to his ability, to each according to work"), leading to the dictatorship of the proletariat. The latter stage eliminates "the rights of the bourgeois," postulating "from each according to his ability, to each according to his needs." Marx proposed the "Asiatic production mode" in his early years, whereas in his old age he proposed the "way of the development of Eastern society." In his research regarding the Russian "agriculture commune," Marx pointed out that all fruits produced by the capitalist system could be incorporated into the commune by Russia. However, to save the Russian commune, a Russian revolution was necessary.[15] It should be noticed that Marx sublated the previous form of universal argument in the argument of "stage theory" and "national conditions theory" and used a special form that has had a significant impact upon the movement of international communism and socialism. But the "stage theory" and the "national conditions theory" lead to an attitude of "suspension" (of beliefs and ideals), which results in a conservative attitude that justifies the existing world rather than propounding critique and revolution.

From utopian socialism to scientific socialism, from theoretical socialism to practical socialism, and from the form of "life theory and practice theory" and "historical conception and natural conception" to the form of "stage theory and national conditions theory," the theory of socialism has changed a lot. On the one hand, it fits the development of reality; on the other hand, it exposes the contradictions between theory and reality.

There is a basic paradox in Marxism and the international communism and socialism practice of every country. According to the general principle, Marx and Engels predict that socialism should be realized first in some developed countries (e.g., Britain, the United States, France, Germany, etc.). In fact, socialism was first realized in undeveloped countries—Russia and even a semicolonial and semifeudal country such as China. It is hard to resolve this paradox with the explanation of "the history conception" and "the natural conception." No matter whether we base our explanation upon the frame of historical necessity or the frame of actual social power, the problem of realizing socialism and communism is more maturely resolved in the West than in the East. This paradox can be resolved by turning to the explanation frame of "the life theory and "the practice theory." The revolution, in certain cases, is decided not by historical necessity and the maturity of actual social power, but by the deterioration of human living conditions. Therefore, theoretically, socialism is the result of the development of capitalism, but in reality it is the consequence of undeveloped capitalism.

After the Paris Commune, Western European capitalist society moved into a peaceful period of development. Marx and Engels noticed the historical fact that along with the peaceful development of capitalist society, the revolutionary storm lulled gradually. When Engels described the British situation, he pointed out that the British proletariat was, in fact, becoming increasingly bourgeoisified.[16] Later the particular phenomenon in Britain became the common phenomenon in Western Europe. Apart from revolutionary trends in the two world wars, the Western proletariat, with the improvement of their living conditions, became less revolutionary and more conservative than before.

When the Western revolutionary storm gradually subsided, the storm began brewing in the East: "The West does not shine but the East becomes bright." Puzzled by this fact, Marx and Engels turned their eyes from the West to the East, from Western Europe to Russia. Marx put forward the theory of the "Asiatic production form" and "the Eastern social development path." Subsequent history has confirmed this prophecy. Russia (the Soviet Union), along with China and some countries in Eastern Europe, East Asia, and Central America, achieved the victory of the proletarian revolution and built a socialist system. Marxism originated in the developed countries of the West (Western Europe) and prevailed in some developing countries in the East (Asia, Africa, and Latin America); when the proletariat in the developed countries became indifferent to Marxism, it was embraced by the poor people in the developing countries. This historical fact is inconceivable with the explanation of "the history conception" and "the natural conception" but reasonable with the explanation of "the life conception" and "the practice conception."

Therefore, Marxism-Leninism was introduced to China, gradually becoming the mainstream ideology, not because of capitalist factors in Chinese society and the degree of proletarian maturity, but because of the bad living conditions of the Chinese people.

Today, we need to reexamine the various forms of justification for socialism. Utopian socialism, let alone scientific socialism, has not lost its historical significance. Socialism, which is an institutional arrangement coupled with principles of justice, is designed to enhance people's happy lives. This is the essence of the form of "life theory" and "practice theory." However, scientific socialism has always been interpreted as a form of "historical conception" or even "natural conception." Indeed, there is no doubt that interpreting human social history using two basic social contradictions or fundamental historical driving forces, like productive forces and production relations, or economic basis and superstructure (e.g., "the incompatibility between the social production and the processes of capitalism," "the opposition between the proletariat and capitalists," "the opposition between the organization of production in each factor and the anarchy state of social production"), has inspired us to grasp the objective conditions and material basis for realizing socialism. However, if we believe that realizing socialism is a "natural" history decided by some "iron laws" (social laws and even natural laws), we will, as history has proven, no longer take humans as the purpose but as the tool, which moves toward some kind of totalitarianism. Therefore, we should weaken the formula of "historical determinism," in particular of "natural determinism," but strengthen the formula of "life theory" and "practice theory." We must understand that socialism is a process that is chosen, constructed, and created by human beings freely and consciously and that it takes the human as the purpose rather than the tool. As for the formula of "the theory of stages and national conditions": on the one hand, it makes socialism more realistic because of its particular concerns; on the other hand, it moves socialism away from the ideal because of its lack of universal concerns. In fact, socialism, on the one hand, is an ideal of universal value that transcends every historical stage and all national conditions; on the other hand, it takes the ideal of value as the paradigm to adapt the system to the design of every historical stage and national condition.

Paralleling the paradox between theory and practice, there is a basic paradox between revolution and construction. Given the deterioration of their living conditions, the proletariat and laboring people devote themselves to the revolution for improving their living conditions. However, when people change their living conditions, they change their revolutionary spirit fundamentally. Therefore, there is a conflict between Marxism and its premise of "theory of life" and "theory of practice."

The basic tendency of dogmatic and deterministic Marxism is to utter blindly Marxist words, but remain indifferent to Marxism's basis in the "theory of life and practice." Hence, Marxist political philosophy becomes a purely abstract political philosophy. Therefore, the remedy for dogmatic Marxism is basing Marxist political philosophy again upon the "theory of life and practice" and restoring the Marxist fundamental spirit, which cares about the living conditions of the proletariat and laboring people. The key point is that the Marxist fundamental spirit expresses its concern not only about the living conditions of common people but about proletarian living conditions particularly. If we are only concerned about upper-middle-class living conditions but neglect poor people's living conditions, we depart from Marxism. Only if we regard Marxism as a discourse for people living at the lowest level of society can its vitality and vigor be restored.

Notes

1. *Collection of Marx and Engels* (in Chinese), 4 vols. (Beijing: People's Press, 1995), 1: 79–81.

2. Ibid., 4: 2.

3. Ibid., 1: 73.

4. *Complete Works of Marx and Engels* (in Chinese), 60 vols. (Beijing: People's Press, 1972), 31: 588.

5. Ibid., 47: 64.

6. *Collection of Marx and Engels,* 1: 9.

7. Ibid., 1: 15–16.

8. *Collection of Lenin* (in Chinese), 4 vols. (Beijing: People's Press, 1995), 1: 91–92.

9. *Collection of Marx and Engels,* 1: 57, 307.

10. *Collection of Lenin,* 1: 526.

11. Ibid., 1: 83.

12. *Collection of Marx and Engels,* 1: 67, 78–79.

13. *Complete Works of Marx and Engels,* 1: 75, 87.

14. Ibid., 3: 366, 740.

15. Ibid., 3: 765, 773.

16. Ibid., 4: 552.

Contributors

Cheng Guangyun is professor and dean of the Department of Philosophy at Capital Normal University in Beijing. He specializes in political philosophy, cultural philosophy, and foreign Marxism studies. He serves as chief editor of the *Yearbook of Chinese Philosophy* (in Chinese), sponsored by the Chinese Academy of Social Sciences, Institute of Philosophy.

Chen Ming is professor of philosophy at Capital Normal University in Beijing. Among his publications are *Ru Zhe Zhi Wei* (The dimensions of Confucian thought) (2004) and "The Reconstruction of Confucianism to Incorporate Constitutionalism" (in Chinese, 2007).

Ci Jiwei, a graduate of the University of Edinburgh, is professor of philosophy at the University of Hong Kong. He specializes in moral and political philosophy. Among his publications are *Dialectic of the Chinese Revolution: From Utopianism to Hedonism* (1994), *The Two Faces of Justice* (2006), and "The Moral Crisis in Post-Mao China" (*Diogenes*, 2009).

Cui Zhiyuan is professor of political science in the School of Public Policy and Management at Tsinghua University in Beijing. He is considered one of the leaders of the Chinese New Left. Among his publications is the important article "Zhidu Chuangxin He Di'erci Sixiang Jiefang" (Beijing, 1994), which examines the "shareholding-cooperative system."

Fred Dallmayr is Emeritus Packey J. Dee Professor of Political Science at the University of Notre Dame (United States). He specializes in modern Western philosophy, Continental philosophy, comparative philosophy, and political theory. He is a former president (2004–2005) of the Society for Asian and Comparative Philosophy (SACP) and executive cochair of the World Public Forum "Dialogue of Civilizations." Among his publications are *Beyond Orientalism: Essays on Cross-Cultural Encounter* (1996), *Alternative Visions: Paths in the Global Village* (1998), *Dialogue among Civilizations: Some Exemplary Voices* (2002), *Peace Talks: Who Will Listen?* (2004), *In Search of the Good Life: A Pedagogy for Troubled Times* (2007), *Integral Pluralism: Beyond Culture Wars* (2010), *Comparative Political Theory: An Introduction* (2010), and *The Promise of Democracy: Political Agency and Transformation* (2010).

Frank Fang (Fang Shaowei) has been director of the Institutional Economics Center in Chicago and serves as a visiting professor at Huazhong University of Science and Technology. He graduated from the School of Economics at Peking University in 1988, worked at the Chinese Academy of Social Sciences (1989–1993), and served as deputy director of the Unirule Institute of Economics (1993–1994). Among his publications is *China Fever: Fascination, Fear, and the World's Next Superpower* (2007).

He Baogang is professor and chair of international studies in the School of Politics and International Studies at Deaking University in Australia. He specializes in Chinese and international politics, comparative politics, and philosophy. Among his publications are *The Democratization of China* (1996), *The Democratic Implications of Civil Society in China* (1997), *Balancing Democracy and Authority* (with Lang Youxing, 2002), *Multiculturalism in Asia* (with Will Kymlicka, 2005), *The Search for Deliberative Democracy in China* (with Ethan Leib, 2006), and *Rural Democracy in China: The Role of Village Elections* (2007).

Ji Wenshun served as senior research linguist from 1959 to 1977 in the Center for Chinese Studies at the University of California, Berkeley. Among his publications are *Ideological Conflicts in Modern China: Democracy and Authoritarianism* (1986, 1992), and *Readings in Chinese Communist Documents* (1963). He died in 1984.

Liu Shuxian is research professor at the Institute of Chinese Literature and Philosophy at the Academia Sinica in Taipei, Taiwan. Among his publications are *Understanding Confucian Philosophy: Classical and Sung-Ming* (1998), *Essentials of Contemporary Neo-Confucian Philosophy* (2003), and *Harmony and Strife: Contemporary Perspectives East and West* (with Robert Allinson, 1988).

Ni Peimin is professor of philosophy and chair of the Chinese Studies Program at Grand Valley State University in Michigan. He holds a BA and an MA from Fudan University and a PhD from the University of Connecticut. He specializes in Chinese and comparative philosophy. He is the founder and former president (1997–1999) of the Association of Chinese Philosophers in America (ACPA) and the past president (2008–2010) of the Society for Asian and Comparative Philosophy (SACP). He is the author of *On Confucius* (2002) and *On Reid* (2002) and coauthor (with Stephen Rowe) of *Wandering: Brush and Pen in Philosophical Reflection* (2002). He is also an accomplished Chinese calligraphy artist.

Wang Shaoguang, a graduate of Cornell University, is chair of the Department of Government and Public Administration at the Chinese University of Hong Kong and professor in the School of Public Policy and Management at Tsinghua University. He taught at Yale University (1990–2000) and is chief editor of the *China Review.* He is widely regarded as one of the leaders of the New Left in China. He specializes in political economy, comparative politics, and processes of development and democratization. Among his publications are *Rationality and Madness: The Masses in the Chinese Cultural Revolution* (1993), *Failure of Charisma: The Cultural Revolution in Wuhan* (1995), *Challenging the Market Myth* (in Chinese, 1997), *The Chinese Economy in Crisis* (with Hu Anang, 2001), *Lessons from the Progressive Era of the United States* (in Chinese, 2002), and *Four Lectures on Democracy* (in Chinese, 2008).

Zhang Feng is a lecturer in international relations in the School of Social Sciences and Humanities at Murdoch University, Australia. He previously taught in the Department of International Relations at Tsinghua University in Beijing. He specializes in the study of international politics and has published numerous articles in that field.

Zhao Tingyang, a graduate of Renmin University, is a researcher at the Chinese Academy of Social Sciences and a professor at Capital Normal University. He specializes in metaphilosophy and ethics. Among his publications are *On Possible Life* (1994), *One or All Problem* (1998), *All-Under-Heaven System* (2005), and *Studies of a Bad World: Political Philosophy as First Philosophy* (2009) (all in Chinese).

Zhou Lian is professor of philosophy at Renmin University of China. He received his PhD from the Chinese University of Hong Kong (2005). His area of specialization is political philosophy, but he is also interested in epistemology, the philosophy of language, and ethics. His book *The Foundation of Modern Political Legitimacy* (in Chinese) was published in 2008 by San Lian Press. In addition, he has published a number of articles and reviews on a variety of topics in several journals.

Index

Asia in the New Millennium

Series Editor: Shiping Hua, University of Louisville

Asia in the New Millennium is a series of books offering new interpretations of an important geopolitical region. The series examines the challenges and opportunities of Asia from the perspectives of politics, economics, and cultural-historical traditions, highlighting the impact of Asian developments on the world. Of particular interest are books on the history and prospect of the democratization process in Asia. The series also includes policy-oriented works that can be used as teaching materials at the undergraduate and graduate levels. Innovative manuscript proposals at any stage are welcome.

Advisory Board

William Callahan, University of Manchester, Southeast Asia, Thailand
Lowell Dittmer, University of California at Berkeley, East Asia and South Asia
Robert Hathaway, Woodrow Wilson International Center for Scholars, South Asia, India, Pakistan
Mike Mochizuki, George Washington University, East Asia, Japan and Korea
Peter Moody, University of Notre Dame, China and Japan
Brantly Womack, University of Virginia, China and Vietnam
Charles Ziegler, University of Louisville, Central Asia and Russia Far East

Books in the Series

The Future of China-Russia Relations
Edited by James Bellacqua

The Mind of Empire: China's History and Modern Foreign Relations
Christopher A. Ford

Korean Democracy in Transition: A Rational Blueprint for Developing Societies
HeeMin Kim

Inside China's Grand Strategy: The Perspective from the People's Republic
Ye Zicheng, Edited and Translated by Steven I. Levine and Guoli Liu

Challenges to Chinese Foreign Policy: Diplomacy, Globalization, and the Next World Power
Edited by Yufan Hao, C. X. George Wei, and Lowell Dittmer

CPSIA information can be obtained at www.ICGtesting.com
Printed in the USA
BVOW061843120612

292459BV00001B/1/P

9 780813 136424